THE YOUNG MAN AND THE SAGE

Book One

THE HERALDS TRILOGY

NORA SPINNOR

The Young Man and the Sage

The Herald's Trilogy © 2025 by Nora Spinnor All rights reserved.

No part of this publication may be reproduced, stored in a retrieval system, or transmitted in any form or by any means—electronic, mechanical, photocopying, recording, or otherwise—without the prior written permission of the publisher, except in the case of brief quotations used in critical articles or reviews.

This is a work of philosophical fiction. Names, characters, dialogue, and events are used allegorically. Any resemblance to actual persons, living or dead, is purely coincidental or metaphysically intentional.

First Edition

Published by **Netism**

www.netism.org

ISBN: 9798280011830

Printed in the United States of America

1 2 3 4 5 6 7 8 9 10

Cover design by Netism Interior layout by Netism

For information, permissions, or special orders, please contact: Netism Publishing info@netism.org

This book is an alchemical text presented through fiction. Each chapter is intentionally structured around key stages of the alchemical process, guiding the reader through a symbolic journey of self-realization and metaphysical insight. As a living codex, its meanings will continue to unfold through repeated contemplation, offering deeper layers of understanding with each return.

    Approach this work with an open mind. Let its symbols and ideas sink beneath the surface of thought and settle into the subconscious. Reflect on its messages as they relate to your own journey. When you have set it aside, return again and notice how your interpretation has changed. As your spiritual resonance evolves, so too will the insights this text reveals.

The Great Seal of Aturn

Contents

Foreword — vii

1. Beginning — 1
2. Death — 19
3. Illusions — 39
4. Cycles — 59
5. Sanity — 77
6. Salvation — 99
7. Vibrations — 129
8. Unseen — 137
9. Identity — 167
10. Journey — 197
11. Chaos — 209
12. Unity — 227
13. Passage — 243
14. Downpour — 251
15. Completion — 261

ALCHEMICAL AND SYMBOLIC INTERPRETATION

Ascent of the Prima Materia — 267
Illumination Beneath the Infinite Vault — 271
The Scales of Judgment and the Speaking Flame — 275
The Dwelling of Discord and Devotion — 279
The Seekers — 283
The Celestial Mirror and the Lion's Cry — 287
The Flame Within the Triangle — 291
The Covenant Beneath the Mirror — 295
The Tempest Within the Silence — 299
The Mind of the Big Fish — 303
Order Within the Root of Chaos — 307
Descent of the Storm Called From Within — 311
Evaporation of the Wounded Waters — 315

Storm at the Gate of Return	317
The Great Current of Becoming	319
About the Author	321
Also by Nora Spinnor	323
About Netism	325

Foreword

WE ARE ABOUT TO ASK YOU, our reader, to depart on a journey with us. Before complaints or excuses arise, we assure you that you do not need a ticket aside from this book. No luggage is required, nor is there a need to arrange for vacation time with an employer. You won't need to travel to an airport or wrestle your way through traffic jams; you won't need to hop onboard a vehicle of any sort. You won't even need to put on a pair of shoes. Our journey is a different sort. The destination is here already; it is a journey of self.

What could one possibly find that is valuable that is here already, within the self? A better question is, what value does one hope to find in running everywhere and anywhere else? So many spend so much time focusing on what is in front of their eyes that they forget that closing them often provides far deeper truths.

Pay attention to the emotions that arise at the proposition of this journey. It is common to get excited about a vacation. It is even more common to be afraid of facing oneself. Our journey is that of a hero; it is not a vacation. It is the arduous path only a few set out on, and it is designed to be painful because that is what makes a person great. Only when the journey is complete can one earn the title of 'hero,' the coveted title granted only to the few individuals who were determined enough not to let failure stand in the way of their visions for themselves.

Are you afraid of what you might find when you journey into your soul? We encourage you not to be because it is already there. Do not run into yourself with prejudices but rather understanding. It is reasonable to want growth for oneself; it is unreasonable to expect growth to happen without confronting what we fear. There is nothing within ourselves we can run from and expect good results. If anything, the longer we run, the harder it will become to face.

Do not begin with a saddened heart. Though the trials we face are never easy, we should be grateful that we have the opportunity to overcome them. The pain that pierces our hearts is not permanent, nor is it useless. Pain can propel one to fantastic heights. Just like we can have no conception of light if we have never known darkness, so, too, will we never be able to recognize true happiness if we have never known pain. A person born into wealth takes little joy in residing in a small, run-down living space. A person who has known extreme poverty, instead, revels in every comfort that the dilapidated space provides. We must ask ourselves who possesses more wisdom: the financier who scoffs at the material of his dinnerware or the beggar who is grateful for the meager meal it contains.

Our journey is that of perception, particularly in how we perceive ourselves. It is most likely with illness of mind and sickness of spirit that we do so. For this reason, we should regard our impending travels with eager anticipation. Should we allow this journey to mold our characters, we will most certainly enjoy the benefits at its completion.

Before we begin, take a moment to breathe in the self. Pay attention to all doubtful thoughts that arise; take note of them. When we depart from each other's company at the end of this book, we hope these doubts will be transformed into memories. In their place, assurance in each reader's unique life experiences will provide enough confidence to make their arguments obsolete. Long-standing fears dictated by real or imagined societal standards will no longer be relevant. Instead, an unshakable peace of mind will dominate all mental faculties. No one will be able to control anyone who accept this book as a valuable ticket towards freedom of self.

FOREWORD

As we start this journey, let barriers slip from our grasp. Let definitions no longer define us. As we propel ourselves forward to ever-greater heights, we learn how to become things we never thought we could be. As we awaken to our divinity, we realize that any state has the potential to become its opposite. One state is only as good as it is to propel us to the next stage of development.

Anything that is stagnant for too long rots, and so we must cherish one value only:

Our Evolution.

Ascent of the Prima Materia

Beginning

All roads have led me to this one; let me be strong in taking this path, Laolys thought as he placed one foot in front of the other, lifting himself over jagged rocks, pushing through thorny bushes, and scaling steep ledges. He wasn't an athlete, but he wasn't out of shape either. His firm determination and ever-present anxiety carried him through each obstacle, though it was never easy. Still, he always found ways to resolve his problems, and this time, he would do it again.

All for a better purpose... if I can find my answer in the end. Laolys had debated his decision to make this climb up the treacherous mountainside, but he had agonized twice as much about the information the man at the top of the mountain supposedly possessed. That information could change the world in the right hands, and Laolys believed he had the hands to make that change happen, if he could just find him and become his student.

The mountain towered above Laolys's town, yet it received almost no visitors. Dangerous rocky cliffs dominated its landscape, but so did lush fields and rich pine forests. It was a terrain fit only for wildlife, too rugged for man to wield his hammer and carve out an easier way of living. However, the town's aversion to the mountain had less to do with its harsh terrain and more to do with its lone inhabitant.

The elusive man Laolys was searching for was both an innovator and a fugitive. Rumors about him ranged from absurd tales of madness to whispers of otherworldly wisdom. Though most dismissed him as unfit for society, a few, in hushed voices, described him as a sage possessing peculiar magic. They said he held the knowledge that could open the gates of the universe, but that none could possess it without also going mad. Laolys was convinced this man held answers of great importance. His father's relentless efforts to stop him was clear evidence; no one devoted such effort to suppressing someone who was merely insane.

Laolys had never imagined he'd be on this mission. Then again, he never had much of a chance to imagine anything for himself. His father, a well-established politician, had decided Laolys's path at birth as soon as he was declared male. But his birth-ordained career had never felt natural to him. He sometimes doubted if he even belonged in his family. They were at peace in the political world, where their reputations preceded them. They found enjoyment in social events and making appearances. Laolys, rather, was a ball of nerves everywhere he went.

He paused to catch his breath, squinting at the distant outline of his town, backlit by the low rays of the afternoon sun. Memories of countless late nights spent pondering the mysterious man his father pursued flooded his mind. His father had referred to him only as *the leak*—a name signifying the forbidden knowledge the man supposedly possessed. He spent many nights eavesdropping on his father's conversations, but they were always coded. All he could determine was that the leak held information capable of altering the populace's mindset—information his father believed must be suppressed at all costs. Disillusioned by the entire political system, he vowed to uncover these truths. If they could change the world, as his father feared, he had to find out what they were.

Just a bit further. Laolys stepped onto a narrow footpath that twisted through a rocky incline. Each step sent sharp protests from his weary feet, but he ignored their complaints. The rocks would have to be passed over, regardless of his pain. In time, and with enough persistence, the soreness would transform into calluses, and his struggles would be replaced by an unshakable inner peace. For now, however, much tribulation lay ahead. So, with a determined will, he pressed on despite the aches.

He turned the bend and froze in place, letting out a small, involuntary shriek. Directly before him, an old, thin, scraggly man was perched on his toes atop a tall rock, balancing precariously on a tiny flat surface. He remained still, staring at him with an irate expression, framed by a mane of wild grey hair that emanated from all directions. His expression suggested he had been waiting for Laolys for some time.

The sage's appearance exuded a mystical sense of duality. His aged features seemed to mock his posture—one that even the youthful would have to rigorously train to maintain. His unkempt, matted grey hair grew wildly around his head and neck, yet his eyes held an intensity that could intimidate even the most sophisticated and educated. His simple robe and pants were so tattered and worn to his form that it was clear he had been wearing them for a long time, yet they somehow gave the impression of a costume. His presence radiated something powerful and otherworldly, and yet, the man was undeniably human.

"State your business and be gone, intruder!" he bellowed from atop the rock. A flock of birds squawked and flew off, startled by the sudden noise.

Laolys's chest tightened with anxiety, and he began sputtering out words as quickly as he could breathe them. "I—I'm Laolys and I'm here on a very important mission! I've just been elected to political office. I want to do things—change things! And who else but you, wise sage, should I ask for guidance?"

He forced a bow, though his muscles quivered in protest. A part of him wanted to flee back down the mountain, but he gritted his teeth and gazed back at the sage with a pleading expression.

The sage's eyes burned with a fire that steamed out of him as he glared at Laolys, unmoved from his perch on the rock. "A man from the government? I pushed my home all the way up this godforsaken mountain to avoid the government! I'm a simple man on untaxed land. Now, go!"

Laolys's stomach churned. He hadn't climbed this far just to be turned away. "Please! No, you misunderstand! You see, I'm not here for political business... I mean, if they knew I was here... No, this is personal. I want to learn from you. I'm going into office and I want to help—"

"Silence!"

Laolys's breath stopped short as he stared back at the man who loomed above him.

"I can't help you."

"What? Why not?"

"You're a politician."

Laolys's heartbeat quickened. "And I'll be in a place to help—"

"I can't help you." The sage's words cut through the air like glass, straight into Laolys's soul.

Laolys clenched his fists. He couldn't bear being turned away so quickly. "You won't at least hear me out?"

The sage's scowl deepened. "You can't help other people through government, not through my wisdom. You're in the wrong place. Now leave."

Laolys took a deep breath. His heart was pounding so hard he could hear it, but his feet and legs were locked into position. He wasn't going to leave, not after he got this far. "Please! I can't just go away with nothing! Just a little of your time?"

The sage remained unmoved in his perch. "Why?"

"Why should you help me?"

"Why do you want to know?"

Laolys's nerves spiked as he thought of his father, the many years he stayed up late at night listening for clues about this man and his wisdom. "I... want to make the world a better place."

The sage's eyes burned as he stared back at Laolys. "Then I can't help you."

"Why not?"

"You're a government official."

Laolys swallowed. "Well, it wasn't really my decision. There's protocol in place, I have to be one—for my family."

"Then I can't teach you."

A spike of panic shot through Laolys. Though he had been warned about the sage's erratic behavior, he hadn't expected to be shut out before he even had a chance to speak. A lump formed in his throat as he contemplated the possibility of descending the mountain without gaining any new insights.

Laolys drew a slow breath. "Just an hour of your time... No, not even an hour, half an hour! I can't go back with nothing. I climbed such a long way to be here!"

The sage looked as if he were about to erupt. "*You've* climbed a long way? *You've* climbed a long way, and yet, not once on that whole climb did you think about how far *I* had to climb to escape the likes of you. But no, no, go on, keep telling me about how far you've climbed. I'll continue not to care."

Laolys's gaze dropped to the ground, and his cheeks burned with embarrassment. *He's right*, he thought. *I only thought of my own journey.* But another part of him seethed, refusing to let the man's scorn drive him away.

"Up here," the sage continued, his voice loud and commanding, "I teach a different type of student. These students listen without argument, and they carry my teachings across the world without complaint. They don't ask for anything in return, not even praise. Tell me, why should I ignore such favorable students to teach the very type I climbed so far up a mountain to escape?"

"I—I'm sorry, sir, I didn't realize you already had students." Laolys suddenly felt unsure of himself. His heart was pounding so fiercely that it left him lightheaded. He stole a quick glance upward, and in that instant, the sage's intensity made him feel like a child caught in a lie.

"Aye, so you can go now." The sage made a dismissive shooing motion with his arms, still perfectly balanced on his toes atop the rock.

"But sir, maybe I can join one of your classes! You won't even know I'm there!"

"Impossible! Students like you always find a way to disrupt and distort the message. No, I've done away with humanity entirely—now be gone!" The sage shut his eyes and began a low, meditative chant.

Laolys's mind raced. He cast a frantic look at the narrow footpath behind him. The thought of trudging back down empty-handed twisted his stomach into knots. Even if the sage was half-mad, there had to be something valuable in what he knew. Otherwise, why would Laolys's father have feared him for so many years?

Reflecting on the rumors, Laolys recognized one common thread: the sage had an insatiable love for knowledge. Once a revolutionary in the academic world, he had mastered numerous subjects, thriving by blending seemingly unrelated fields to uncover truths that applied across disciplines. No matter where his thirst for knowledge had taken him, he had carried it with him well into old age. Laolys swung his bag from his back and began rifling through it, searching for the book he'd stowed beneath his clothes.

The sage's eyes remained closed, but he stopped chanting long enough to bellow ominously, "Bribery will get you nowhere. I have plenty of food, and I've no use for gold or trinkets."

Laolys ignored the sage's protest and continued rummaging. His hand closed around something at the bottom, and with a firm tug, he pulled out a thick book from beneath his clothes and supplies. He placed it carefully on the ground before the rock where the sage was perched. Though the sage's eyes remained closed, Laolys noticed the subtle way his posture shifted; there was no way he could have known what had been placed before him.

"I happen to have something that, I believe, is more valuable than gold. I know you have a love for knowledge, and you once made great waves in the academic world. I also know that you've been in isolation for the last twenty years. Well, many incredible discoveries have been made since then. They're in this book. It's yours for just one hour of lessons. One hour for one book."

The sage's eyes snapped open, locking onto the book with interest. Then, in a movement so quick it was almost a blur, he sprang from his perch, snatched up the book, and leaped back onto the rock. He resumed his former position, cradling the book tightly against his chest, his fingers gripping the edges like a predator protecting its kill.

"We have a deal." The sage's expression remained stern, but his eyes glowed with excitement. "A fair trade, considering how many decades—though I won't specify a number—are going into the hour of lessons I have in store for you."

"Then let's not waste any more time!" Laolys exhaled a deep sigh of relief, but his breath caught again as the sage immediately began speaking.

"Tell me what it means to be a man in power." The sage's voice carried as if he were addressing a large lecture hall. There was no introduction, no warning—just the sudden start of the lesson. For someone who lived isolated from society, he seemed unusually pressed for time.

Laolys blinked, caught off guard. He grasped for the answer that had been drilled into him during his political training. "It means taking responsibility for the welfare of all those governed."

"Tell me then, what if two men are at odds, both claiming ownership of the same property? How do you intervene in a matter that you have no knowledge of or business in?"

"Well... you set up a court of judgment."

"And what if the court you appoint doesn't know either man or the property?"

"Then they have each man state his case clearly, without interruption, and answer all ensuing questions."

"And what if one man is honest and the other a practiced liar?"

"Then they have to have witnesses."

The sage raised one eyebrow. "And if the liar brings forth false witnesses?"

"They have to have evidence!"

"And if there isn't any?"

"Then... neither man will lay claim to the property!"

"So, the state robs both men—one honest, the other a thief?"

Laolys threw his hands up. "But how could anyone be certain?"

"Why get involved at all?" The sage remained completely unmoved in his spot atop the rock.

"But if no one stops the criminal, society will become his slave!"

"Yet, in trying to stop one criminal, you can create a network of criminals, all working together to line their pockets."

Laolys stared at the sage, taken aback. "What do you mean?"

"Those who seek power often do it for control, not to serve. The moment you create a system to judge others, you open the door for people to take those seats of power—not to uphold justice, but to manipulate the system for their own gain."

"So what then? We do nothing? Just let criminals run free?" Laolys was starting to wonder if the sage actually had answers or if he just enjoyed making things difficult.

"Not exactly. It's about weighing the cost of action versus inaction. Failing to enforce consequences for things like violence or theft would make the world a much more dangerous place. That's why every government, no matter how different, has some kind of justice system. What I'm saying is, the moment you put a structure in place, you also create an opportunity for corruption. Balance has to be considered in everything, especially government."

"Even if corruption is inevitable, surely, having a government—flaws and all—is better than not having *any* government?"

"Aye. That's why most societies have governments."

"They'll never be perfect!"

The sage shrugged. "Nothing ever will be."

"So, we shouldn't aim for perfection?"

"We should always aim to improve, to seek harmony and balance. But know your limitations. Assume that whatever you create with good intentions will eventually be used for something else. Sometimes, in a flawed system, the best action is inaction, because trying to fix it could lead to even bigger problems."

Laolys felt a pang of frustration, but he couldn't deny there was truth in the sage's words. He had seen firsthand how power was abused; he had grown up under his father's shadow, watching it happen. Even if he managed to implement real, meaningful changes, there was no guarantee the next person in power wouldn't twist them into something harmful.

"But if governments can't help society, what can?"

The sage shrugged. "Who says society can be helped?"

Laolys took a deep breath, trying to slow down to process his thoughts clearly. He knew the sage wasn't some cynic who had given up on the world. If he really believed society was beyond saving, he wouldn't have spent his life teaching people how to live differently. He looked up at the man, his figure now a dark silhouette against the fading light in the sky, and asked, "You really think it can't be helped?"

"Not if it doesn't want the help or doesn't think it needs it."

Laolys glanced around at his surroundings—rocks, bushes, and endless sky. Humanity, however, was a sparse commodity. "With all due respect, sir... how can you claim to be so wise about society when you've lived apart from it for so long?"

The sage glared at him. "I'm wise about it because I'm removed. You, along with the rest of them don't know any different. You're blind on the matter. Distance grants clarity. I've found that, more often than not, it's best stay out of other people's affairs."

"And live as a hermit? Not everyone has the luxury!" Laolys's thoughts drifted to his family. A wave of guilt rushed over him as he imagined his parents' disappointment and his fiancée's confusion. If they knew where he was, they'd be devastated.

"The luxury is free to all!" The sage threw his arms out, startling a small flock of birds into flight. "Just walk far enough, and you'll see most of the problems you used to face don't matter anymore."

Laolys took a deep breath. "Sure, maybe up here I don't have to answer to them, but they're still worried about me. I have to return to them."

"Why?"

"Why? Well, they'd worry!"

"Don't they have feet too?"

"Of course they have feet!"

"Then, if they want to stop worrying, they can do the same—walk until they find peace."

Laolys shifted his stance, his sore muscles protesting. He fought to keep his composure, unwilling to let the sage see his frustration. "But everyone can't just live as hermits! Societies help people in a lot of ways!"

"Well then, it's a good thing people don't have to physically remove themselves from them to stay out of other people's affairs!"

The sage scowled and continued, "There are only two types of people who concern themselves with other people's business. The first type does so out of necessity because they depend on other people for survival. The second does so willingly, because they enjoy power and recognition. The second type always preys upon the first."

"But there's a third type!" Laolys argued. "Some people who help out of genuine kindness! They get involved in things all the time—not for power or necessity, but because they feel responsible for making the world a better place."

The sage shook his head. "There is no third type. If I asked you to name someone who fits this description, you wouldn't be able to. Think about it. If someone truly helps out of pure kindness—not for any other purpose than to help that specific person—their deeds remain unknown. And they're never really wrapped up in anyone's affairs unless they choose to be. People who make sacrifices for their reputation complain. People who make sacrifices because they want to? They don't complain at all. They don't see any burden."

"I see... you're saying they could exist, but most people don't know about them. They're invisible."

"That's right. The moment someone advertises their own generosity, it stops being true generosity. Real kindness doesn't need an audience; it's enough to simply know you helped."

"And you don't think people perform selfless acts?"

"No, some people do. But the moment kindness is advertised or leveraged for personal gain, it loses its meaning. It becomes a currency. That's what I saw in society before I left—people helping only when they stood to benefit. That's not morality. That's just the desire for good favor."

Laolys looked up at the sage, a bony old man with intense eyes and a scowl, still perched on his toes. He imagined that even in his younger years, society would've noticed he was something different. For that reason, his experience must have been more trying.

"But if people are really as selfish and immoral as you say they are, isn't that an argument for a stricter government? People need to be kept in check."

The sage's scowl deepened. "Quite the contrary, actually. Tell me, what kind of people do you think fight the hardest to claim those high authority positions?"

Laolys hesitated, thinking back on all the politicians he had encountered in his life—far too many. As a child, he had overheard countless private conversations between officials, enough to know that very few of them had what he would consider strong moral character. "People who are willing to step on others to get there, I suppose."

The sage nodded. "Correct. Only the morally corrupt seek that kind of authority. They will always end up in positions of power; it's inevitable. That's why the government should be restricted in its ability to create laws. It should, ideally, merely represent them."

"Merely represent them? But it has to enforce them too!"

The sage shook his head. "No, it wouldn't be fair. The citizens have to do that, too."

Laolys stared at him. "The citizens police themselves?"

"Yes."

"So if the government isn't writing the laws, and it isn't enforcing them, what is it doing? Just representing them?" Inside, Laolys's blood was boiling, but he tried to maintain a calm demeanor.

"Ideally, yes. A government's main role should be foreign diplomacy, protecting its people who self-organize."

"And for that, they'd need to keep and maintain troops."

"Only in emergencies!" The sage waved his arms dismissively. "Otherwise, they're just stockpiling an army with no purpose, draining resources in the process. And when a government has a standing army, it'll always find a use for it—one that benefits its own power, not its people. Citizens will defend their land when they believe it's worth defending. If a government serves them well, they'll fight for it without needing to be forced."

Laolys threw his hands up. "But if power is as corrupting as you say, why allow anyone to hold office at all? If the people who seek it are the most likely to abuse it, wouldn't it be better to do away with government entirely?"

"Because otherwise, the worst, most violent man will claim it. It's better to put someone in power with checks and balances than to leave the seat open for the strongest brute to seize. If you can convince him, too, that the only way to keep his power is to be liked, then he'll at least pretend to be honorable. That alone is better than unchecked tyranny."

The sage's eyes glinted as he studied Laolys, and his lips widened into a smile. "Your question makes me think... You're already a little different than you were a few minutes ago. Tell me again, what is it to be a man in power?"

Laolys blushed and cast his eyes toward the ground. "It means, I suppose, to accept responsibility only as it's called for."

The sage clapped his hands together. "That is the mark of a good man in power, if such a thing exists." He locked eyes with Laolys.

Laolys's heart pounded; he felt like the sage was peering straight into his soul.

"Now we're making progress," the sage continued. "It's time to get to business. Tell me, why do you want to better humanity?"

Laolys's breath caught in his throat. "Why wouldn't I?"

"Because it doesn't concern you."

"I say it does. It's in everyone's interest to better society."

The sage tilted his head. "That may be true, but that's not why people try to do it."

"Then why do they do it?"

"For recognition. To be remembered."

"I suppose that's true for many..."

"Almost all."

"But is that such a problem? If the end result is the progression of humanity, does it matter why people do it?"

The sage threw his arms out wildly. "But the result isn't the same! It's tainted! It's hardly a fraction of what it could be! You have no idea how much knowledge the human race has lost simply because people insisted the world had to be a certain way and feared how they might appear if they discovered it wasn't."

Laolys looked at the sage in fascination. "Are you saying people have discovered things—amazing things—and intentionally kept them secret out of fear of ridicule?"

"I'm saying they're too afraid to even be capable of making such discoveries."

BEGINNING

The sage studied him, a glint of interest in his eyes. Laolys turned his gaze toward the mountains, but he still couldn't shake the feeling of those piercing eyes locked onto him.

"I'm going to make you an offer. I will teach you my wisdom—secrets I have learned throughout the years. They won't bring you wealth, or power, or status, but they'll bring you peace. And, if you share them, they could even change the world."

Laolys froze, barely believing what he was hearing. His mind instantly flashed back to the night he heard his father shout, *If he convinces enough people with these truths, it will change the world!*

"I'm only asking for one thing in return." The sage's expression was stern, unreadable.

Laolys could barely bring the words to his lips. "What?"

"That when you descend this mountain with your knowledge intact, you share this wisdom with anyone who asks."

"That's it?" Laolys's jaw dropped open. "Well of course I accept the offer!"

"Listen to my words! I said you have to share these truths with *anyone* who asks. When you descend the mountain, people *will* ask."

Laolys let out a deep exhale. "Oh." His mind instantly flashed to his father asking him where he had been. That wouldn't be a pleasant conversation.

"It will cost you nearly everything, I'm afraid."

Laolys imagined once word got out about his journey, everyone he knew would ask. As a recently elected official, he was well-known. His heart sank. It *would* cost him nearly everything.

"They... will call me a madman."

"Aye. People always fight progress. Great innovators are rarely praised for their work. One day, these truths will become commonly accepted, but by then, both you and I will have long passed. You will never be recognized by name for your work, but by spreading the message, you will eventually change the world."

Laolys stared at the ground in front of him. The future scorn of his parents locked his knees into place.

"Is this an offer you're willing to accept?"

Laolys took a deep breath and turned his focus back to the sage. "How do I know you won't fill my head with nonsense? How do I know it will actually be helpful?"

"You have my word, that's it. My reputation brought you up here, your heart has to decide the rest. Is this what you want? Are you ready for it? Can you leave with this knowledge intact?"

Laolys's mind spun. It was all happening so fast. Though he had spent countless nights mulling over where this journey might lead, none of it had prepared him for this moment. Could he descend as a changed man? Could he live with himself if he walked away?

"I... have to share it?"

The sage nodded. "That's all I ask."

Laolys pictured his family, the contempt of the government he had been groomed to serve. Yet, the promise of real knowledge—knowledge so profound it had driven this man into hiding—lit a fire inside him. If the rumors were true, if the sage truly held the path to enlightenment, how could he turn away?

"I want to learn your secrets." He forced the words out before his doubts could stop him. "I need to. For the sake of humanity—for anyone who seeks a better path."

The sage didn't move. His piercing eyes stayed fixed on Laolys. "Why?"

Laolys took another breath, feeling the weight of his decision settle over him. "Because, despite your arguments, I believe that true wisdom can't be ignored. I need to learn what you have to teach—not just for myself, but for everyone willing to listen."

The sage gave a half-nod. "That'll do."

Laolys exhaled and his shoulders released tension he was unaware he was holding.

The sage looked toward the horizon, watching the sun dip below the valleys. "But there's much to be done first. Too much to be done. Too much time has already been wasted." Without another word, he leaped from the rock and almost instantaneously disappeared into the trees.

Laolys stood frozen, unsure if the sage's proposal had been a test, a trick, or a genuine offer of forbidden knowledge. He felt oddly exposed—stripped bare by the old man's scrutiny, only for him to vanish without explanation. A cool breeze brushed against his cheek, reminding him that he was alone again. The sage was the only other human on the mountain.

He sank down onto a nearby boulder and let out a long exhale. The sage's behavior was so bizarre, it bordered on madness; yet Laolys couldn't ignore the razor-sharp intellect behind those intense eyes. *Was I doing him a favor by accepting?* he wondered, or *did I just throw myself into a path of no return?* He glanced over his shoulder, half-expecting the sage to leap out from behind a tree and berate him for moping, but there was only silence.

His gaze drifted to the distant town, barely visible below. *They'll offer me little comfort when I return,* he thought. *If I return at all.* The idea sent an anxious tremor through his chest, reminding him of the night he'd first realized who might dwell on this mountain.

It had been a casual evening with friends, a few drinks shared in good humor, when someone excused himself for the restroom, saying he needed to "take a leak." Jeremy had laughed a little too loudly. "Don't say that around here," he'd teased, "or that man on the mountain might think you're after his mirror!"

Everyone else shrugged off the remark, but Laolys had felt a jolt of curiosity. "What man on the mountain?" he'd asked, heart thrumming with sudden hope.

Jeremy explained the rumor: there was a hermit who referred to his 'mirror' as a *portal*, a so-called "leak" into other dimensions. Most people considered it drunken legend. But the name—*the leak*—snapped Laolys to rapt attention. He could still recall how his father had railed about *"that leak who could undermine everything."*

Later that night, Jeremy confided that the hermit was more than a mad recluse; he was a fugitive from society who'd uncovered truths governments suppressed. "They say no one returns from the mountain sane, if they return at all," Jeremy had added, eyes flicking uneasily to Laolys, as though daring him to test the legend.

Now, as the last rays of sunlight smeared the sky with orange and purple, Laolys replayed Jeremy's words. He tried to ground himself by focusing on the forest's gentle rustle, but the memory of that conversation pulsed in his mind. *I had to come,* he reminded himself. *If I can't change a broken system, maybe this sage—the so-called leak—can show me how.*

A shiver ran through him as a brisk gust ruffled his clothes. The sage might have offered lessons, but that didn't mean he'd stick around to teach them. Perhaps he was gone for good, and Laolys was a fool, waiting for a man who was only interested in keeping his solitude.

Still, he felt an inexplicable sense of reassurance on the mountainside, amidst the towering pines. All around him, the forest darkened, and the sky began to sparkle with tiny twinkling stars. First, just a few arrived, then the trees and rocks around him turned into shadowy forms and more came to grace the sky. It was as if the curtain was closing on one great act of nature only to open a second act on another stage, offering a nonstop performance to any traveler who might decide to take a seat.

Not long into this second act, exhaustion overwhelmed his weary mind and body. He determined he could no longer stay awake waiting for the sage. If his fears of abandonment were correct, he would have to investigate in the morning. He permitted himself to close his eyes, and sleep overcame the young man almost immediately.

Illumination Beneath the Infinite Vault

Death

"Your birth was not a true beginning; your death is not a true end. The only result anyone has ever obtained with certainty in death is life, just as the only certainty one can claim to possess in life is death."

The words startled Laolys awake. Opening his eyes, he was met with an impenetrable pitch-black void. The darkness that surrounded him here was deeper and denser than anything he had ever experienced in his town. There, even in the dead of night, a faint sliver of light from some distant window or lantern always cut through the gloom. These tiny slivers accumulated down there like a second moon that never fully disappeared. But here, up on the mountain, everything felt more intense, and the darkness was no exception.

"E-Excuse me?" Laolys called out, his voice trembling slightly. He wondered if he was dreaming. Logic suggested that if the sage were truly nearby, there would be some sign of him—a flicker of light, perhaps a small fire illuminating a corner of this dark world.

"Your birth was not a true beginning; your death is not a true end. The only result anyone has ever obtained with certainty in death is life, just as the only certainty one can claim to possess in life is death," the sage's voice echoed, calm and unwavering, repeating the words exactly.

So it is the sage, Laolys thought as his heart rate spiked with anxiety. He had heard tales of the sage's bizarre habits, but none of the rumors had prepared him for the reality of interacting with him.

"Y-yes, but shouldn't we discuss this in the morning?"

"Now."

"But why?"

"The birds are my students in the morning."

Laolys blinked, struggling to make sense of the bizarre circumstances. The sage had mentioned having students earlier; did he mean the birds? A wave of doubt washed over Laolys, and he began to question his decision to come up here. Maybe the rumors were true, and the sage was simply mad. But it was too late to turn back now. He had to see this through, no matter how strange the lesson might be.

"You're starting our class now... in the middle of the night... so you can teach the birds in the morning?" Laolys asked slowly, hoping that speaking the absurdity out loud might somehow make it more comprehendible.

"Yes."

So the sage is mad, Laolys thought. There was no other explanation for such bizarre behavior. Still, what could he expect from a man who had lived in seclusion for the last two decades? No rumor, not even the ones praising his wisdom, had ever mentioned the sage being normal or particularly friendly. *Perhaps I should cut him some slack when it comes to social matters,* he mused, but his train of thought was quickly interrupted.

"No words? No thoughts? No arguments?" The sage seemed full of boundless energy. Laolys sensed the soft scrape of a stone to his right, then to his left. He couldn't be sure, but it felt as if the sage was jumping around the rocks surrounding him. He tried to shake the image from his mind; there was no way anyone could navigate such actions safely in the pitch darkness.

"No fire?" Laolys wiped the sleep from his eyes. The night was moonless, and everything before him was shrouded in mystery, no matter how badly he wished his eyes would adjust.

DEATH

"I don't want anything to detract from the lovely darkness in which we're indulging!"

Laolys sighed, reasoning that any questions regarding the sage's behavior were pointless. He decided to steer the conversation elsewhere. Recalling the sage's initial statement, he asked, "Why should I take your word on what happens to a soul after a body dies?"

"Why wouldn't you?"

"No one knows these things."

"I do."

"How can you say that?"

"I have died many times. I have lived many lives before this one." The sage's voice faded softly into the darkness.

"That you remember? Anyone would say a person's mad who says such things!" Laolys could feel his heart pound in his chest. The stress of the moment, compounded by sleep deprivation and the disorienting pitch-black night, was pushing him to his limits. He could feel himself barely holding it together.

"Didn't I warn you of exactly that?" The sage's voice seemed to materialize from one spot, now alarmingly close—just a foot in front of Laolys's face.

Laolys swallowed as nerves began to rise in his throat. "Yes, but how am I supposed to repeat your claims if I have no reason to believe them myself?" The weight of his decision made only hours earlier, to carry the sage's wisdom to the world, now felt heavy on his mind.

"Then tell them you have lived many lives and died many deaths."

"But I haven't."

"Indeed, you have."

"But I can't remember them."

"Then remember."

Laolys sighed. This wasn't going to be an easy undertaking. He had no idea what kind of truths the sage expected him to uncover, what would be asked of him next, or what consequences might follow if he failed to meet the sage's expectations. Still, he closed his eyes and attempted to remember, as directed. After only a brief pause, he opened his eyes and said, "I can't. I can't remember anything before this life."

"Sure, you can."

Laolys could still sense the sage right in front of him; the scent of his breath made the hairs in his nostrils stand on end. "But how?"

"First, you must believe that you can. Then, I will tell you how."

"But how can I believe that I can if I don't know how it's possible?"

"The method relies on whether you believe in your abilities."

"But nobody's supposed to have these abilities! I want to know how they can be obtained!" Laolys felt as though he were shouting his frustrations into the empty air, though the sage replied immediately.

"No one believes they can have such abilities, that's all. The method is simpler than you think. Try again."

Laolys exhaled and closed his eyes, though he could hardly see much with them open. He tried again to focus, letting his mind drift, while the sage remained silent. To his surprise, images began to flash through his mind—rocking a baby, the faint scent of lavender, the sound of gentle cooing. He let these visions play out for some time before pulling himself back to a wakeful state.

"Well?" the sage asked the moment Laolys opened his eyes.

"I don't know. I saw myself rocking a baby in a room full of people, but I've never even held a baby before."

"No, you've held a baby many times. You remember it now."

"But how can I trust this memory?"

"If you can *feel* it. It's more than a visual, it's filled with emotions. It seems tangible."

Laolys reflected on the vision. It was an all-encompassing experience, he felt the stuffiness of the room, the sweat of those around him, the baby clawing at his shirt, or her shirt in that case. The vision gave a strong impression of belonging to a female. Still, it all seemed too easy. "Is there anything else I should look for?"

"Look for things you couldn't have imagined, like technology you've never seen before, or customs that are completely unknown. Also, if you can verify through historical facts—death records and the like—you have good indications of a true, unfabricated experience."

Laolys nodded. He couldn't recall specifics from the vision but resolved to try again, knowing what to focus on, if he could even see anything more. A wave of unease rose in his chest as he remembered the promise he had made only hours earlier to share these teachings.

"But I can't just say I know all these things, people are going to think I'm mad!"

A silence followed, and the sage cleared his throat. "You came to learn from me, correct?"

"Y-yes." Laolys's heart raced. He had known this would be challenging, but he hadn't expected it to feel this insurmountable.

"Well, I'm telling you that life goes on after death and that you've lived many lives before this one. I've even shown you that you can access some of the memories. Your response is that you want more proof." He exhaled. "I'm starting to think you're being difficult on purpose."

The words jolted Laolys with a tinge of outrage. "What? Me? You think *I'm* being difficult?"

"Yes, quite frankly, I was beginning to suspect you wanted out of the deal. If you're no longer interested in my lessons, it's fine; you can leave."

Laolys felt his heart skip a beat. He wasn't ready to leave, he was just getting started. "No! Forgive me. I'm not trying to be difficult; I just..." He took a deep breath. "I need to understand these lessons. When I teach them to others, they're going to ask so many questions."

"I'm showing you how to find the information yourself, but you'll never be able to if you keep questioning your integrity."

"What? How am I questioning my integrity?"

"You don't believe your own memories, your own instincts. You doubt the information that comes to your mind as having any relevance, despite the fact that it arrived under focused intent. You feel the truth of the lesson, but you doubt you can teach it, so you, in turn, doubt me." The sage's tone held no anger nor any frivolity. Laolys sensed that he may be wearing on the sage's patience, a thought he hadn't considered until now.

"I'm sorry, but how could you possibly know that life continues after death?"

"Because energy can't be created or destroyed. You and I are both energy. We didn't arise from thin air or mere biological processes. Our consciousnesses have a history with memories that we can access."

Laolys's breath caught short. "But... what if that's just imagination? How are you so sure?"

"If I told you the answer now, you wouldn't believe me. Maybe, if you stick around, you'll have more details. For now, though, you'll just have to take my word for it."

"Just take your word for it?"

The sage sighed. "Yes, until you can verify the reality—I mean live it yourself—you'll have to take my word. If you listen, maybe you'll see it too. But that depends on whether you truly listen."

"Verify it?" Laolys's interest was piqued. "Have *you* verified it?"

"Aye. But you'll never see it for yourself unless you learn how to listen."

Laolys stared at the black world in front of him, reflecting on the idea of reincarnation. It wasn't a foreign concept; he had always sensed that life continued in some form after death. He had been raised in a monotheistic faith that emphasized one God and an eternal afterlife but had never fully believed it held all the answers.

"So, if there is a cycle, and not one life..." He paused. "What does it mean to escape it?"

"It means a complete shift in a spirit's resonance." The sage's breath brushed up against his nostrils, alerting him to his close proximity.

Laolys shifted uncomfortably.

"No more fear, anxiety, anger, greed, none of that," the sage continued. "All those pains have to be transcended. Once we do that, we're free to traverse the Cosmos, unchained to any single world. Until then though, you'll keep coming back to a body somewhere among billions of worlds and dimensions all over the multiverse."

"Billions?"

"Billions is an understatement, really. A single world has many parallel realities, each completely separate from the others. Then, if you consider the habitable planets in our universe alone, the number is in the quintillions. But that's just one universe, ours. The multiverse has a non-quantifiable number of universes. The number of places we could end up isn't infinite, but it's certainly more than billions."

"But why don't people have memories of them?"

"Different worlds might have very strange forms and customs. Different universes have different laws of physics. If we were to see some of these places..." The sage let loose a small, barely audible chuckle. "Well, some of them we wouldn't even know what we were looking at."

"Like what?"

"Try imagining a universe where everything is expanding and collapsing so frequently that all life forms are composed of a gel-like fluid."

Laolys envisioned a planet with only gel-like globs, separated from one another by thickness and color.

"Now," the sage continued, "imagine conducting commerce in that world."

Laolys laughed. "I can't!"

"Exactly. Your mind can't grasp it. It's too strange. But you could have lived in a world like that at some point. Back then, you would've understood that reality well and to catch a glimpse of your current one... Well, you'd have no idea what to make of it."

"I can't imagine!"

"If we had all our past life memories, we'd be overwhelmed. Too much information, too many perspectives—it'd be impossible to function. Each life has its own focus, its own lessons. We need that fresh start to really absorb what we're here to learn. But when we ascend, we're no longer tied to just one life, one place. We can move freely across the Cosmos."

"So... ascending is kind of like heaven, but in the Cosmos?"

The sage sighed. "Not like heaven. It's not eternal bliss. Honestly, I'd find that pretty boring after a while. The Cosmos isn't some paradise, it's just a vast existence without the physical limitations we have here. Picture endless worlds, some similar to this one, others completely alien. This place—this world—it's not perfect, but it's not hell either. Most people are decent enough, but some do horrible things. Life here has some predictability, but wild, unexpected things happen too. The spiritual realms? They're the same way. There's no telling what you'll run into."

Laolys listened closely, trying to commit every word to memory. He'd never heard life after death explained this way before. The idea of traveling between worlds as a spirit fascinated him. "Is it hard to navigate?"

"It's natural, like dreaming. I don't have all the answers for you yet, but I can tell you this—ancient religions all saw the afterlife as a journey, not just some final destination. The underworld was always dangerous. That's why so many traditions had people memorize prayers, and why families left offerings to help their loved ones navigate it. Nobody just died and woke up in paradise or torment, there were steps, trials. And those who earned a place near the gods? That wasn't just a reward. It came with responsibilities, expectations. They had to help maintain Cosmic balance. It was an honor, but it was also work."

"Maybe I should just stay here," Laolys joked. The sage's descriptions of the afterlife were overwhelming, especially in the pitch black.

"For a while! The good news is, you can't get there until you're ready, whether you're alive or dead."

"Then I won't worry," Laolys said, though his tone carried more sarcasm than he intended.

"Don't waste time worrying. Prepare, sure, but never worry. Worry just drains your energy. If the bad thing never happens, you worried for nothing. If it does happen, then you spent all that time making yourself miserable in advance."

"That's one way of looking at it!"

"It's the only way of looking at it if you actually want to enjoy the present moment—which, by the way, is all we ever really have."

"So from what you're saying, it sounds like life just keeps going. But what about people who do terrible things? Is there any kind of punishment?"

"There's an unavoidable moment of reflection after death," the sage began. "A spirit has to confront every major moment of its life—all of it, with absolute clarity. And it doesn't just see its actions; it sees the full effect of those actions rippling outward. If someone lived selfishly or hurt others, that moment can be excruciating. They have to face exactly how much damage they caused. Then, when they've finally reckoned with it, they take another vessel somewhere in the vast multiverse and try again—another lifetime, another chance to get it right."

"Do people usually do better the next go-around?"

"Ha!" The sage let out an emphatic burst of laughter, a sharp sound that seemed to arise from both his throat and nose at once. "Most people just repeat the same mistakes, life after life. They start fresh in a new body with no memory of their past lives or their time between them. But their spirit? That carries the same resonance they left their last life with. A bitter, angry person doesn't just wake up kind and enlightened in the next round."

"So, no growth happens between lives?"

"No, we can learn everything there, but we can't apply it. The only chance to work on our faults is here, now, while we're alive. And if you've been given enough awareness to seek ascension, seek it with everything you've got, before it's too late."

"But wouldn't it help if we could remember at least *some* things?" Laolys pressed.

"The spirit remembers differently. It's not like the brain; it doesn't store facts or dates. But it remembers feelings."

Out of the darkness, a hand tapped Laolys's chest. It was gentle, though, and he wasn't startled by it.

"This," the sage said, "is what we carry. It's your raw essence, before the world told you what to be."

Laolys thought about his spirit. What had he brought into this life? All he could remember was feeling afraid when he was younger, but that could have easily been tied to his upbringing. "I don't even know what that is."

"You think too much, that's all. The brain conflicts with the spirit. The spirit knows; the brain argues."

Laolys had no counterargument. His brain was always arguing, usually with itself. "But what about past mistakes? Is there any kind of karmic retribution in the next life? Do people become victims of their former crimes?"

THE YOUNG MAN AND THE SAGE

He imagined some kind of divine Cosmic judgment hall, where people were assigned their next life based on their past deeds. A greedy profiteer who exploited workers might return as an underpaid laborer. Someone who lived honorably but never ascended might be born into a secure and happy family.

"Nothing so organized," the sage said. "For nearly everyone, the next birth is completely random. We can't look at someone's life and assume it's a direct consequence of a former one. It doesn't work like that. There are too many souls, too many worlds and dimensions, too many variables involved. More often than not, when a soul is ready, it's swept into the next life without any say in the matter."

Laolys nodded. It made sense that things were more chaotic than he had imagined. "Some aren't random?"

"Some souls have advanced far enough to choose. This happens in the spirit world, and it's not usually about picking the most comfortable life, but the one that offers the best opportunity for ascension. The spirit is given the answers, then it's tossed into another life to wake up as a blank slate again."

"A continuous cycle..." Laolys mumbled. He wasn't sure whether he liked or disliked the idea, but it made sense.

"Until you rise to the next. Whether you know it or not, that's really your ultimate goal."

Laolys reflected on the lesson. The sage saw reincarnation with a sense of urgency. It wasn't just another turn on the wheel, it was something to transcend, to evolve past. This would be a hard sell to his people, who believed they had only one life and one chance at heaven.

"What you're saying makes sense to me," Laolys began cautiously, "but this won't go over well with my townspeople. They're firmly rooted in the belief that God, heaven, and hell are absolute truths that aren't up for debate."

The sage sighed, letting a brief silence settle between them before responding. "The idea that a soul's eternal fate is decided after just one lifetime... it's hard for me to wrap my head around. I've spent decades wandering through my own pasts, far removed from the world. Remind me how it goes again."

"The concept of eternal salvation or damnation?"

"Yes."

"Well..." Laolys's mind flashed to childhood memories of sitting in church. Though his family wasn't truly religious, they wanted to appear that way, and attended semi-regularly as he was growing up. "The idea is that this life is our one chance to prove our devotion to our creator. As long as we follow basic laws and remain faithful, we can enter heaven after death."

Silence stretched between them before the sage asked, "What if we don't hear the laws, or fail to understand the need for devotion?"

"Then, I suppose, we go to hell."

"And where do all the souls come from? The new ones, born with every life?"

"According to the theory, God makes them."

"Each time?"

"Yes."

Low, unintelligible murmurs escaped the sage, as if he were working through a complex calculation in his mind. Finally, he asked, "But afterward, there are all these souls who aren't going anywhere?"

"Well, I'm not exactly sure... only that they aren't recycled," Laolys admitted.

A few more moments of silence passed before the sage spoke again. "I'm just not following the math."

"I never really thought about the math behind it."

"According to the law of conservation of energy, energy can't be created or destroyed. Consciousness is energy; so is the soul. Where is consciousness generating from if it doesn't continue into another life after this one?"

"I suppose... God has infinite power," Laolys offered, struggling to articulate the finer details of his religion.

The sage grumbled softly. "No, reincarnation is the only mathematical plausibility. With or without divine interference, there's no room in my calculations for infinite creation."

"But God goes beyond the confines of math!" The words burst from Laolys's mouth before he realized the thought. It was impulse more than reason.

The sage sighed. "Even if we recognize everything as a creation, we have to accept that absolutely everything within that creation follows mathematical laws. Whether it was a divine plan or simply the only way life could organize in this universe, everything is governed by physical laws. So tell me, how does everything around us adhere to these laws, yet somehow we're exempt? That our souls are created for only one lifetime, one test, with eternity following death as the final exam?"

Laolys's mind raced. Until now, he had taken his beliefs for granted. It was what everyone he knew believed. No one had ever challenged it, and he had never thought to question it himself. But now, for the first time, he saw things differently. His heart skipped a beat as the realization hit him—*now he* would be the alternative.

Anxiety swelled through his body. The disorienting darkness, the sage's erratic way of teaching, and now this—imagining himself standing before the people, professing these radical ideas. It was overwhelming.

He took several deep breaths. The sage waited patiently as if he could read Laolys's internal struggle in the thick, blanketed darkness.

"But where would God fall into the concept of reincarnation?" Laolys finally asked.

"That's entirely up to the individual to decide. I can't dictate what another should believe."

"But you don't believe in God?"

"Not as they do, that's certain. I see the mathematical purity of nature, the significance of the smallest microbes, and the interconnectivity of every species in the ecosystem. To me, that's far more awe-inspiring than what they sing about in church. I also value unpredictability; the idea of an omnipotent deity with a preordained plan doesn't resonate with me."

"You don't fear you could be wrong?"

A soft chuckle escaped the sage. "If only you had lived my life, or knew my story, and believed it, you'd understand my certainty in this matter. There is organization in this universe, but that alone, to me, is not God."

"You don't think there's anything higher?"

"There are many, many beings who have advanced far beyond my level. The Cosmos is teeming with life. But I don't name anything as my god. Instead, I seek to unify my spirit with the planet and the Cosmos. For me, spiritual fluidity and unity are the paths toward those higher beings."

"Do you think there could be some truths in religion?" Laolys had, at times, found comfort in religious rituals during moments of distress. The idea of relinquishing all of that felt overwhelming, especially here in the dark woods, speaking with the sage, who was wise, yet undeniably mad.

"All religions have truth in them," the sage said. "That's why they resonate with people. They all carry seeds of real phenomena, divine inspiration, and spiritual insight. But they are all very human, too. Each religion is an attempt to understand spirituality from a human perspective. We can't avoid this. We shouldn't look to religion for infallible answers; not even the divine are infallible. Instead, we should find the truths that resonate with our spirit, always remembering that we, too, are constantly changing."

"Not even the divine are infallible?" Laolys repeated, surprised not only to hear the sage speak of divine beings but also to call them fallible.

"If there's one way to determine a truth, it's this: as above, so below. The macro mirrors the micro. Beings at every level of existence are learning, growing, and evolving. This is true in the lower cycles, and it's true in the higher cycles—on and on until infinity. When we ascend, we're not done learning. Instead, we're exploring entirely new terrain, with entirely new ways to make mistakes. The multiverse holds infinite possibilities. I'd say the only thing outside the realm of possibility is perfection."

Laolys swallowed as a lump formed in his throat. He liked the idea that life went on after death, but he also found comfort in the notion of a simple afterlife—a place where he could reunite with loved ones, where the trials of the material world would finally ease. "Is it possible to see our loved ones after death?"

"In between lives lies a realm of timelessness. There is no set period for a spirit to reincarnate; they do so when they're ready. It's possible to see some spirits who have passed on, particularly those still clinging to their former lives."

"But not in heaven," Laolys mumbled.

"Not as many imagine it. The spiritual realms are vast, varied, and far more interesting than I believe heaven—as most conceive it—could be. Eternal bliss isn't realistic, but I don't desire it anymore. I find great joy in overcoming challenges. Sisyphus was not so cursed; from another perspective, he was blessed to always have a challenge before him. To work towards something is to delight the spirit."

"Sisyphus?" Laolys repeated, unfamiliar with the name.

"From the Greek mythos—he was an evil tyrant who faced strict punishment in the underworld after his death. His sentence was to push a large boulder to the top of a steep hill. But every time it neared the top, it was fated to roll back down again. So, for eternity, he always has the same problem before him: getting the boulder to the top of the hill."

"Aren't you being a bit hypocritical?" Laolys began hesitantly. "Why retreat to the woods if not to escape the ills of humanity? I mean, in this very action, aren't you running from challenges?"

"I face a good number of challenges simply in survival out here. But I never claimed to be above others. I know the struggles of my fellow men because I share in them."

Laolys's heart rate quickened. "Y-yes, that's true. You've never boasted about yourself. I have no idea what struggles you've faced."

"Nor have you asked."

"Forgive me!" Laolys felt his face flush with embarrassment. He was grateful, now, for the cover of darkness.

"There's no need for forgiveness." The sage's tone was gentle, perhaps even slightly amused. "I offered you a deal, and you accepted. Nowhere in that offer did I suggest a pretense of friendship."

Though the sage's voice was untroubled, the fact that Laolys couldn't see his expression made him worry he had committed a terrible social blunder. "But I should ask out of kindness, not out of pretense!"

"Do you remember what I said when you first told me where you came from?"

"You asked me to leave, saying you owed no taxes. But you misunderstood me!" Laolys's heart raced as he silently pleaded for the sage to overlook his social blunders.

"I misunderstood nothing; I simply didn't care to understand."

"But now you know so much more about me, and I still know nothing about you!"

"That's only because it's in my interest to teach you, and you won't stop talking!" The sage's voice carried a trace of amusement; Laolys could tell he was smiling.

"But it would still be kind of me to ask about you."

"Do you really care that much about knowing me?"

"I—well, not if you don't want to share." Laolys had no idea how to respond.

"Good, because I find it quite laborious to talk about myself when people are inclined to hear it. It is even more bothersome when they're not so inclined, yet still, I must pretend that they are. If it's fine with you, I'd like to leave societal pressures at the bottom of the mountain with your countrymen."

"It is more than fine with me," Laolys said, though something in the air shifted. The space around him felt calmer, emptier. He suspected the sage had left, though there had been no sound of his departure, no farewell. Still, it would be in character for how he had presented himself so far.

Laolys waited for several minutes, then leaned back against a rock and shut his eyes. Though the lesson had raised many life-changing questions, his mind was too exhausted to process them now. His body ached from the week-long climb up rugged terrain, and soon, he drifted into a light, troubled sleep.

He awoke the following morning to the sound of the birds in full chorus. Their music filled the surrounding air like a symphony, some strange orchestra that had a rhythm only to them. The trees were host to hundreds of them by the sound of it, and there were no competing noises to detract from their songs. It was as if every ear in the forest leaned in to listen to their daily hymns to nature. The mountain stood still in serene silence as the birds pierced the atmosphere with sweet vibrations.

The sage was nowhere in sight. Laolys smiled, imagining him perched somewhere in the trees instructing the birds on the matters of life, death, and enlightenment. He briefly debated whether to stay put or search for his elusive teacher. He glanced around, noting the steep pitch of the mountainside. The rocks offered a modestly flat space to sit, but he still felt exposed to the elements. A sharp drop-off only a few yards away kept his nerves on edge. He had already pushed himself beyond his comfort zone during this climb, but he wasn't prepared to wait indefinitely in such uneasy proximity to a deadly fall—especially for a sage who might never return.

He stood up and gathered his belongings. If the instructions he had been given to find the sage were correct, it was only a little further up the mountain until the land would flatten into a small valley with a small grove of trees. Amidst those trees, he was told, the sage had constructed a tiny hut he called home. This would not only be a safer place to rest but also his best bet of finding his missing instructor.

As he began to pick his way through the rocky landscape, his muscles complained obnoxiously. Grunting, he lifted himself from rock to rock, foothold to foothold. Curiously, his largest concern was not the credibility of the sage, who may or may not be completely mad, it was his own aptitude for the task before him.

He took a deep breath of the mountain air. It had a serenity he had never felt before. He had never been this far removed from other people. Whenever he had been alone in the past, someone else was always just around the corner. Here, it was just him. The sage was somewhere unknown, and he had a way of making his whereabouts invisible until he was right there, staring you in the face. He seemed to blend into the landscape, becoming one with it.

Fortunately, the directions proved to be accurate. After a brief but steep climb, the terrain transitioned to a gentle incline before flattening out entirely into a valley. Nestled at the far end of the valley was a small grove of trees. Beyond the trees, the mountain rose sharply again. Adjacent to the grove was a steep drop-off, creating a small, wooded sanctuary in an otherwise nearly impassable mountain. Laolys continued toward the trees and there, nestled among them, he discovered the legendary hut—the tiny one-roomed home the sage had handcrafted.

The word *hut* was not doing the structure a disservice. From the outside, the structure resembled little more than a make-shift shed. It was not designed to impress. It was not designed for anything more than a small reprieve from inclement weather. It looked like an afterthought of the sage, rather than his only home for the last 20 years. It was put together without any acknowledgment to form or symmetry. Logs of all sorts and shapes were stuck together with mud and sap, and only a few precious nails poked out of corners, locking the logs into place without concern for appearances.

Laolys knocked on the door and stayed silent, listening. The stillness of the air assured him there were no other humans for miles, if that. He then unfastened the latch on the door and shoved it open. The door responded with a loud creak, and he was bombarded with a cloud of dust and dirt as the door rattled the logs of the hut upon opening.

Stepping inside, he felt as if he were entering a musty storage room rather than someone's home. Jars, boxes, bags, books, and small odds and ends overwhelmed the tiny room. Only one corner hosted a small livable area with a nest of bedding. The rest was populated by belongings stacked without clear organization or respect for structure. Pots and pans, clearly dirty, were strewn about the area. Only a couple looked to be used for their intended purpose. Some held dead plants and herbs, others held odd assortments of collections, like tiny army figurines and thread spools with the thread long missing. Laolys was surprised by how many things the sage had accumulated so high on the mountainside. But, considering that this was what the man had left after a long lifetime on this planet and two decades as a fugitive from society, it seemed much more sparing.

"Hello?" he spoke to no one, out of practiced courtesy, as he stepped into the small room. He knew the sage wasn't here, and he felt a twinge of guilt looking through his things in his absence. Still, his curiosity was insurmountable. The sage was so far removed from anyone he had ever encountered; he had to understand him better.

I suppose a bookshelf isn't a commodity the sage feels the need for in his soli-

tude, he thought as he peered at the titles the sage kept near his bed. The Odyssey, Plato's Republic, and The Meditations of Marcus Aurelius sat stacked on top of a few unrecognizable books. Lifting the top ones, he saw the name Paracelsus printed on two of the underlying books. The last one seemed to be missing an author's name. As he flipped through it, he got the impression it was only a manuscript. The pages felt like stiff vellum and looked yellow with age and exposure to the elements. It was full of diagrams that made little sense to him, being unversed in the symbols of Alchemy.

He placed the books back as he found them and continued to scan the room. History books of countries no longer in operation seemed to be a theme the sage liked to collect. He also had two books on geometry, three regarding herbal medical remedies, countless books by famous and obscure philosophers, and a book that focused only on counting systems used throughout world history. Amongst all of these, classic fictional works populated the room as though they were old friends shining kind eyes between the less friendly glares of the more daunting reads.

What kind of life leads to this conclusion? Laolys wondered as he exited the hut. What cruel inflictions did society bear upon the sage to lead a highly educated man to seek solitude in nature for the remainder of his life?

Perhaps I was not kind enough to him. Laolys reflected on his interactions with the sage so far. He was so thrown off by the sage's strange behavior that he had forgotten the many kindnesses he habitually bestowed upon others.

Vowing to make a conscious effort to show more care towards the sage, he peered around the woods for any sign of his new friend. The landscape showed no sign of disturbance that any other person was or had been near in some time, but would there be any? The sage blended seamlessly into the environment. He seemed to arise and disappear as if ripping the seam of the earth itself, so akin was he to his surroundings.

Should I go back to the rocks where we met or stay here? Laolys wondered. He figured that going back to the rocks would give the sage every chance to avoid him if he so chose. Staying here, the sage could avoid him for some time, but eventually, he would have to return to his home. *I suppose I'll stay here*, he thought, though he wasn't sure the sage was avoiding him at all.

The day wore on without incident as Laolys watched it pass from outside the hut. As the sun neared the horizon, he began to consider his initial fear that he had been abandoned with more weight.

Soon, however, a familiar form gave rise to a shadow in front of the setting sun, and Laolys knew it was the sage.

"I suppose nothing in the universe remains fixed in position. I should know better than to expect a bipedal creature to perform such a miracle!" he shouted as he approached Laolys. He was walking quickly, clearly bothered.

Laolys smiled. "I awoke and went looking for you."

"Not a wise decision out here. You could have gotten lost, you could have gotten eaten, or you could have turned up in a number of alternate dimensions!"

"What?"

"Not my concern anymore now that I've laid eyes on you. But from here on out, you stay put, okay?"

"Yes, sir, my apologies. I'm sorry if I made you worry."

"You can spare the formalities out here; waste of breath." The sage stood in front of Laolys, breathing heavily and staring at him with a caring expression undercut with irritation.

Laolys let loose a sigh of relief, grateful his instructor had returned. "As you wish."

The Scales of Judgment and the Speaking Flame

Illusions

"This world is the illusory one. You are currently asleep. Very few ever wake up to this fact until their death."

The sage's voice boomed across the clearing, making Laolys flinch. He stood just a few paces away from Laolys, his lean frame backlit by the late afternoon sun. A faint breeze rustled the pine needles overhead, carrying the echo of his words through the trees.

Without warning, the sage sat down before Laolys, leaning forward with wide, unblinking eyes. His intensity made Laolys's stomach twist with unease. While he was grateful this lesson would take place in the daylight, he couldn't help but find the sage's intense eye contact a bit unnerving.

"What do you mean? Do I awaken when I sleep?" Laolys averted his eyes to the mountainside.

"No, you're sleeping, of course. But, while you're dreaming you're more receptive, so in a way you may be more awake when you're asleep."

"What do you mean?"

"When you dream, your normal consciousness is dormant. This

allows you to access parts of your consciousness that are closed off during waking hours."

Laolys stared back at the sage, puzzled. "But dreaming isn't awakening?"

"Dreams are a window into your consciousness, not a door. They might give you insight, sure, but that's not the same as waking up. To awaken is to see the illusions for what they are, illusions. It's seeing that everything's the way it is only because that's how we perceive it. When we dream, we can see things differently than when we're awake. We might catch flashes of the truth, but it's not awakening."

Laolys reflected on the lesson so far. It suggested that the world was full of illusions that didn't become apparent until after death. He felt trapped. "So I don't wake up until I die?"

The sage shook his head. "No, ideally, you wake up *before* then. But you could also carry many illusions through death, many do."

"So not even death brings awakening?"

The sage shrugged. "Not every spirit's ready for awakening, so they hold onto illusions, even after death."

Laolys stared at the sage, astonished. If not even death provided answers, what kind of illusions was the sage referring to? "Can you give me an example of an illusion?"

"Money."

"How is money an illusion?"

"Money only works because we all agree it has value. We trust that whatever business we take it to will respect that value, so everyone works to earn these coins. But tell me, what if a business suddenly decides that a coin has no value, or double the value?"

"They'll go out of business!" Laolys exclaimed.

"Okay, but what if *every* business in the province decides that every coin suddenly has no value, or double the value?"

"Then... everyone would have to either find a new currency or adjust to the new value."

"Correct." The sage smiled. "Now, how can something suddenly change its value overnight or become meaningless if it's not an illusion?"

Laolys looked down at his empty hands, thinking of the coins that filled his father's study. "I suppose the value of coin is only as strong as people believe it to be." He glanced back at the sage. "What else is an illusion?"

"Political power." The sage eyed Laolys with a mischievous grin. "You won your seat by popular vote, but what would happen if the people collectively decided to stop recognizing your authority?"

Laolys fought an instinctual flash of anxiety. He could almost feel the phantom weight of official documents in his arms. "But there's protocol..."

The sage shrugged. "Doesn't matter. Let's say they burned all government documents, eradicated everything."

"Then that would be a riot, or a coup, and no government official would have any power!"

"Exactly. The illusion of government would be gone. And what about you, today, in a country that doesn't know the name of your government?"

"Then... I suppose my power would have no sway there," Laolys mumbled.

"That's right!" The sage clapped his hands together once, startling a few birds into flight. "Political power only matters to the people who believe in the illusion of that government. Take that recognition away, there is no power."

Laolys felt disoriented. His entire life had been centered around one thing: get and maintain political power. If power were merely an illusion, his life's work—his family's work—suddenly made no sense. "But people *do* recognize it, so it has to be more than an illusion."

"Many people agree on the illusion, so it stands. The world runs on illusions. That doesn't make them any less illusionary."

Laolys shook his head, trying to grapple with the lesson. "What else is an illusion?"

The sage sat still, gazing at Laolys with an intense glare that made him shift uncomfortably. "Why did you come to learn from me?"

Caught off guard, Laolys felt a jolt of nerves. He dropped his gaze to the ground. "I... I heard you had incredible truths. Some even said that your wisdom could change the world."

"That's an illusion, too." The sage gestured to his surroundings.

THE YOUNG MAN AND THE SAGE

"I'm a man who built a hut on a mountain so that people would leave me alone. I left society twenty years ago and haven't looked back. Now, does that sound like a man who has all the answers to you?"

Laolys felt his insides squirming with anxiety. "I—well, I think there's much wisdom in what you've taught so far. Maybe not all the answers, but... you seem to have many!"

The sage nodded. "So there's truth to the illusion, but it's still an illusion."

"There can be truth to an illusion?"

"There are truths to all illusions. Did you know that two people can see the same event and have two completely different conclusions of it? That is, see two different illusions, and they both would have a truth of the event?"

Laolys leaned in. "Can you give an example?"

"Well, take this lesson right now. I could place another student next to you, and chances are, they'd walk away with a completely different takeaway on this moment. Chances are, the other student would only see a fugitive and a madman... and they'd be right."

"But you are more than those things!" Laolys exclaimed, forgetting himself. "I mean, you aren't a madman."

"I'm both of those things. There's truth to that illusion as well." The sage caught himself mid-smile. "But sometimes madness and brilliance walk hand in hand. You see the brilliance; they only see the madness. There's a reason I put myself all the way up here. It wasn't easy. I find that only the ones who see the brilliance make the climb."

"But if there's truth to every illusion, is anything merely an illusion?"

"Nothing is *merely* an illusion. Any phenomenon is an infinite number of illusions at once, and at the same time, its true self. Quite impressive, actually."

"Very impressive," Laolys said, though the idea still felt like a distant dream. It sounded wonderful, but without any idea how to apply it, it remained abstract. "How do I start seeing things as illusions? How do I awaken?"

"Shift your perspective, as often as you can. Take any event and challenge yourself to see how many different perspectives you can view it from. Find value in things that seem meaningless and see the meaninglessness in things you've placed great value. Push yourself past your limits, safely, until you realize every boundary you thought existed is just an illusion. Prove to yourself that you can do things you once thought you couldn't—or wouldn't. You are a fluid spiritual being."

Laolys thought of all the boundaries he had already broken just to climb this mountain. Now, when he descended, he would have to break even more each time someone asked him about his journey. "It's... a little terrifying."

"That's because you're still holding on to illusions that keep you afraid. You still see power, success, and status as indicators of a person's worth. That's how your parents see the world, and how you were raised to see it. But you're already starting to break free. Otherwise, you wouldn't be up here. If you keep clinging to these illusions after you leave, your life will be much harder than it needs to be. The sooner you realize that approval and praise are just as meaningless as criticism, the happier you'll be."

Laolys's shoulders dropped. He'd been trained his entire life on gaining approval as a political figure. If praise and criticism were meaningless, what exactly had he been working towards? His mind flashed to a future vision of himself, teaching the sage's wisdom to people who scorned him. Anywhere he went, he would likely be recognized and shunned.

"It's hard not to listen to people when they're shouting their disapproval at you. Public figures don't get the discretion of etiquette afforded to everyone else."

The sage's eyes softened. "If that's the case... listen to them. Hear the truth in their illusion. Everyone has some truth in the way they view the world, even if it's only a spec of the entire view. Then, see how each and every illusion is absolutely meaningless. The only ones that matter are the ones you choose. That's waking up."

Laolys stared at the ground in front of him, reflecting on the lesson. It was about seeing illusions for what they were—and in doing so, freeing oneself from their hold entirely. It required a constant shift in perspective, a conscious mastery of perception. And through that, by choosing to see the beauty in things, unbothered by the fear that came from faulty illusions, he could at last know inner peace.

He turned to the sage with a glint of awe. To the world, he was a madman, but he had found a way to delight in that illusion. "So, you choose many of the illusions you see now?"

"Indeed... but that's just a fancy way of saying that I see the possibilities in things and pick the one most to my liking."

"Didn't that interfere with other people's way of seeing things? Did your perspective ever cause problems when you lived in society?"

"Actually, yes, in a way." The sage's gaze turned distant as he stared at the landscape. His usually vibrant eyes appeared glazed, detached from the present.

"I, um, didn't mean to pry." Laolys blushed. "I'm sorry if my question was out of line. I won't ask about your past if you don't want to speak of it."

The sage's focus snapped back to the present and his usual brightness returned to his eyes. "Don't apologize. Curiosity is natural. You'd hardly be human if you didn't wonder about me. But digging into old history doesn't always give us the clearest understanding of how things are today."

"Our past actions shaped us into who we are now."

The sage drew his hand to his chin. "You know, I thought the same thing until I saw the other timelines. Then I saw how many different outcomes could arise from the same event all altered by my reactions. I watched all sorts of scenarios play out. Then I realized that we can blame our defects of character on any number of things, but in most cases, it has nothing to do with the external. That's when I finally realized how to free myself from myself."

Laolys stared back at the sage blankly. "Other timelines?"

The sage's brows twisted upward in confusion. "Yes, the other timelines. There are many, many timelines."

"Timelines of what? Right now?"

"Of anything."

"Well, where are they? What makes them different?"

The sage leaned back. "Well, they exist in parallel realities. They're happening right now, just as they happened in the past, and will continue in the future. Usually, they branch off at major decisions, but even the smallest choices can create a split."

Laolys's mind raced through the biggest decisions of his life. He imagined all the terrible outcomes that could have resulted if he had chosen differently. "So... there are other timelines playing out right now? Other versions of me making different choices?"

"An inconceivably large number of them, yes."

Laolys's breath caught short. "How... how does that even work?"

The sage gestured toward a narrow trail winding through the distance. "Imagine you're standing at a crossroads. You have four options: left, right, forward, or turning back. Each choice leads you down a different path, creating a unique chain of events. You can only pick one, but the others still exist. They continue without you."

"They just go on?"

"Aye. But you have to pick one or else you'll just stay put."

"But where do they lead?"

"Let's say left takes you to a new city, straight leads to a market, and right takes you into a forest." The sage locked eyes with Laolys. "So, what'll it be?"

Laolys's heart rate spiked, even though he knew it was entirely hypothetical. "Uh—left!"

The sage grinned. "Are you sure about that?"

Laolys hesitated, suddenly second-guessing himself. "Well, I suppose so. It's just a thought experiment, after all."

"Left it is. But the other three choices don't just disappear. They still unfold, just not for you. They exist somewhere, whether as parallel realities, thought forms, or unrealized potential. Some paths become actual worlds, running alongside this one, while others remain ideas, mere potential."

Laolys's mind spun. He couldn't help but envision all the terrible things he'd avoided over the course of his life, and how things could have turned out if he had chosen differently. "So... do our choices even matter? If every option plays out somewhere, then even if I choose wisely, the bad choice still happens in another reality."

The sage cast him a sharp glare. "If you look into those parallel timelines, you'll see *exactly* how much our choices shape reality."

Laolys stared at the mountainside, trying to ground himself. He didn't want to imagine how else things could have been. He was already too busy worrying about his future. "They really continue?"

The sage's eyes softened as he looked at his student. Somehow, he seemed to understand his struggle. "So do you want to know what happens?"

"Hmm?"

"You chose left. Don't you want to know what happens?"

Laolys shrugged. "I suppose."

"You arrive in an unfamiliar town and stop outside a closed shop. When you ask a man standing nearby why it's shut down. He tells you he used to own it but lost everything due to a series of unexpected misfortunes. His story teaches you about the struggle of material pursuits, the cycles of hope and loss, and the need to sometimes rethink your values.

"As you listen, you reflect on your own life—your battle to succeed in politics when your heart desires something else. You and this man trade stories about your family struggles. Your situations are different, but there's common ground. He gives you a rare perspective on your father, which helps you to forgive him for some of his actions.

"But the biggest change in this timeline isn't for you." The sage locked eyes with him. "Your decision to stop and listen—to ask questions, to value his experience—creates an echo. I see him wandering through the other timelines. He passes you, notices you... and then keeps going."

Laolys felt a strange mix of nervousness and excitement. "Is he looking for me?"

"He doesn't know to look for you. He doesn't even know who you are. But when we profoundly affect someone, our timelines connect in ways we don't always understand. That connection vibrates through the others."

"So... he doesn't recognize me, but he still notices me?"

The sage nodded. "Just for a second. It's rarely something the conscious mind catches. It's a pull from the subconscious."

"Just because I talked to him?"

"You changed the course of his life. Why would you assume you had any less of an impact on him than he did on you?"

Laolys hesitated, reflecting on the scenario again. "I guess that makes sense. I just never really thought of myself as someone who could influence another person like that. I never gave myself that kind of importance."

"Yes, much of what we do can get lost in the sea of normalcy if we remain unengaged, complacent. But in that moment, you were neither. Acts of kindness, meaningful connections—they travel far. Would you like to hear what became of the stranger?"

Laolys straightened. "Yes, of course."

"He was in a dark place. His family had shut him out emotionally, and he had lost his livelihood. He was looking for reasons to end his life. Your conversation didn't pull him out of depression, but it made him start searching for reasons to live instead."

Laolys's heart skipped a beat. "It really went that far?"

The sage nodded. "That's why, in the other timelines, his unconscious mind is looking for you. His conscious mind doesn't understand it, so the thought never reaches full awareness. But in all three alternate timelines, he walks by you on the street, notices you for a brief second... then never thinks about you again."

"I'm glad I chose that timeline!"

The sage smirked. "Your fixation on illusion and imagination is either a great blessing or a great curse... depending on how you use it."

"What do you mean?" Laolys suddenly felt embarrassed for having gotten so caught up in his imaginary self's success.

"Well, up until now, you've mostly been using your mind against yourself, imagining all sorts of worst-case scenarios. But under the right mindset and guidance, you could create incredible things."

"You mean like magic?"

"I mean, you could live a happy, peaceful life and positively impact the lives of many others. You just have to imagine it for yourself, vividly and often enough that you actually start living it." The sage chuckled softly and shrugged. "*Some* might call that magic."

Laolys reflected on the lesson. The sage had introduced so many new concepts that it would take time for them to sink in. The concept of alternate timelines still baffled him. "Is time an illusion?"

"Time is real—measurable, inextricably linked to space. In our three-dimensional awareness, it isn't an illusion. But when we transcend to higher planes of consciousness, we transcend both space and time. We do this when we dream, when we astrally travel in meditation, and, of course, when we leave this plane in death. So, like everything else, time is both real... and an illusion."

"Three dimensions? I thought time was the fourth dimension."

The sage shook his head. "Maybe in some systems, but time is linked to *every* spatial dimension. The first two don't exist outside of time; they flow right along with it. Same with the higher spatial dimensions—time touches every aspect of the material realms."

"So... we can't escape it."

"Not until we transcend the material realms entirely. That only happens after death."

Laolys stared at the mountainside. He didn't want to think about death. Turning back to the sage, he asked, "Can you see the other timelines of yourself right now?"

The sage gave a single nod. "I can."

Laolys stared at the sage, wide-eyed, waiting for him to continue. When it became clear the sage wasn't going to elaborate unprompted, he asked, "What kind of things do you see?"

"Right now?" The sage paused. "I see myself dead in a field after a bear attack. I also see myself eating berries. In another, I'm riding a mule—no idea where I got it. And then there's one where I've sprouted a large fin on my back. Not all of these are realistic in this world."

Laolys blinked, trying to process the strange images. "You see all this happening right now?"

"Only when I try to, and only in quick glimpses."

"Can you see the future?"

"I can, but it's just a vast array of possibilities. There are so many that predicting the future is nearly impossible. I don't even see all of them. I can narrow it down by ignoring the ones that don't apply to this universe, but in my line of work... Well, there are far fewer I can rule out than for your average person."

"So you can see the future, but you can't predict it," Laolys noted.

"Exactly. I'm often surprised by what manifests, even though I already know the possibilities."

"Can you see other people's future timelines?"

"Certainly." The sage fell silent, his gaze fixed on the mountainside.

"Well, can you see mine?" Laolys's voice was tinged with both tension and excitement. If the sage's claims were true, it was astonishing. Even if they weren't, he was eager to hear what he might envision.

The sage turned his eyes to Laolys, studying him with an intensity that seemed to stretch endlessly, then abruptly looked away. "No. Not a good idea."

"What? Why? What did you see?"

"Possibilities. That's all they are right now. But if I tell them to you, they'll get logged into your mind and turn into probabilities. Your mind is too permeable. The second you lock onto a future vision of yourself—especially one you fear—it becomes a very real expectation."

"What? How?" Laolys eyed the sage suspiciously. Was he avoiding the question? Maybe even lying about his ability to see the future?

"Your mind has far more power to manifest reality than you give it credit for. Everything—your health, your misfortunes, even your general disposition—are manifestations of your expectations. We get what we believe we deserve, and most people don't believe very good things about themselves. If we fear we'll hurt someone, we often do. If we believe we won't be good at something, we fail right away. If I tell you a future timeline, you might turn it into your destiny."

"My destiny?" Laolys repeated, old fables surfacing in his mind.

"Yes. Destiny is an illusion. We manifest what we truly believe will happen. Your mind is responsible for the reality you live in. It filters everything you see, only allowing in what it believes you need to pay attention to. And what do our brains fixate on? Danger. Fear. If you live in fear, you'll constantly find proof that it's justified, and people can stay trapped in that cycle forever. If I told you this particular future, I might as well be sending you straight to the asylum."

Laolys's breath caught in his throat. "Is it that bad?"

The sage grimaced.

Laolys couldn't help himself. His anxieties about the future were too overwhelming. "Oh, please, just tell me."

The sage let out a long, weary sigh. "Well, don't say I didn't warn you." He closed his eyes, his expression settling into deep concentration. A minute passed in silence before he opened them again and began to speak.

"When you leave here, you return to your hometown and haven't the slightest clue how to reintegrate. The world that once bored you now astonishes and baffles you. This becomes such a disability that you can't even leave your house. Your family sees you as confused—crazy, even. Soon, you find yourself alone, unemployed, and with no prospects, a man in a poor position indeed!

"You remember how I instructed the birds during your studies here, so you leave your family and build a new home in the trees. You develop an innovative method for using birds as message carriers, but no one will listen long enough to let you demonstrate. Eventually, you convince one person to look past your reputation and see the value in your skill. However, because you've lost all social ability when it comes to people, you're completely incapable of teaching your methods to anyone else.

"Just as you're about to give up, you see a beautiful woman feeding birds on the street. You fall in love instantly. You send her love letters via your birds. She confesses her admiration for her mysterious admirer and agrees to meet. But the second she lays eyes on you, she recognizes you—calls you a heretic and a coward, a man who shirked his political duty. She leaves you heartbroken, worse than before.

"And then!" The sage leaped up, eyes sparkling with a mischievous glint. "Your psyche fractures into two! One part regresses to the consciousness of your childhood. The other..." He flapped his arms wildly and began running in circles. "Believes you *are* your carrier bird!"

Laolys burst into laughter as the sage ran past, slapping him on the back while flailing his arms. "That can't be real, can it?" he asked, his laughter fading as the sage sat back down beside him.

"Somewhere, in some universe, it may happen." The sage resumed his calm demeanor, gazing at the mountainside with a serene smile.

"There are many other possibilities though, right?"

The sage shrugged. "There are many timelines where you don't make it that far. This mountain is no stranger to predators. In many timelines, you end your life here."

"What?!"

"Oh relax." The sage chuckled softly. "You know, I see myself dead every day out here. I've managed alright in this timeline."

"How does that not bother you?" Laolys stared at him, baffled.

The sage tilted his head. "Why should it?"

"It's your *death*! Most people are terrified of death!"

"That's like being afraid of going to sleep. Or eating!" the sage replied, amused.

"I'm terrified of dying. How can you say you aren't?"

"Because death is an illusion. Nothing really dies, it just... moves on. We say people are dead because they don't come back, we can't see them anymore, but they're alive somewhere else. It's just a transition."

Laolys shook his head. "I understand the concept, but the end of the body is so real... and so final. How can it be an illusion?"

The sage bent down and picked up a fallen leaf, turning it over in his fingers. "Look at this leaf. It's left the tree, never to return. But does it just *vanish*?" He held it up for Laolys to see before letting it drop. "No. It decays, it becomes part of the earth, nourishing the soil, feeding the roots. Eventually, it helps give rise to new life. Death is just part of the cycle—it's not an end. The leaf lives on in another form. In time, it even returns to the tree."

Laolys watched the leaf settle among the others on the forest floor. "So... death is just part of the cycle, like waking and sleeping?"

"Exactly. Physical death is a transition, not an ending." The sage dusted his hands off. "People fear death because they think this life, this body, is all they are. But you're much more than that. Just like you don't mourn the end of the day when you go to sleep, you don't need to fear the end of a lifetime. It's just a passage into another state of being."

"It's less terrifying when you put it that way, but it's still death. It's still a mystery my current consciousness has no experience with."

"Death is a natural process of life. We've all died many times before, and we'll all die again. This isn't something we should dwell on. There are some things we can choose in life; there are many more things we have no say in. Death is most often the latter, so we shouldn't waste too much time trying to make it the former."

"But we should have some fear of death. Otherwise, wouldn't we just waste our lives?"

The sage turned, his sharp gaze meeting Laolys's. "Is loving something only possible through fear of losing it?"

"I suppose not."

"Then we can love life every day without fearing death." The sage smiled broadly as he took a deep breath, holding it as if savoring the moment.

"I suppose we can," Laolys admitted, "but I can't let go of this fear so easily. I've carried it my whole life."

"Most people have. But maybe you can get used to the idea that for every day you've lived, at least one version of you has died. Every one of those deaths was unavoidable. And yet, here you are, alive and well. Here I am too, alive and well. I may as well have been eaten by a bear in that field over there…" The sage gestured toward a valley in the distance. "But I wasn't. Here we both are. Incredible, isn't it?"

"Quite incredible, actually." Laolys looked at the valley. He felt an odd gratitude to be here, in this moment, with a teacher who still lived.

"Every circumstance is incredible," the sage continued. "Out of infinite possibilities, this is the one we've been given—this one, and every other we've gotten to experience. Whether we enjoyed them or not, all circumstances are equally incredible improbabilities."

"I guess that means I need to decide exactly what I want for myself now," Laolys mumbled, trying to shake the mental image of himself as a homeless birdman.

"That'd be the wise thing to do, otherwise you'll end up with the future you fear the most."

Laolys hesitated. "One thing I always imagined I'd have in life is a loving wife."

"Not a wise decision." The sage's tone was cold, slightly abrasive.

"Why not? I'm engaged." Laolys's thoughts drifted to his fiancée back home—the scent of her breath, the warmth of her touch. But as he lingered on the thought, a new unease crept in. How much of his world would change by the time he returned?

"You can't choose a destiny that depends on someone else. It's negated by their right to free will."

"Not even if it's vague?" Laolys liked the idea of true love someday, even if it wasn't with the woman he envisioned now.

"It's not advised."

Laolys lowered his gaze. "Then maybe I don't even know what I want."

"Not power? Not to be the savior of humanity?"

"I could hardly be humanity's savior. And power seems more trouble than it's worth." A heaviness settled into Laolys's chest. He felt suddenly incapable of the path he'd set out on—one that had unexpectedly reshaped itself upon meeting the sage. Right now, he just wanted to hide, to stay on top of the mountain forever.

"But your career is in politics."

"That doesn't seem to be the case anymore... given our deal."

"Not necessarily," the sage said. "A man in a good position could teach many things."

"But the truths I'll teach will ruin my name. People aren't ready for them." Laolys tried to imagine a hopeful future, but anxiety bled into every scenario. He couldn't yet envision a life where he was both happy and successful.

"That doesn't mean your words won't reach them."

"But they'll curse my name and damn me to the farthest place they can think of!"

"And such is the fate of many who earn the title 'savior,'" the sage said gently.

"I never asked to be one!"

"Then why did you come to learn from me?" The sage glanced at him, raising an eyebrow.

"I was about to take office; I wanted to be a good leader."

"You could have learned that from your father."

Laolys flinched as his father's furious outburst regarding *the leak* flashed through his mind. "No," he said, shaking the thought away. "I wanted to do more than he did. I actually wanted to help people. All my father cared about was securing their money and their obedience." The words left a bitter taste in his mouth. He had always seen so much potential in his position; potential that was constantly sacrificed for profit and power.

"Then you never really wanted a position in government," the sage replied, reminding Laolys of his first lesson. "A government should be limited. It should protect its citizens, not interfere in their lives. A government can't improve a person's life unless that person is a refugee seeking asylum."

"Maybe I did want to be some sort of hero..."

"And in many futures, you are. Only, most don't know who you really are."

"Then how am I their hero?"

The sage locked eyes with him. "Who is your hero? A man of history?"

"Yes, you could say that."

"Then you don't know your hero. He's been turned into a figure, an idol, far removed from the pains and struggles of the man he really was."

Inside, Laolys's emotions swirled. He could imagine no future for himself, now, that wasn't full of pain. Everywhere he went, he'd be scorned.

"But if no one knows my name, I'll never be remembered! I'll never be immortalized!" Laolys's outburst surprised him, it came out of his mouth faster than he could think it.

"Becoming an idol doesn't make you immortal! It doesn't mean a thing! It's just a name in a book that people twist and attach to whatever ideas suit them!" The sage's voice rose to match Laolys's, and his face held a scowl that few would tempt.

Laolys shrank back, ashamed. He looked at the ground and took a deep breath. "Then... how *does* someone achieve immortality?"

"As far as I know, it's a given." The sage resumed his calm demeanor, staring at the mountainside with a serene expression. "Live, then die, then live again. Rinse and repeat. Forever and ever, until ascension."

"I don't know which sounds worse: mortality or immortality."

The sage chuckled softly. "Humans are an ill and curious lot."

"You say that as if you aren't one of them."

"Oh, I've made my fair share of foolish mistakes! No, I've earned my humanity, and I've got the scars to prove it."

Laolys studied him. "So, what did *you* want for your destiny? Was it this?"

The sage let out a yelp of laughter, coughed a few times, and cleared his throat. "I must do a good job of making things seem glamorous! No, living as a hermit, an outcast in the mountains, wasn't always in the game plan!"

"What was?"

"Oh, the usual: love, money, to find the philosopher's stone..." The sage trailed off.

"So, pipe dreams."

The sage shook his head. "Oh, no, I got all those things. They didn't make me happy."

Laolys's eyes widened. "The philosopher's stone?! The great myth of alchemy?!"

"Yes, but it's not for transmuting gold. That is, indeed, a myth. No, it's more like a mental key. It lets you see things as I do, understand the things I know."

"Can I find it, too?"

The sage sighed. "Yes, but you must do so on your own. I will not play a part in that journey—*that* I am too old for. I'm retired from it, permanently."

"I would like that to be my destiny, or at least my quest: knowledge."

The sage smiled at him. "You've chosen your quest already, hero; knowledge from me is part of that."

"Yes, but I'd like to see things too. I want to find the philosopher's stone."

"I'll do my best to discourage you from that quest, but I understand the temptation all too well." The sage turned his gaze to the mountainside, his eyes distant, nostalgic.

"But knowledge made you happy. It gave you peace out here, peace with yourself."

The sage shook his head. "No, wisdom did. Hard-earned wisdom from a hard-lived life. I had to face my pain and choose to love myself enough to grant myself my own freedom. Knowledge had nothing to do with it."

"What do you mean?"

"I could teach you everything I know, but it wouldn't mean a damn thing unless you tested it yourself—lived it, suffered through it, and came out on the other side. You can't overcome your inner turmoil just by reading books or learning from a mentor, no matter how well-intentioned. Wisdom isn't something you inherit. It's something you unlock by exploring the hidden corners of yourself, stepping into the unknown, and especially facing what you fear the most. Knowledge alone won't bring you peace."

"But your knowledge means something!" Laolys was sure the sage was dodging specifics on purpose, being intentionally difficult to work with.

"Again, I must make things look glamorous without intending to. Maybe you've already turned me into an idol. I'll give you one more well-intended warning—this life you imagine for yourself, of fame, of glory, of heroism... it comes with more trials and pain than most other lives."

"But shouldn't I strive to do great things?"

"You should strive to do many great things, but their success shouldn't be determined by other people's opinions."

"Hmm. You know, that's all politics is—and my future was always in politics—I never thought about defining success any other way." Laolys wondered if perhaps his upbringing had caused him more anxiety than he previously realized.

"Well, think about it differently from this moment forward. You define what it means to be great. You choose your heroes, and you make them into who they are in your mind."

Laolys took a deep breath. "I suppose you're right. I've always been in control of myself and my vision for my future."

"Of course I'm right."

Laolys opened his mouth to reply but stopped, realizing the sage was no longer seated next to him. Nor was the sage anywhere off in the distance that could still be seen in the last rays of sunlight. This trend was becoming familiar to Laolys, who reclined back down on the forest floor in silent contemplation. The sage had given him a lot to think about, and he supposed that was his only option, having been instructed to stay put.

Soon, it was dark, and there was no sign his new friend would be returning for the remainder of the night. Laolys stayed outside the hut, just in case, and drifted into a light, troubled sleep. Illusions he had held of himself were peeling away, leaving him feeling raw and exposed. He was not the polished politician he was expected to be, nor did he feel worthy of the title 'hero' or 'savior.' The sage had already confronted him with several hard truths about himself. By challenging him to live up to his own claims of merit, the sage was forcing him to face his fears. It was all for the best, but it was painful, as growth always is.

The illusions we cling to—money, reputation, prestige—offer little nourishment for the spirit. If we spend our lives chasing them, it could be said we have lived little, if at all. When death announces the final curtain call and the blindfold is lifted from our eyes, we will see these illusions in their bare form. Only then, it will be too late to make any changes.

It is easy to become distracted by illusions; humanity everywhere is consumed by illusionary pursuits. If we should catch even a glimpse of them in their true form, we should kindle that realization, no matter what popular opinion insists. The more we see the world in all its varied forms, the more we will come to understand our power as observers.

The Dwelling of Discord and Devotion

Cycles

"Life surrounds us everywhere. From the planet itself to the tiny microorganisms that cover every surface, life persists."

The sage's booming words jolted Laolys awake. At first, he couldn't see more than a blanket of deep night overhead, with only the faintest glow gathering at the horizon to signal the coming dawn. He felt a cool breeze graze his cheeks and realized, somewhat disoriented, that he had fallen asleep outside the sage's hut.

Shaking off the last of his drowsiness, he rose and wandered toward a small, crackling campfire, settling beside it. The sage crouched beside him, steadily turning two skewered animals above the flames.

"Good morning." Laolys rubbed the lingering sleep from his eyes. As he eyed the roasting figures, his stomach churned. He swallowed a wave of unease and reminded himself that food on this mountainside was a rarity.

"I suppose you call every morning a good one." The sage's eyes gleamed with fervor as he turned the skewers. "Meaningless chatter. Did you hear what I said?"

Laolys inhaled the crisp air, noticing how the pine-tinged

breeze mingled with the smoky scent of cooking. "Something about life?"

"This is important!" the sage bellowed, causing Laolys's heart to skip a beat. "I will repeat myself, but I don't like making it a habit. Life surrounds us everywhere. From the planet itself to the tiny microorganisms that cover every surface, life persists."

"Yes, I suppose it does." Laolys yawned, still groggy. The sage's relentless passion at this early hour both impressed and unnerved him.

The sage kicked a smooth pebble across the ground which landed near Laolys's foot with a dull clack. "Take this rock, for example." He nodded to Laolys to pick up the rock.

Laolys bent down and grabbed it, noting how cold and damp it felt against his palm.

"That tiny rock you're holding is host to an unfathomable number of tiny organisms. And think further, the molecules themselves are teeming with life. Even if an object appears still, it's really composed of countless molecules all swarming about, bumping into each other and interacting with their environment."

Laolys looked at the rock, trying to muster the same enthusiasm. "Yes, I suppose so."

"And the planet!" The sage yanked the skewers away from the fire, waving his arms in the air. Sparks flew upward, swirling in the early-morning gloom. "The planet is a living, breathing organism! The trees are its lungs, the rivers its veins, and birds act as the neurotransmitters! It's the macro that is host to the micro!"

Laolys took a moment to glance at the shadowy outlines of trees encircling the hut. They were kind, stable guardians, circulating air molecules by photosynthesis. "Hmm. I guess the trees *do* breathe for the world, converting carbon dioxide to oxygen."

"They speak to each other, too," the sage added, returning the animals to the flame.

"I'm sorry, you'll have to explain that further." Laolys stretched again, trying to bring his brain up to speed. Some of the sage's worldviews took a lot of mental energy to understand.

"Not verbal speech. They speak through impulse, like how one part of our body speaks to another. Underneath the soil, their root systems form a network of fungi. Signals of distress, such as drought, fire, or insect invasions, are carried underground to every other tree in the network."

Laolys turned his attention back to the trees towering above him. They were more than mere bystanders circulating air; they were communicators, too. They had their own language system—a telegraph composed of chemical signals—which any tree connected to the network could receive. "And the birds?" he asked, noticing a few of them gathering near the sage. "How are they like neurotransmitters?"

"Think about it; they greet the sun each morning, and their songs stir the world awake. When the light arrives, they liven the world with their music, like dopamine and norepinephrine flooding the brain. They follow the sun with the seasons, carrying their messages to whoever can interpret them. Without them, I believe the earth would be in a state of depression."

Laolys smiled at the metaphor. He'd never seen birds in this light. Their early chirps, rising to a gentle crescendo, infused the air with a hopeful energy that soothed the heaviness in his heart. "Are all animals part of this... planetary system?" His gaze drifted to the horizon, where the sky glowed with faint orange and pink.

"Yes, though they each have their own consciousness, they all play a role in the planet's body. The whole ecosystem is connected, like our organs and cells. Carnivores keep populations in check. Herbivores prevent vegetation from overgrowing and help maintain biodiversity. Every species—insect, bird, fish—has a crucial role in keeping the whole network healthy."

Laolys's thoughts turned inward. A wave of guilt settled over him as he considered humanity's impact on the world. "Even humans?"

"No, not humans. We're more like a virus. We damage the system."

Laolys's heartbeat quickened. The word virus, applied to humanity, struck a chord deep within him. "Maybe we can change?"

The sage grimaced. "Unlikely, but I hope people at least *try*."

"Do you think the planet's trying to get rid of us?"

"Without a doubt. A good virus stays undetected. We passed that point long ago. Maybe if we reverse course, start healing the Earth instead of harming it, it'll let us stay. That'd take effort from all of us, but in theory... it could work."

Laolys lifted his gaze toward the night sky. "Are we just a virus... or are we part of something more?"

"We're part of the planet while we're here. Well, we should be, anyway." The sage gestured with his stick, sending sparks flying in the direction of Laolys's town. "In other lives, we were part of other planets, other star systems. No matter how much people down there deny their connection to the Earth, they're still woven into its system. Everything is."

Laolys eyed the forms on the end of the sage's sticks with unease. "We're... *all* interconnected? Animals too?"

The sage gave a half-nod, transfixed by the fire. "Aye."

"Well... do they travel across the galaxies too? When they die, I mean."

The sage shook his head. "No, not the animals. They always come back to the same planet, same species even."

"What? Why?"

"Resonance." The sage turned the skewers slowly, watching the flames lick at the charred bodies. "A squirrel doesn't know how to be anything other than a squirrel. That's the level of its soul's development—its resonant tone. It can't go anywhere else until it evolves further."

"Not other planets?"

The sage shrugged. "As far as I'm aware, they always come back to the same one."

Laolys swallowed against the lump of unease rising in his throat. The sight of the scorched animals made his stomach turn, yet at the same time, he was undeniably hungry. He decided not to ask what they were, figuring it might be easier to eat if he left it a mystery.

He forced his attention back to the sage. "So if a squirrel always comes back as a squirrel, I guess there's no chance of humans and animals ever switching?"

"It's all about resonance. We've moved beyond the animal cycle—we've already learned those lessons. Now we think, dream, and question. We can engage with the spirit realms. Animals can't do any of that."

"The cycles... they decide what kind of bodies we take on?"

"Exactly." The sage poked at the fire, sending embers drifting into the air. "Each cycle vibrates at a specific frequency, like a harmonic pattern. A soul can't enter a body unless it matches that vibration. It's like trying to open a lock with the wrong key. It won't work. Everything within a cycle moves together, resonating at the same range."

Laolys imagined human spirits produced chaotic waves, pulsing erratically, full of contradictions and unpredictability. Animal spirits, by contrast, moved more fluidly—faster, steadier, without the constant inner conflict of human thought. Their patterns didn't match, so they couldn't cross into each other's cycles.

"I think I get it," he said slowly. "Human spirits vibrate within a certain range, and animals within another. They can't switch between them because their frequencies don't align."

The sage nodded. "To make a major frequency jump, you'd have to shift into an entirely different cycle. That means altering your fundamental vibration to match a new range. Each cycle is its own self-contained reality. Everything within it—matter, energy, consciousness—resonates in harmony with its core frequency. As above, so below: the macro mirrors the micro."

Laolys stretched his hands toward the fire, letting the warmth seep into his fingers. "So what other cycles are there? Besides animals and humans?"

"It starts small. The String Cycle, then the Subatomic and Atomic Cycles. Those lay the foundation for the Microbial and Multicellular Cycles. Then you get what we already covered—the Zoological and Anthropogenic Cycles—which span from simple flatworms all the way to highly advanced species, some far beyond humanity."

He gazed up at the sky, still speckled with fading stars. "Then there are the spiritual, formless cycles. And beyond those, even larger ones—the Planetary, Cosmic, Multiversal... and beyond that, cycles we can't even begin to understand."

"So the planet and the universe cycle too?"

The sage lifted a stick and gestured to the landscape around them. "The Earth isn't just a rock floating in space. She's alive. She has a spirit, a consciousness. Everything on her—the animals, the plants, even us—is part of her body. She was born long before any of us, and she'll still be here long after humanity is gone. That's her cycle. It's longer than ours, but compared to the universe, her cycle is short. Even the multiverse cycles."

"Does everything cycle?"

"I can't think of anything that doesn't. Even the void cycles."

Laolys turned to him. "The void?"

"The void. The origin of our multiverse. It existed before anything else, and eventually, everything will collapse back into it. It breathes, just like everything else." The sage pulled the skewers away from the fire, inspected the meat, then placed them back into the flames.

"So... everything is part of a cycle," Laolys mumbled. "And even if different cycles share the same space, they don't mix because of resonance."

"Exactly. Think about the cells in your body. They live and die much faster than you do, operating on an entirely different vibrational scale. Right now, millions are replicating and dying inside you, but you don't notice it. They exist within you, but their world is separate from yours. Just like we exist inside the planet, and the planet inside the universe."

Laolys let the idea settle. It was simple, yet the way it applied to everything was overwhelming. "So, we all exist together, but because our vibrations are different, we don't interfere with each other."

The sage leaned back, gazing at the forms with satisfaction. "We've already passed through all the cycles below us. That's why we experience the world the way we do. Believe it or not," he gestured to a nearby tree, "we once knew what plants know. Their lesson is simple: grow in response to the world around them. But even that takes complex coordination. They rely on the cycles beneath them to function. Everything is woven together. It starts with the strings and builds up from there."

"Strings?"

"The strings came first, before anything else." The sage pulled a stick from the flames, checked the meat, then placed it back. "Not literal strings; think of them as aethereal fibers, vibrating motion that exists before even quarks. That's the first cycle our soul enters."

"And what's after that? Atoms?"

"Not yet. Before atoms, there's subatomic energy."

"What comes after atoms?"

"Cells." The sage smiled. "Think about it. The jump from a single atom to a single cell is massive. A cell has structure, autonomy, the ability to replicate. That level of complexity takes countless lifetimes of development to reach."

Laolys placed his hands near the fire and watched the firelight dance across his skin. For the first time, he saw his body not as a single thing, but as a vast collection of tiny lives. They didn't think; they persisted through impulse—an irrefutable drive toward life.

"So, the cycles have to follow a set order? Each one depends on the ones before it."

The sage nodded. "There's no other way for things to unfold."

"What's after cells?"

"Plants. They start as tiny seeds and grow," he gestured with a stick, sending sparks flying toward a thick-trunked tree, "into massive trees like this. But trees are more than just living things; they're the information hubs of the forest. They send messages to each other, pass nutrients to younger, struggling trees, all through their underground fungal networks."

Laolys looked at the tree in a way he never had before. He had always thought of plants as passive, but the sage made them sound like quiet architects of their environment. "Still, plants can't move or interact with the world like animals. That's a huge leap."

The sage shrugged. "It happens gradually, almost seamlessly. Worms, for instance, are like roots that finally escaped their mother's grip. They tunnel through the soil wherever they please... free at last."

Laolys smiled at the metaphor. "I guess that makes sense. And animals progress for a while... all the way up to species that are nearly self-aware."

"*Nearly* being the keyword. Once a species truly becomes aware of itself, it enters our cycle—the Anthropogenic Cycle. That leap is rare, which shows just how long it takes for a soul to move through the cycles." He tilted his head slightly. "Then again, time doesn't really mean anything to a soul. A soul exists beyond the material realms, where time is irrelevant."

Laolys glanced up at the sky, still heavy with stars. Their cold, distant glow made Earth—and himself—seem impossibly small in the grand scheme of things. "What comes after this? The formless cycles?"

"Once we ascend, we enter the Guardian Cycle. That's when we begin exploring the Cosmos—not as physical beings, but as spirits. We've touched these realms before—when we dream, when we die, when we drift between lifetimes—but it's different after ascension. Then, the entire multiverse opens to us. It takes a while just to find our footing."

"I... can't imagine."

The sage smiled. "You'll live it eventually. Everyone will."

"What's after that?"

The sage slowly rotated the sticks over the fire. "The cycles keep going through the aethereal realms. I don't know where they end—just that, eventually, they loop back inward, back to the void."

Laolys imagined himself soaring through the stars, a formless being of light drifting between galaxies. It was a tempting vision. He could understand why the sage had sacrificed so much, why he had devoted himself entirely to this path. "So, when you say the universe is teeming with life, you mean there are all kinds of lifeforms we can't see—beings we aren't even aware of."

"That's right."

Laolys looked at the rock in his hand again. After considering formless energy in space, he thought of the tiny energy in the rock in a new light. At the atomic level, he realized he was holding an immense network of tiny particles constantly bumping each other. They intersected not only with each other but with his hand as well, continuously engaged with the surrounding environment. On its outermost surface, other tiny microorganisms crawled about, investigating the crevices. They arrived and departed at all hours and traveled with the rock. This rock, he realized, was a foundation of life, a microcosm of the universe's ceaseless expansion.

Laolys felt the sage's piercing gaze and turned to see him staring with wide, unblinking eyes.

"Step outside of the concept that all forms of consciousness look like you or like animals." The sage lifted the sticks toward the sky and turned his gaze upward. "Consciousness permeates all kinds of forms... or no form at all."

"I'm still having trouble wrapping my head around that," Laolys said. He was slightly embarrassed about his struggles next to the sage, who seemed almost otherworldly in his wisdom.

"Then you're still clinging to too many illusions—one of them being that your vessel matters. Your consciousness only attaches to a body for a short time. One lifetime is nothing in the full span of your soul's existence." He pulled one of the roasting animals closer, inspecting it before returning it to the fire.

Laolys's gaze lingered on the skewered figures, their charred edges outlined in the flickering light. He still wasn't entirely sure what they were, and, up until now, he'd been too afraid to ask. *No more fear*, he reminded himself. Clearing his throat, he asked, "So... what's for breakfast? Is that... a squirrel?"

"Close enough. Vermin of another kind."

"Vermin?" Laolys's face twisted in disgust before he quickly masked it.

"Don't look so offended." The sage cast him an amused glance. "I've watched this family grow near my hut for years. I just killed the two fattest ones for us."

Laolys felt his stomach turn, his face paling as he scrambled for an appropriate response. "Ah, my apologies! I... uh, I'm used to a different diet. But I appreciate the meal, truly."

"As you should. I won't apologize for my lack of attire for guests. I never planned to entertain up here."

"And yet, you're a natural at it." Laolys pulled his lips into a weak smile. "Truly, you put on quite the show."

The sage erupted into a fit of laughter, coughing between chuckles as if it had all gotten caught in his throat at once. "I do make it seem quite glamorous, don't I? Perhaps I should think about locking the door to my hut, before someone else gets it in their head to steal it!"

Laolys chuckled softly, not gleaming near the amusement of the old man.

The sage breathed a satisfied sigh and resumed his normal, calm demeanor. "But, when you eat one of my old friends here, you should reflect on the sacrifice, but also on your place in the cycle. Everything must die. If death ceased to exist, nothing would transition, nothing would grow... and nothing would eat."

Laolys looked at the forms again. Eating did sound good. "Death inevitably leads to new life," he mumbled.

"Exactly. But cherish your life. Use every second of it. Learn from it. Take the good with the bad and learn how to shift your perspective. Sisyphus's hell is an injured man's dream."

"And I'm sure Sisyphus envies the injured man who can lie in bed all day," Laolys added.

"That's right! Everyone's pining for what they don't have, ignoring the plate right in front of them. If one man's trash is another man's treasure, maybe we all have very little trash."

Laolys glanced at the roasting animals, their charred forms turning slowly on the sticks. "That... not-squirrel there... many would consider that trash."

The sage shrugged. "Not someone who is hungry. Perhaps most people don't know hunger like they think they do."

"No, but everyone thinks they have it pretty bad off. Even the rich are always bitter about one thing or another; they think the world is out to get them."

"Maybe it is. They have too much."

"How much should a person have?"

"Enough. That is all one needs. Most have enough, but many others don't. And the ones who have too much can't see it's causing them more pain than it's worth."

"Having too much causes pain?" Laolys had always known that wealth didn't guarantee happiness; this was plain in the faces of the adults he'd grown up around. But the idea that wealth could cause suffering was a new and unsettling notion.

"Indeed! Wealth doesn't give a person happiness, but most people think that it does. When people obtain wealth and still aren't happy, they think they just need more of it, or need to spend more of it, or whatever. All the while, they miss out on the things that actually give a spirit pleasure."

Laolys looked at the sage with interest. "What gives a spirit pleasure?"

The sage looked up from the fire to meet Laolys's gaze. "Breathe, my friend, and know pleasure."

Laolys took a deep breath.

"Close your eyes and breathe deeper."

Laolys did as directed.

"Keep going, slowly, and don't open your eyes."

Laolys took several more slow, deep breaths. He cleared his mind and watched, as a passive observer, what entered his mental view. He noticed shapes shift and move from behind his eyelids. Then patterns began to jump, and lights of all colors and shades surrounded him. He felt a deep sense of serenity as he breathed deeper and drifted further into his mind's eye.

A tunnel formed as he ventured increasingly inwards. Blackness lay ahead of him, but he was not frightened of it. It seemed to hold every single light in the universe, and he felt compelled to join it. He was also a light, one among many, approaching this strange black magnetic field. The other lights grew fuzzy as he drew closer, and he felt warmth from those nearby who were radiating heat.

"Now wake up."

Laolys jolted upright, startled back into the present moment. "What? Why? What's happening?" He rubbed his eyes, still caught between realms.

"Breakfast." The sage grinned and shoved a skewer toward him. On the end of it, well-scorched vermin awaited Laolys.

"Uh... thanks." Laolys forced a polite smile. He swallowed the lump forming in his throat. He was starving, but his palate was nowhere near as rugged as the sage's. Next to him, the sage was already tearing into his meal with unrestrained enthusiasm.

The sooner it's over with, the better, Laolys thought, and dug into his breakfast. He tried to bypass his mouth as quickly as possible, sending the morsels of food down to his stomach without focusing on what it was.

The sage, having already finished, leaned back and watched Laolys eat with a wide grin. "So, do you think our little friend there is grateful to be rolling around in your belly?"

Laolys grimaced. "Uh, I... I suppose not."

"Well, you suppose wrong."

"You think he's happy about it?"

"I don't think he's thinking about it at all."

"Why not?"

"He's dead."

Laolys set down the bare carcass of his meal and met the sage's gaze. "But you said life goes on after death."

"It does."

"Then why isn't he thinking about it?"

The sage lifted his picked-clean skewer, gesturing vaguely toward the sky. "Because he's somewhere else now. Thinking about something entirely new."

Laolys glanced down at the small carcass beside him, a pang of guilt washing over him. "You don't think he wants to come back?"

The sage smirked. "Few do. Most find more peace in the first moments after death than they ever did in life. But all vermin return, and almost all humans do as well."

"Why do humans keep coming back?"

The sage's gaze drifted toward the horizon, now streaked with soft gold and pink. "Because they rarely do what's required of them. They have to step outside their comfort zones, face their fears. Most aren't willing to do that."

Laolys lowered his eyes, guilt rising in his chest. He had spent most of his life in fear, making decisions that felt safe. Until now, he hadn't even known there was another way. "I think most people are just misguided," he said. "They don't know any better. No one knows what enlightenment even is, let alone how to get there."

He looked at the sage with admiration. "Except you. You're the only person I know who's achieved even a semblance of peace."

The sage shrugged. "I paid a steep price for my peace. I'm sure most people wouldn't endure a fraction of what I did. But I imagine there's a simpler way."

"How'd you figure it out?"

"I wanted it. I kept looking. I didn't give up. Most people called me mad for even trying. That's their problem. They don't think they're capable of enlightenment, so they never bother to look."

Laolys stared into the fire. Was he even capable of enlightenment? "I think for most people... it's overwhelming to even start."

The sage's gaze softened. "Overcoming yourself is a daunting task. But real transformation only comes from real effort. You can't avoid the hard things and expect results."

Laolys kept his eyes on the fire. Part of him wanted to chase awakening, but another part felt completely incapable.

"Starting is the hardest part," the sage continued. "At first, it feels like everything is out of control, like breaking the first barrier might send you over the edge. But once you push through, you'll be able to look back and see that the things that used to terrify you are nothing now. And that makes it easier to keep going, though it'll never really be easy."

He locked eyes with Laolys. "You're not as far off as you think you are. If you keep at it, one day, you'll see things just like I do."

Laolys's heart skipped a beat at the intensity of the sage's gaze. He quickly looked away, tilting his head toward the stars. Next to the sage, he felt small, like he was still struggling to grasp even the most basic ideas. "You really think so?"

"This goes far beyond think. This one, I know." The sage winked and turned his gaze back to the fire.

"What was it like for you when you started out?"

"Oh, I struggled in many of the same ways. I had to fight through many sleepless nights until I learned how to laugh at the people who laughed at me. The one thing I had going for me was that no matter what, I just kept searching for enlightenment. Eventually, I stopped caring what they thought. I had found truths they wouldn't believe if I told them, so I carried on. I taught those who were willing to listen, and everyone else—well, they were just missing out."

"I see, it's hardest to start." Laolys's gaze drifted towards his town in the distance. Though the thought was daunting, it was also freeing. If the hardest part was at the beginning, then the rest of the journey would come easier.

"You hold onto too many illusions. Let go of them, and you'll be a happier man."

"How do I let go of them?"

The sage shrugged. "Is greatness only great if people recognize it?"

"No, of course not."

"That's right. You know, most of the most famous paintings we know today only became famous after the artist died."

"That's tragic."

"The painter could have wallowed in despair when his first few paintings were ignored. He could have given up or changed the way he painted. But if he had, we wouldn't call it art. Art doesn't need to be recognized. It's an expression of the soul in the most vulnerable way. If the painter only painted for approval—to hang his work in palaces and please clients—he would've lost the very thing that made his art real."

The sage paused, and a flicker of pain crossed his face. "Your soul is the same way, you know. If you treat yourself as a commodity—acting to please others, instead of living by your true nature—you're robbing yourself of your soul's growth."

Laolys's breath caught short. "I... never thought of it that way."

"No one else can die for you. Just remember that. Not a damn person on their deathbed has ever said they were glad for the chances they *didn't* take, especially for fear of other people's opinions. Only you can claim your ascension."

Laolys looked up at the sky, taking note of how the pink hues stretched up the horizon. The birds had ramped up their calls to each other, beckoning every sleepy member of their flock to arise for the encroaching dawn.

"I'd like that," he said softly. "To ascend."

"As would I." The sage followed Laolys's gaze toward the horizon, and his expression changed from one of pain to determination. "This experience—this existence—has been a very harrowing one. I'm not interested in repeating it, so I'm doing everything I can to ensure I ascend."

Laolys studied him, intrigued. "What exactly are you doing?"

"The details of my daily practices would only confuse you at this point. As your mentor, my job is to keep you from unnecessary distractions."

"Then... how do I ensure I ascend?"

"There is no way to ensure your ascension. Few things in this universe are certain. And something as complex as the evolution of a soul? Well, forget it. These lessons will give you the keys to unlock many doors, but you still have to unlock them. These blockages are within you; no one else can do it for you."

The sage paused and made eye contact with Laolys. "That's why, eventually, you must leave here. You'll have to take everything you've learned and apply it to the world. Otherwise, it's all meaningless."

Laolys took a deep breath. "Whatever they say about me is meaningless too."

The sage nodded. "Political power, popular approval—they're illusions."

"I see... we need to see past the illusions?"

"Rather, see all the illusions, then choose the one that suits you best." The sage leaned in towards Laolys, his rancid breath making Laolys cringe, and lowered his voice. "Do you know why you see my lifestyle as somewhat glamorous?"

Laolys glanced around. By most standards, this was hardly a glamorous existence—living alone in a hut on the side of a mountain, eating whatever could be caught. And yet, there was something undeniably peaceful about it. "Because... you make it seem that way?"

"No." The sage chuckled. "Because I believe it is. And I radiate it outward. You see it. The birds see it too."

As if on cue, Laolys noticed the small flock that had gathered nearby, their morning calls growing louder. He had seen this before, how they seemed to gravitate toward the sage as if he were one of them.

"But if I didn't believe it," the sage continued, "if I didn't see the beauty in the nature that surrounds me, if I didn't see that even though my plate is sparse, I have plenty because I have enough, if I didn't like the person I find behind my eyelids... then no one would see glamour or beauty in my lifestyle. I'd radiate sadness, and no one would climb a mountain to seek my advice."

Laolys sat with this statement. The peace of the morning air and the wise words of the sage were too pleasant to disrupt just yet. The sage sensed this too, and for several minutes both sat in silent meditation, breathing in the moment.

The sage sighed deeply. "I'm not a special man; at least I shouldn't be, anyway. I'm simply a man who found beauty in the world, in the most ordinary places, and wanted to learn all he could about it. In this, I found all the varying illusions and layers of the seen and unseen worlds. In the end, I chose to live up here because it's simple. It's elegant in its removal. It's not easy, but I've acclimated myself to the hardships so that I barely notice the difficulties anymore." He paused, swallowing, and a range of emotions flickered across his face.

Laolys struggled to comprehend everything the sage had experienced to gain both his knowledge and his predicament. None of it, neither past nor present, appeared easy.

"You have a little while before you return to other people, to a normal life," the sage continued, nodding to him. "And you must return... When you do, know that your life is fully in your hands. How others respond to your words may not be, but what you radiate out to them is. If you believe their harsh words—and sometimes it will be *all* harsh words—you'll crumble. You'll prove them right. But, if you don't believe them... in time, they won't believe them either."

Laolys nodded but felt a strange emptiness beside him where moments before, the sage had been. When he turned to look, the sage was gone, and only the gentle breeze and a flock of birds remained in his place. Laolys sat in silent humility, watching the life of the lower cycles around him stir at the light of the sun. It arose in harmony with the planet, tuned to its Cosmic rays. Humans were the exception to this. The sage's mannerisms—his affinity for the birds—were beginning to make more sense. He wanted to blend in with nature. Humanity, in its current state, was more like a virus.

Laolys let the songs of the birds drown out his thoughts. Perhaps he was better off taking a lesson from the life around him than trying to solve all the possible problems that could arise in his future. The sage, though his entire life had been trying, thought of none of those things now.

The first rays of light shoot into the air with vigor each morning, regardless of who is or isn't around to see them. We believe their jubilation is justified; they have won a great victory. Though we can't see the sun over the course of the night, it doesn't fade from existence. It travels through the unseen world and faces the unknown, just as we do, without its light. Take joy when the first rays claim their victory; you have claimed a victory too. No matter the trials of days past, no matter whether we slept soundly or not at all, when the sun graces us with its presence over the horizon, we breathe in another day.

The sun rose high in the sky, and after several hours of quiet contemplation, Laolys took the liberty of borrowing some of the sage's literature to pass the time. As the day progressed, he read and re-read some of the more famous works of various souls long separated by history. Their words were timeless. The pains and struggles of the human soul have existed since its conception. Ancient philosophers, separated from the modern age by millennia, struggled with the same concepts as modern man: love, loss, and mortality. We will never escape these questions, but we should never stop asking them. We should never assume we have all the answers or that we know best. We should question ourselves and reassess our values daily. If they change, we should applaud ourselves for achieving growth, for everything is meant to change in time. If they stay the same, we know that we have questioned all angles and that our sentiments have solid integrity.

Sanity

"We define madness as a descent into the dark regions of the unconscious mind. A man who has thus arisen from the other side, however, only believes it mad to never have begun."

The sage's statement echoed through the tranquil afternoon air, breaking the silence that enveloped Laolys as he hunched over one of the sage's many books on Alchemy. Before the announcement, the only sound he had heard for hours was the gentle rustling of leaves and small, sporadic chirps of a few nearby birds, making the sudden intrusion of words jolting. Startled by the sudden noise, he sprang upright, sending the book tumbling to the moss-covered forest floor.

"What? Can you say that again?" He bent down to retrieve the fallen book and dust it off.

The sage, still standing behind Laolys, sighed audibly, then repeated his words exactly: "We define madness as a descent into the dark regions of the unconscious mind. A man who has thus arisen from the other side, however, only believes it mad to never have begun."

Laolys placed the book on a rock and rose to face his mentor. The sage's solemn gaze met his, but he remained silent, apparently waiting for something.

"Do you think I'm mad?" Laolys's brows knotted into a look of concern.

"Do you think I'm qualified to answer that?"

A soft chuckle escaped Laolys. "I doubt either of us is. You're up here, living as a recluse, and I—" he spread his arms, gesturing to the surroundings, "—I'm barely faring better, living up here with you, listening to all your advice!"

"Well then, we ought to carry on as we please, rather than concern ourselves with what's mad and what isn't." The sage sat down on a rock next to the mountainside, overlooking the landscape, and Laolys followed, sitting adjacent to him.

The setting sun ignited the sky with shades of red and gold. The light in the sky was similar to when they last sat together at sunrise, but the air was vastly different. It bore a weariness that the morning did not, a readiness for darkness to once again draw the day to a close and tell all the creatures of the forest that they have done enough, and work was done for the day.

"So madness..." Laolys said, "You define it as a descent into the unconscious mind?"

"Yes that's one way of describing it. When we open the door to our unconscious mind and allow unusual thoughts and strange visuals into our conscious awareness, it can feel quite disturbing. Memories of past lives or visions of alternate timelines are blocked by our consciousness for a reason. It can confuse our sense of self and loosen our grip on reality."

Laolys shivered, though the day's warmth still lingered. Like everyone, he carried buried parts of himself—things he feared to confront. He was just barely holding himself together. He wasn't sure what might surface if he opened the door to his unconscious.

"Anyone who awakens has to come to many terrifying realizations about themselves," the sage continued. "It's inevitable to go through a period of what many would call madness before you sort yourself out. Struggling with identity isn't easy, and it'll last until you realize that your identity can't be defined. You have to forgive your past mistakes and realize that your triumphs are equally meaningless. We're fluid, all-encompassing spiritual beings, and we can only be defined by unity."

"So, madness is an unavoidable part of awakening?"

The sage glanced at Laolys, his eyes shining with a light that was as enchanting as it was unsettling. "If by madness we mean, as most people do, to see realities that extend beyond the traditional, then yes, madness is an unavoidable part of awakening."

"Genius is mad, sometimes." Laolys considered the sage the inspiration for this thought. He considered him a genius, and he was clearly quite mad by most people's standards.

"Aye, genius is misunderstood, so genius is mad."

"Mad is misunderstood?"

"Yes, that's the simplest way to put it." The sage's expression darkened, though his tone remained light. "Most revolutionary ideas were labeled mad at their inception. Every genius idea begins as madness, then becomes brilliance, then eventually turns into the standard. By that point, though, if the innovator is still alive, they've already moved on to more 'mad' endeavors."

Laolys exhaled, releasing tension he was unaware he was holding. "So being mad, as they call it... It's not so bad, then."

"It's all a matter of perception. People fear what's different; that's why madness carries a bad name. But madness is also the spark of brilliance, the thing that sees what others overlook. Humanity's progress depends on it. Without madness, nothing ever changes."

"All the great inventions of history... they were all considered mad, weren't they?" Laolys thought of Leonardo da Vinci, Copernicus, the Wright brothers—brilliant minds that could have been lost had they listened to those who dismissed them.

"Nearly by law." The sage's expression turned wistful. "But here's the thing about madness, the standard changes over time. What people once did—like using leeches for medicine—we now call mad. It was once madness to believe in germs. Madness, when properly applied, is just thinking ahead of the curve." He shrugged. "But what do I know? When I think back on the life I lived in society... it all seems mad."

"You think the way you used to live down there was mad?" Laolys glanced toward the town at the mountain's base. The rumors he'd heard before leaving—calling the sage a wild madman—felt both true and ironic.

"Aye, quite mad." The sage leaned towards Laolys. "And that realization—that's what I mean by coming out the other side. Once you're there, you see the madness of your life before the journey began. And then," he drew a deep breath, "it becomes curious that everyone doesn't undergo a similar journey."

Laolys glanced at the sage with admiration. He had found a way to make his madness an asset, not a hindrance. Madness wasn't as simple as people made it out to be. Much of what was deemed madness was only different. Still, he felt that true madness could exist for some. "What about those who, whether by malady or some genetic cause, struggle with uncontrollable delusions? Are there people who are truly mad?"

The sage stroked his chin. "We could say yes, but in truth, we have no idea how to qualify it. We label madness as existing in a reality separate from our own. But consider this, if someone is deep in conversation with someone we can't see, who's to say that the other person isn't really there, existing in a parallel dimension? Perhaps what we perceive as madness is simply someone coexisting in two realities at once, caught between worlds."

Laolys's jaw dropped. "That can happen?"

"Quite easily here, actually. Our planet is home to an unusually high number of overlapping realities, far more than most other planets. Each exists unaware of the others. Now imagine the disorientation of someone who sees two at once."

"Terrifying." Laolys shuddered, picturing the loneliness of such an existence. To live that way would mean only living in half-worlds, people fading in and out like ghosts in both realms.

"Indeed! We know nothing of their reality, only that it differs from the status quo. Most people believe that if a lot of people can agree on something, it must be true. Not only has history proven otherwise, as in the popular consensus of where our planet resides in the solar system—with so many dimensions packed together, we really can't be too certain of any particular one."

"What do you mean?"

"I mean, we may argue the case of a particular dimensional reality, not realizing that it doesn't even apply to the one we're in now. It's not uncommon to accidentally cross into another."

"What would that be like?" Laolys looked around nervously. The sage, the infamous *leak*, was known for his inter-dimensional portals.

"Not as fantastic as you imagine. These parallel realities are all very similar; only minor alterations set them apart. Are you familiar with the Mandela Effect?"

"The Mandela Effect..." Laolys searched his memory. "It's when a group of people remember something incorrectly, right? A collective false memory—when a bunch of people swear they recall something a certain way, even though it supposedly never happened?"

The sage nodded. "It's named after the confusion surrounding Nelson Mandela. A lot of people remember hearing that he died in prison, but he was actually released and lived for many years after. Enough people were convinced they had read about his death that it became a phenomenon.

"The explanation is fascinating. What it really points to is dimensional crossovers. At some point, two nearly identical parallel dimensions, each with slightly different timelines, merged, and a number of people unknowingly crossed into this one."

"So that's it? They're just in another dimension now?"

The sage shrugged. "Happens all the time—at least, here anyway. Humanity rarely notices because they don't know what to look for. Most just assume they misremembered something, never realizing they crossed a dimensional plane."

"Yeah, people tend to blame their own memory first," Laolys said.

"It's an easy explanation," the sage continued. "And sometimes, that *is* the case. But often, these shifts involve minor details—things that don't disrupt the overall timeline for the person crossing over. The outcome of a distant sports match, for example. Or something even more trivial; the color of a cereal box mascot's shirt, or the spelling of a street name, like Cherry Creek Drive and Berry Creek Drive."

Laolys laughed. "The poor postal workers who have to deal with these crossovers."

"Aye," the sage grinned. "The mail would still find its way to the correct address in its proper dimension. But the worker—well, he'd be questioning himself at every stop. 'I *swear* I delivered to Cherry Creek yesterday, but here I am at Berry Creek. Maybe I'm losing it. I really ought to get my eyes checked.'"

"So, what would it be like for someone to exist in two adjacent dimensions at once? You mentioned that earlier."

"It would vary depending on the person. Some might see the world shift around them, subtle changes they can't quite explain. Others might be haunted by strange apparitions—real people from adjacent dimensions. Left unchecked and unguided, these glimpses of dimensional drift could lead to paranoia, tangled thinking, distorted views..." The sage exhaled sharply. "And then, to help such people, society calmly tells them that all their experiences are just tricks of the mind, only deepening their turmoil."

Laolys studied him, intrigued. "So... should we give people suffering from delusions more credit?"

"In an ideal world, we wouldn't dismiss them outright. We'd try to understand exactly what they see and help them make sense of it. We should listen—not as though they're plagued by false realities, but as people witnessing something real that they can't make sense of."

Laolys reflected on the lesson. Reality, as the sage described it, was universally subjective. Most people limited themselves to viewing similar planes and having similar experiences. But one's sense of reality could stretch farther, seeing beyond what most believed possible.

"Why are some people wired that way, to see things differently?" he asked.

"Call it luck of the draw, in some cases. It wasn't always a disadvantage. In ancient times, those who could perceive beyond the usual boundaries—who could see what others couldn't—were valued as spiritual leaders. They were shamans, seers, and priests."

"Do you think people we call mad today might have some kind of religious significance?"

The sage shook his head. "Importance is only importance when it's rightfully claimed. Some of our ancestors—those with heightened perception—were trained to harness it, to direct it with purpose. They understood it better than even our most advanced psychologists do today. To them, the Cosmos, the extra dimensions, the higher planes of consciousness—they weren't abstract theories. They were the foundation of their religion."

"And you don't think we can do that today?"

"Today, we're lost in confusion but refuse to admit it. Instead, we cling to certainty, and when something defies our logic, we panic. We expect the world to fit our narrow understanding, and when it doesn't, we reject the world instead of expanding our perception. We've grown so accustomed to improvement—always imagining how things could be better—that we refuse to let anything *be*. Not ourselves, not others, not even the world around us."

The sage closed his eyes and inhaled deeply, holding his breath for what felt like an eternity. Laolys sat in quiet fascination, watching. Something about the moment felt charged, weighty, as if the air itself had stilled in reverence. The sage's unkempt hair swayed lightly in the breeze, his expression one of absolute serenity.

The sage exhaled and opened his eyes. "This planet, the one we so carelessly exploit, is special—a jewel within the multiverse. Our brief excursions here demand not only appreciation but reverence. For in nurturing Earth, we are tending to the wellspring of universal consciousness itself."

Laolys inhaled deeply, enjoying the cool mountain air. The forest around him breathed with wildlife. Everywhere, birds, squirrels, and insects went about their afternoon activities, enlivening the mountain with a constant hum of life. Even the rocks had lifelike qualities, somehow adding to the vibrations even though they were still. This planet was incredible; he had never considered life anywhere else.

"It is wonderful," he said, "but what makes it so unique? Unlike other worlds?"

"We have so many dimensions packed together here. As far as planets go, it's a dimensional access point of magnanimous proportions. Other planets usually have far fewer. Of the ones that have this many dimensions and are hospitable to life, our Earth is one of only four, in all the galaxies, all the star systems in the universe we reside in."

"One of four?" Laolys repeated, astonished. He didn't know the details of how the sage had come by this knowledge, but something in him sensed it was too important to dismiss.

"Yes, we are very fortunate to incarnate here. If humanity weren't at each other's throats all the time, it'd be the prime place for ascension."

"We have an advantage here? Different from other worlds?"

The sage nodded. "Yes. Not in terms of life itself—people are not kind to each other, so life is hard—but in terms of spiritual advancement. Here, reaching the higher realms is easier. The dimensions are packed so closely together that they're more accessible."

He gestured toward the sky. "Imagine the spirit as a musician. With the right training, it can tune itself to different frequencies and experience other dimensions. Most planets, less fortunate than this one, are like guitars. Six strings, a broad range, but ultimately limited. A skilled player can create incredible music on a guitar, but this planet..." He paused, a smile stretching across his lips. "This planet is a piano. A full scale of notes, an immense range. Frequencies that simply don't exist elsewhere."

Laolys had never thought of Earth that way. No one seemed to give it the reverence it deserved—probably because they weren't aware of it in the first place. "What gives us the advantage? Why does our planet have so many dimensions?"

"Simply the location." The sage's gaze drifted toward the horizon. "There are many convergence points in the universe, but very few with planets. Even fewer with planets hospitable to life. And even fewer that can sustain advanced life." He exhaled, his gaze drifting toward the valleys below. "It's rare. Almost a miracle that places like this exist at all."

"Almost?" Laolys eyed the sage curiously.

"Well, given the sheer size of the universe, it's inevitable that some habitable planets will drift into these axis points from time to time. In our universe alone, it's a mathematical certainty that at least one life-supporting planet will emerge within these dimensional domains. But there are never many. If we have the chance to be here, we should use it to our advantage."

"How do we do that?"

"These dimensional axis points give life a real shot at evolving to the next cycle. They allow all sorts of things to occur. Even to the less aware, they offer glimpses into fantastical and bizarre realities. To spiritually minded people, they make the higher planes of consciousness more accessible and make it easier for the inhabitants of those planes to reach us."

The sage leaned back. "You know, we have something very special here. Stories of dimensional crossovers, strange happenings, and unexplained disappearances seem to be as old as humanity itself."

Laolys's eyes widened. "Are you saying some of the strange creatures and events from myths and legends could be real? And that it's because of how many dimensions are stacked here?"

The sage nodded. "Some. Certainly not all, but a few may be actual accounts of real phenomena. Just because an event can't be replicated or only a handful of people saw it doesn't mean it didn't happen. When dimensions press together and pull apart, sometimes there's a glitch—something that shouldn't slip through does... but only for a brief moment. Then it's gone. Never seen again."

"Incredible," Laolys mumbled.

"Incredible, beautiful... and at times, terrifying," the sage added. "Now, what do you think happens to most people who witness such things?"

"I... I'm not sure. I imagine they'd start questioning their reality."

"They *should* question their reality. But most don't. Instead, they question *themselves*. They doubt their own minds. They stay silent, burying the experience beneath layers of denial instead of letting it open the door to new discoveries."

"So you're saying these bizarre occurrences—these dimensional shifts—are far more common than we realize, simply because people refuse to admit they've experienced one?"

"Without a doubt," the sage said. "They're afraid. Afraid of what others might think, afraid they might actually be crazy... or worse—afraid that they're *not*. Because if they aren't, then their entire worldview collapses. So instead, they dismiss it. 'It was just a trick of the light. A lapse in awareness. A poor night's sleep.' Anything but what it actually was. Accepting what they saw means reassessing everything they thought they knew. Most people aren't willing to do that."

"Then... how do they break free?"

"They have to let go of their fear." The sage paused, and his eyes locked onto the fading blue and gold sky. "People cling to their illusions because uncertainty terrifies them. It's easier to believe in some divine plan, some grand order, than to face the truth—that the real nature of existence is Chaos. But if they want to see things as they are, if they want to grow, then sooner or later, they'll have to step into it."

"I suppose I can understand why so many people react with fear to strange phenomena. But I've always found glimpses of other realities, or dimensional drifts, as you call them, fascinating."

"And that," the sage said, gesturing toward the distant valleys, "is why you're up here with me instead of down there with the rest of society."

Laolys smiled. "Just the two of us seems a bit lonely for witnessing the true nature of the multidimensional universe."

"Aye, so it is. Good thing you'll be teaching them about the other realms when you descend the mountain. Or better yet, explore them yourself and show others their reality."

"Me?" Laolys's eyes widened. "I don't know how to access them!"

"It's easier than you think. You're already halfway there. First, you have to believe they exist. Then, you must want to experience them. The last step is just rigorous study, meditation, and an unrelenting drive toward the unseen world. Godspeed, my student!"

Laolys gave him a blank look. "Are you going to give me any actual guidance?"

"It's irrelevant. You have to find the path on your own." The sage turned his gaze toward the mountainside. "You're already off to a good start. Not only did you climb the mountain to find me, but you stayed when I warned you the journey wouldn't be easy. That alone tells me you'll find any realm you seek, so long as you don't give up trying to reach it."

He winked, the sunlight catching his eyes in a way that made him look both unsettling and strangely warm. "You have just the right touch of madness."

Laolys laughed. "You *do* think I'm mad!"

"You have to be, to be up here with me. But remember, mad is also genius."

Laolys paused in consideration of the lesson. "So to be mad is, essentially, to see things differently from others?"

"Precisely. There are varying degrees of madness, but at its core, mad is exceptional, brave, and, at times, irrational. It unsettles people, but it's usually the first tidal wave in a tsunami of change. What was once madness becomes the norm, until something madder comes along to reshape it again."

"So mad is always cast out, even if it's brilliant?"

"Yes. Any spark of true brilliance is first called madness, then it's genius, then finally, it becomes the standard."

Laolys smiled. "You know, everyone down there says you're mad. But I think you're a genius."

"I *am* quite mad by their standards. And I'd be lying if I said I wanted to be anything else!"

"You don't want their recognition? To move from madness to genius in their eyes?"

"Never! Do you know why?"

"Because... you don't like their mindset?" Laolys imagined the sage had a difficult time conforming to societal norms while living among people. His scraggly friend may have had a slightly more kempt face then, but his intense eyes were a dead giveaway that his spirit was amiss, someplace elsewhere and higher.

"No, I like them just fine. But by their standards, I'll always be mad; I'll always be an outcast. So, I embraced it. I loved it. I took it to the extreme. I became so mad that they couldn't ignore me. And, on occasion, people still climb all the way up here to find me." The sage grinned, clearly proud of himself.

"How often do you get visitors?"

The sage shrugged. "Time isn't something I'm good at measuring with a calendar and clock. Up here, it's hopeless. It might be once a year or once every two years." The sage's gaze went blank as he stared at the landscape, his consciousness slipping into the realm of memories.

Laolys studied the sage with fascination. "You've still made quite a name for yourself."

"Oh? What name is that?" The sage turned to him with a fixed glare—friendly yet charged with something that made Laolys uneasy. His presence had a way of making the smallest gestures feel intense.

"You know," Laolys hesitated, suddenly unsure of himself, "no one down there actually knows your name. And now that I think about it... you never gave me one either." He searched his memory, trying to recall their introduction. He had been so nervous, so caught up in the sage's strange behavior, that he'd never thought to ask. Or perhaps he had assumed he should have already known it.

"Good. Let's keep it that way," the sage said, cutting off Laolys's train of thought.

"You won't tell me your name? Why not?"

"Names assume too much. If I tell you my name, my real one, you'll assume far, far too much about me."

"I would know who you are?"

"Who I *was*, without a doubt."

"But you have to tell me!" Laolys couldn't contain his curiosity. The mystery surrounding the so-called leak had only deepened since his arrival. The sage, full of contradictions, kept revealing more layers to what had seemed like a simple existence.

"You'll find out one day, on your own." The sage's tone was firm, almost abrasive. "And when you do, you'll know it's time to return home."

"But why?"

"I can't tell you. It'll make sense later; that's all I can say."

"But now I won't be able to stop thinking about it!"

"Let it go. One day, you'll understand. Today is not that day." The sage scowled as he stared at the mountainside.

"But how am I supposed to stop thinking about it?" Laolys's frustration overwhelmed his better senses. He knew the sage wouldn't budge, but that didn't make it any easier.

The sage turned to him, eyes sharp. "Understand this: a man is only as poor as his desires. If he desires much, he remains poor, no matter how much he possesses. A man like me, who has little and desires little, isn't poor at all."

"So, just stop wanting things? Is it that easy? Shouldn't we want to be better, stronger? To push further?"

"We should have some desires—but only for things that are within our grasp, for things worth having. Fantastic things, even. But we must choose wisely."

Laolys stared at the sage, dumbfounded. He didn't expect him to be the type to say people should limit themselves. Or maybe he was—the sage had done nothing but surprise him since they met. "But shouldn't we push past our limits? Ignore the people who say we can't have something?"

The sage shrugged. "Sometimes yes, sometimes no. There are few, if any, absolutes. Everything has a positive and negative pole. Everything shifts. Balance is key; it should be applied to all things."

He grew quiet, his demeanor darkening. Something lingered beneath his words, something he wasn't saying.

"And sometimes," the sage's breath caught, "sometimes you spend your whole life chasing something, wanting it with everything you have, only to realize, in the end, that it was never worth the struggle. Sometimes, it's better to walk away entirely."

Laolys caught a flicker of something in the sage's eyes, something painful, lost. "So... I should just give up trying to guess your name, then?"

"Yes." The sage's demeanor brightened, and the usual glint returned to his eyes. "But I already told you, when the time is right, you'll have my name. Now is not that time."

"When will it be time?"

"When you've learned enough, and you're ready to go home."

Laolys nodded; he figured he should stop pressing it altogether. He wasn't ready to go home. His prior life seemed like a distant dream, and he felt he could remain in this world forever. It felt nice here; it was serene. He had never had this feeling before; he was used to always pressing onward for the next big moment. Not here. Here, the whole world seemed to stand still. Perhaps it was the center of everything, one solid point around which everything else in the world spun.

"You've learned a lot in a short time," the sage said, breaking Laolys's train of thought. "But you're not ready yet. So, if you don't mind, I'd like to share my findings from today with my new friend."

He reached into the fold of his robe and pulled out a small bag. When he opened it, Laolys could see it held an assortment of leaves, berries, and nuts.

"All edible, I assure you." The sage grabbed a handful and shoved some into his mouth. "Haven't perished yet!"

"Not in this timeline, thankfully!" Laolys grinned as he reached into the bag.

"You're catching on quickly!" The sage flashed a grin. "But you wouldn't believe—in another timeline today, I got the berry harvest all wrong."

Laolys froze mid-chew and stared at him with wide eyes.

The sage erupted into howls of laughter, spewing crumbs from his mouth as he tumbled off his rock onto the forest floor.

Laolys felt heat rise to his face, realizing too late what had happened. Embarrassed, he joined in the laughter. Yet, a small part of him still wondered—was the sage actually joking?

"Anyway," the sage said, stifling his laughter as he climbed back onto his rock, "back to the lesson at hand. Don't be afraid to explore a rabbit hole. You're midway through a rather perturbing one right now."

"What do you mean?"

"Don't be afraid to ask questions. Dig into yourself. And more importantly, don't fear the answers when you get them. Allow both the fantastic and the mediocre to be true."

"I'm midway through a rabbit hole?"

"A tunnel of self-discovery."

"There's an end?"

"Yes and no!" The sage smiled. "We're always growing, changing, so there's always more to discover about oneself. But there are many rabbit holes. Some of them are not fruitful, while others are essential to explore. Some are simple, and some seem never-ending. And answers... well, they're not always clear either. Many are rabbit holes in and of themselves."

Laolys studied the sage, intrigued. "Now that I've had time to reflect on some of your statements, I've noticed you often convey multiple meanings in just a few words."

"Layers!" the sage exclaimed. "There are many, many layers to the universe! Endless layers! My words only scratch the surface. But the universe..." He paused, watching the sun dip below the horizon. "Now *that* has layers."

"If only I could see the world like you do, with your passion for things most people overlook. It's fascinating."

"You can see things this way in time, if you apply yourself. I was quite a wreck at your age."

"You were?" Laolys tried to picture the sage as a young man. He imagined someone reckless, always entangling himself in situations he had no business in.

"I didn't develop my appetite for the bizarre and the occult in old age, I merely refined it. You could say I always had a knack for finding trouble... though not in the usual ways."

"Like what?"

"I was nearly boiled alive. I was locked inside a chapel on an inaccessible mountain. I've had to brandish my sword against the most formidable of men. I've been a fugitive in more nations than one..." The sage's voice trailed off, his gaze distant. For a moment, he seemed absent, lost in some faraway memory, his mind slipping beyond the waking world to a plane far removed from their quiet mountainside.

Laolys hesitated, unsure if he should speak. "I don't mean to pry, and forgive me if this is out of line... but why were you in so much danger?"

The sage's eyes refocused, though his expression remained unreadable. "Because I asked the questions they were afraid to ask. And I found the answers they hoped I'd never find."

Laolys swallowed. The weight of those words settled heavily between them. "Should I... be concerned that I might suffer the same fate?"

The sage shrugged. "Fate is what you make it."

"I suppose. If I can ever decide what I want my fate to be, maybe I'll find out. But who really gets to decide such things? If anyone."

"I'd say most decisions are made by those with the confidence and fortitude to make them. The rest?" The sage let out a short breath. "They're just along for the ride."

"Is it bad if I end up just along for the ride?" Laolys stared at the distant valleys with quiet dread. At that moment, he felt small, incapable, beside the great and serene sage. A man so full of wisdom yet cast out by the world for his teachings. If the world couldn't accept him—a figure as magnanimous as he was intimidating—how could it ever handle someone like Laolys?

"Good or bad, it's all a matter of perspective," the sage said. "Sometimes we get to pull the strings, but more often than not, we're the ones being tugged along. It's true that those who act with force and direction do more of the pulling, but no one's always in control. Even dictators are pulled along far more than they'd admit."

"I understand," Laolys mumbled. "A lot of things are out of our hands."

"But don't let that wither you away, my young student!" The sage's voice rang through the forest with a sudden onset of passion, causing Laolys to straighten in his seat. "The universe is infinite, and Chaos gives rise to endless possibilities. Far more is within your control if you're willing to do the work to claim it."

Laolys studied him. The sage was not without troubles. He simply chose not to let them bother him anymore. "How did you do it? Learn as much as you did?"

"I loved it more than anything—the pursuit of greater understanding, the secrets hidden behind the most guarded doors. I chased it with the desperation of a drowning man gasping for air. I sacrificed everything, over and over again. I proved my worth, then I faced the real tests. Those tests nearly broke me, but they taught me what I needed to learn. And when I had nothing left, I proved my worth again. Eventually..." The sage paused, his expression unreadable. "Eventually, I had some extra help. But above all else, I simply loved."

A long silence settled between them, the weight of the words hanging heavy in the air. Then, the sage met Laolys's gaze. "It all boils down to this: Do you truly want what you came for? And how much are you willing to sacrifice for it?"

Laolys felt the question settle in his chest, knowing it wasn't rhetorical. "I have a feeling it'll cost me everything."

"Correct. At least several times over."

"My original reason for coming... to learn how to help mankind?"

"Still stands—well within your reach now, if you're willing to let go of everything you hold and reach for it instead."

Laolys nodded slowly, fully grasping the weight of the choice before him. His family, his career, his fiancée—everything would be swept away. And there was no telling what lay beyond that sacrifice.

The sage had lived a life of exile, feared and cast out by society. He had become an enemy of multiple governments for no crime other than his teachings. Ideas of self-liberation, of the soul's evolution, though they resonated deeply with Laolys, stood in direct opposition to the prevailing belief in divine authority and societal structure.

The reality of his future was nearly too much to bear. The same scorn his father held for the sage, the infamous leak, would soon be directed at him, along with the full force of the government he had once been destined to serve.

"Nothing is binding you to this path," the sage said, pulling Laolys back into the moment. He was studying him with an expression that held an equal mix of parental sympathy and scientific interest.

"Huh?" Laolys looked back blankly.

"You can walk away now. Keep this knowledge to yourself, try to continue down the path you imagined before. I wouldn't resent you for it, not that it should matter to you if I did."

Laolys stared at him, stunned. "And if I stayed longer but backed out in the end?"

"It would only make things harder for you. Personally, I'd enjoy the company either way." The sage caught himself mid-smile before adding, "But the longer you stay, the harder it'll be to accept simple things as truth. You'll always want more. You'll become, in a sense, like me."

"But I could learn these truths and not share them? Keep them to myself?"

"Yes, well, *learn* may not be the right word in that case. You could *remember* these truths and choose not to share them, but you can't truly learn and embody them while keeping them to yourself. That'd contradict the very message they hold. Evolution isn't a solitary effort; we grow by spreading growth. To reach enlightenment, to see the suffering of the world, and feel no desire to alleviate it..." He grimaced. "Well, I don't think that enlightenment would last long."

Laolys looked toward his hometown, imagining himself going back to his political career, keeping the story of his journey to himself. The thought filled his stomach with a pit of dread. It wasn't what he wanted.

He turned his attention back to the sage and smiled. "Well, I believe it's already too late."

"Oh?" The sage looked up.

"Life down there..." Laolys gestured toward his town. "It's not worth sacrificing my spiritual evolution for. I was miserable. It's not where I'm meant to be. For whatever reason, I'm meant to be here, learning this instead." He took a deep breath and nodded. "When I leave with these truths, I will live by their message. I will share them... because that's what my soul wants to do. Even though it still scares me."

The sage's gaze fell to the mountainside, his expression neutral, unreadable. "I think you're right. It is far too late for you."

Laolys studied him, trying to determine whether he should take offense.

"You're not like everyone else," the sage continued. "And now, you're *really* not like everyone else. Most people alive today will never understand your brilliance. Don't let their cries of madness bog you down."

Laolys felt a cool breeze rustle through his hair, grounding him in the moment. "I will take what lies ahead," he said softly, but something felt off. The air had an odd absence. When he turned, he noticed the sage was nowhere in sight.

Laolys sighed and turned his gaze back to the mountainside. The sage had left him with a lot of things to think about, and for whatever reason, he wondered about his strange disappearances the least. Now that he was alone, words from the lesson swam through his mind, urging him to look further into his internal state.

"You're mid-way through a rabbit hole." What rabbit hole was the sage referring to? The sage had said there was a fine line between genius and madness, perhaps no line at all, only varied perspectives. Was he going mad?"

"A man who has risen out the other side only thinks it mad to never have begun." The more he thought about it, the more absurd it seemed to try to return to his life as a politician and pretend that nothing had changed. In just a short time up here, he had gained an entirely new way of seeing the world. Living as he had before was no longer an option. Unfortunately, he still had no idea how to live any other way.

The last rays of the sun disappeared fully behind the horizon, and another cold breeze brushed against his skin. He stood up and tentatively walked towards the hut. "Hello?" he called out, unsure whether the sage was truly gone or still nearby.

No answer came, and a chill ran down Laolys's neck. *I haven't seen him use his hut yet*, he thought, and pushed the door open with a determined heave, rattling dust and dirt around the doorway.

Without light, he fumbled forward, knocking over several small, unidentifiable items in the process. Fortunately, it was only a few steps before he fell face-first into a nest of bedding thick with dust. He coughed a few times and settled into a comfortable position. Sleep was still far from the precipice. He lay there, listening to the wind outside, its howls adding to his sense of unease. Eventually, he fell into a light, fitful sleep.

Are things easier if we have a choice, or if the choice is made for us? In one manner, we have ourselves to blame for what we consider to be poor circumstances. In the latter, we can blame everything and everyone else. Yet, in doing so, we shirk any responsibility for our personal faults, as well as let go of any hope of a brighter future. We are, in effect, a slave to circumstance when we refuse to accept that our present situation is a result of our own choices.

A bright future is well within our grasp, given the fates don't strip us away from life just yet, but we must be willing to do the work. We can't wish to become an Olympic athlete without training incessantly, sacrificing sleep, good company, and indulgences. We should not desire things we are unwilling to work for, nor should we waste any time not working towards what we desire.

When Laolys awoke, the sun was high in the air and the sage was nowhere to be found. Had he missed him? The forest around him buzzed with life, but it had only a fraction of the enthusiasm that chimed at dawn. He figured it was late morning, and the sage was off doing whatever he did—gathering berries or crossing dimensions.

With no other option than to stay put and wait for the sage, Laolys lay down beneath a tall pine tree and closed his eyes, not to sleep, but to meditate. He took a deep breath, and perhaps by the miracle of the mountain, he felt his astral body lift into the air above him almost immediately.

He drifted effortlessly across the landscape, passing over rocks and trees, following the winding paths of creeks. In an instant, he reached the ocean, traveling hundreds of miles in mere seconds. He hovered there, watching the waves lap against the shore.

People appeared in his vision, strangers in distant lands. He observed them speaking in unfamiliar tongues, going about their daily lives. He studied their movements, their gestures, their expressions, though none held his attention for long. He wasn't steering himself; there was no conscious direction to his travel. Instead, he allowed the world to unfold before him, shifting and revealing itself as he remained still.

He meditated for hours, unaware of time's passage. Up here, it was meaningless. The sage kept no schedule, and there were no obligations. Some nights, dinner came early; other nights, it never came at all. Were it not for the changing face of the moon, he might have questioned whether any days had passed at all.

At times, he felt as though he were in a waking dream, as if the sage had cast some subtle spell over the mountaintop. But in truth, he was just beginning to awaken. It was easier here, away from the noise of the world. Down there, it had been too easy to get caught up in things that should never have concerned him.

It's important to be fluid—to adapt, to shift, to take in new truths and perspectives. Yet if we only mirror our surroundings, how can we ever know our true nature? Sometimes, we must separate from the world to find our true resonance. Each of us has a part to play, a single note in the grand symphony of existence. And we must find that note, that unique vibration, because it is needed. Without each individual's unique hum, harmony can never be achieved.

The Celestial Mirror and the Lion's Cry

Salvation

"There is no ultimate judge. Our hearts are made heavy by guilt and resentment. Clear yourself of your punishment now so that you may ascend."

Laolys's eyes shot open, and he sprang to his feet, excited. He glanced around, searching for the sage, but saw no sign of him. It was mid-afternoon, and the sun illuminated the whole forest. Still, every angle he turned, his friend was absent in the frame.

"Excuse me?" Laolys asked, uncertain if he had actually heard the sage or if he was developing an acute case of psychosis.

Without warning, a pinecone flew out of a nearby tree, barely missing his head. Startled, he spun towards the source. Squinting against the light, he strained his eyes to see the sage perched delicately on one of the upper branches.

The sage, seeing that he had Laolys's full attention, repeated his earlier statement with force, his voice reverberating down through the branches. "There is no ultimate judge. Our hearts are made heavy by guilt and resentment. Clear yourself of your punishment now so that you may ascend."

Laolys nodded, absorbing the words. Then, shading his eyes, he looked back up at the sage, still perched high above, and shouted, "It's a bit hard to converse this way! Mind coming down?"

"Actually, I do mind coming down; otherwise, I wouldn't be up here. Why don't you come up?"

Laolys swallowed a lump of nerves in his throat. "That high? I could fall!"

"And you could get eaten down there, any day out here. In many other timelines, you already have. Now get up here!"

Laolys sighed and reached for the nearest branch. Whether the sage had truly foreseen something or was simply being irrational, arguing wasn't going to get him anywhere. Gritting his teeth, he pushed through the anxiety of his lifelong fear of heights and climbed carefully, one branch at a time. His fingers gripped each branch tightly as his forehead dripped with sweat. Through sheer desperation, he made it up the tree, just a few limbs below the sage.

"This is as far as I go," he said, straddling a branch and tightly gripping the trunk.

"Then that's as far as you'll get." The sage grinned. "Are you ready to start your lesson?"

"As ready as I'll ever be."

"We spoke before about the cycle of life and death, the endless loop of reincarnation. Now, we'll discuss how to escape it through ascension. The trick is rather simple, but its application eludes almost everyone." The sage locked eyes with him. "Can you guess what it is?"

Laolys had no clue. "What?"

"No baggage."

"What do you mean?"

"When you die, you have to let go of everything from your life. If you hold on to anger, guilt, regrets, or attachments you won't ascend. You'll just come back again, over and over, until you finally release it all."

Laolys adjusted his grip on the tree branch. "Release it all... you mean detachment?"

"Exactly. We have to practice that now, in this life. Learn to forgive. Break free of the beliefs and behaviors that weigh us down. Otherwise, we'll keep getting thrown back into new lives, facing the same struggles until we finally let go."

The sage turned his head toward the mountainside. "Ever heard of the ancient Egyptian weighing of the heart?"

Laolys shook his head. The concept sounded vaguely familiar, but he couldn't recall the details.

"The ancient Egyptians believed that after death, a soul was judged," the sage continued. "The heart was placed on a scale and weighed against a feather. If it was as light as the feather, the soul moved on to the Field of Reeds, a paradise. But if it was too heavy, it was devoured by Ammit, and the soul was sent back for another life."

He glanced at Laolys. "Of course, this wasn't a literal scale with a feather. The judgment happened within the soul itself, in the astral realms. The gods oversaw it, but they didn't grant ascension. The soul determined its own fate by how it lived. If it lived in balance, in harmony, it ascended. If it carried burdens like regret, anger, or attachments, it couldn't move forward."

Laolys's mind filled with images from books he had read—scenes of ancient Egyptian judgment, grand carvings of towering gods, a golden scale at the center of it all. He recalled the depiction of a heart on one side, a single feather on the other.

"You believe in the same concept?" he asked, turning back to the sage.

The sage nodded. "I believe the allegory is entirely true for beings in our cycle."

"And what you said about there being no judge?"

"It means no one else determines our fate, only we do. No deity grants ascension. In fact, it's impossible to elevate a soul to a higher cycle before it's ready. It wouldn't be able to sustain itself at that vibrational frequency. It would simply fall back."

"Frequencies..." Laolys echoed, recalling their previous lessons. "Each cycle has a specific frequency range, right?"

"Exactly. And it's up to us to tune our vibrations to match it."

"But how exactly do we do that?" Laolys was at a loss on how to achieve enlightenment for himself. It all seemed too abstract; his disarray was too daunting for him to make solid use of the sage's teaching yet.

"There's no rigid doctrine, no commandments set in stone, except one." The sage held up a bony finger. "The principle of unity. The Law of One."

"The Law of One?"

"It states that all is one. The universal matrix is a single heartbeat. Every individual consciousness is merely a fragment of something vast —so vast it defies comprehension. To live in accordance with this law, we cannot harm another, nor can we live in greed, lust, or obsession with material things. It's a shift in awareness—a spiritual realization that dissolves the illusion of separateness between you, everyone else, the planet, even the galaxy itself."

Laolys's gaze drifted as he considered the implications. "This awareness of unity... is that enlightenment?"

"One and the same." The sage took a deep breath, his eyes following a bird as it fluttered through the branches. "To truly embody unity of spirit has been the pursuit of seekers for millennia. All religions point to it in some form. It is the natural inclination of the soul, but most of us are too lost, too confused, to find our way toward its light."

Laolys reflected on his life. He had never sought unity, never even considered that he could be one with everything else. His focus had always been on competition, on being better, stronger, ahead of others. In that mindset, unity had been impossible. He had measured himself only in terms of separation, in how he stood apart.

"Confusion is an understatement." He turned back to the sage. "How do I achieve unity?"

The sage squinted at him, as if searching for something beyond what Laolys could perceive. "You won't be ready to conceive of unity until you address your maladies of spirit."

"My maladies of spirit?"

"Yes. The illnesses attached to your ego—you have more than a few. They fuel your nervousness, your fear. They are major hindrances to your progression. Your competitive nature, your self-doubt, they are all diseases of the ego."

Laolys felt his face flush. He lowered his gaze, fixing his eyes on the landscape below.

"You're as much a part of the galaxy as you are of this tree you're clinging to," the sage continued. "Death won't end your consciousness. In fact, it'll bring you closer to your source. All the things you ascribe importance to—your ambitions, your status, your fears—are illusions. Until you come to that realization, enlightenment will remain out of reach."

Laolys leaned into the tree and took several deep breaths, trying to calm the trembling in his hands. Slowly, his nerves steadied. He shifted his gaze away from the bark beneath his fingers and took in the view before him.

It was breathtaking. Rolling green hills stretched endlessly, their curves broken by jagged cliffs and valleys bursting with wildflowers. Rivers and creeks wove through the landscape like veins along neural highways, carrying life wherever the land was willing to receive it. Far in the distance, he could barely make out the tiny houses at the outskirts of his town. Life was still moving down there—his household carrying on with its daily activities, its quiet struggles and fleeting joys. His absence had done nothing to halt its rhythm. The town lived on without him. It didn't need his presence, his consideration. Up here, perched in the tree with the sage, he was utterly removed from it. *So why*, he wondered, did he still concern himself so much with the life that continued down there?

"I have full confidence you'll get there," the sage said, interrupting his thoughts. "Enlightenment is a lifelong journey, and you've only just begun. But you're off to a good start—you've gotten yourself this far." He smiled, nodding toward Laolys's slowly relaxing posture. "You're up on this mountain, high in this tree!"

Laolys grinned back, then immediately clenched his teeth as his anxiety came rushing back. He had, momentarily, forgotten where he was. But now, the reality of being suspended so high above the ground made his stomach twist. He took another deep breath. Then another. Slowly, he forced his body to relax, accept the situation, and trust the sage.

"You can't go on insisting on your faulty perceptions forever," the sage continued. "Not when you know a better life exists—one waiting for you, both here and in the Cosmos."

The sage's eyes drifted over the landscape; his expression bore a state of absolute peace. Laolys admired it, but deep down, he doubted he'd ever find it for himself.

"Well, how do I get there?" Laolys stared at the sage expectantly.

"That's exactly what we're here to work on. Most people are lost, stumbling through life without ever learning what they're meant to. The road to enlightenment sounds simple, but it's the hardest road of all. Because to walk it, we have to let go of everything we believe about ourselves. We have to learn to let things be as they are."

Laolys tried to steady his breathing, to still his mind, but anxious thoughts slipped through with every measured inhale. He latched onto a question, hoping to distract himself. "How do we undergo the judgment?"

"The judgment is done by us. During our life review."

Laolys up at the sage in interest.

"As we observe our life, we must be able to honestly say that we've learned from our faults. We will see everything—every action and its consequence, not just in our own life but how it rippled outward. We'll see how a simple smile can send a blessing to the other side of the world, and how a single outburst of anger can shake the roots of another's sorrow."

The sage's voice softened. "If we haven't learned from our mistakes—if we haven't forgiven everyone, including ourselves—we will be sent back, to try again. The cycle continues until we reach a state of true understanding."

Laolys shifted. "What kind of things does a person get cast back for?"

"Anger, failure to live by the law of unity, and lack of humility are the most common. When a spirit believes it has been wronged and demands justice, it's forced to seek that justice in another life. Likewise, if a spirit has harmed another and failed to recognize or amend its behavior, it will have no choice but to confront it after death, in between realms, where denial is impossible."

Laolys swallowed as nervous energy swelled in his throat.

"That spirit," the sage continued, "will then be sent into the next life, where it must either change its nature or continue the cycle indefinitely."

Laolys pictured himself before a massive scale, his life flashing before his eyes. Under honest assessment, he had lived fearfully. Selfishly. His mind filled with moments of anger, pain, and regret, especially toward himself. He imagined the scale dropping lower and lower with each recollection. His hands tightened instinctively around the tree trunk.

"It really is quite simple," the sage said, observing Laolys's anxious state. "It all comes down to living in the spirit of unity and practicing forgiveness. Forgiveness is essential."

"Forgiveness... Is it really that simple?"

"Aye. Every bit of pain you hold—your guilt, your anger—can be extinguished by the simple act of forgiveness." The sage sighed. "But I'm afraid most humans today will not be able to forgive and let go after death. Which means they'll fail the weighing... and be recycled."

"Why do you think it's so hard for us? Forgiveness—it should be simple."

"Fear. Anger is built on fear. Some are afraid that if they let go, they'll become vulnerable. Others don't know how to let go, or don't understand why they should. But forgiveness—it isn't for the one who wronged us. It isn't for anyone else at all." The sage paused and turned his gaze back to Laolys. "Forgiveness is for our peace of mind. It is the key to our own freedom."

"And guilt?"

"Guilt is our anger towards ourselves. Some people have done horrible things, and seeing the consequences of their actions led them to hate that part of themselves. This is anger turned inward. Let your anger only stretch as far as necessary to drive change. When you've transformed from your former sicknesses, you should forgive yourself, not to make your past behavior okay, but to allow yourself to walk forward, renewed."

"Easier said than done," Laolys mumbled.

"Exactly. So today, we will cover anger and guilt individually, as they are huge roadblocks in your way toward ascension. Let's start with guilt." The sage paused, looking down to lock eyes with Laolys. "I'm sure you have many. Name one."

Laolys's heart pounded as anxiety took hold. The first memory that surfaced was from childhood, so he latched onto it. "When I was young, I had a habit of sneaking around and snooping. One day, I got into my father's office and ruined some important documents by drawing on them. When he started looking for them, I panicked and threw them out. He still doesn't know what happened. It turned into a whole political ordeal."

The sage scowled. "You were a child. Children do these things. Don't tell me you climbed all the way up this mountain just to waste my time. What weighs heavy on your heart *today*?"

Laolys took a deep breath and turned inward. Down in the valleys below, people awaited his return, expecting him to come back the same as when he left. But he wouldn't. Many had warned him he would return a changed man, and most would call him mad.

He pictured his father, the pride in his son's election dissolving into outrage and disappointment. His father had spent years preparing him for a path he was about to abandon, rejecting everything he'd been raised to uphold.

"What about all the people I'll let down when I can't fulfill my duties as expected? My selfishness in continuing this journey will cause my family a great deal of pain. My father has been training me my whole life. I'm about to throw it all back in his face."

The sage shook his head. "Walking your own path isn't selfish. That's what we're here to do. True selfishness is forcing someone onto a road that isn't theirs. When we do that, we risk pulling a soul away from the journey it was meant to take. Your path is proof of this. I'm sure your family wouldn't have approved if they had known where you were headed. And yet, unknowingly, it's they who are being selfish— expecting you to sacrifice your enlightenment for their expectations."

Laolys exhaled sharply. "I never thought of it that way... But still, I was given a role, a position to fill. Whether or not I chose it, it's my responsibility now."

The sage tilted his head. "Is it? Or is it your life, your dreams, your journey? Not theirs? Is it fair for them to ask you to give up everything you are so they can see their vision for you fulfilled?"

Laolys hesitated. A weight he had carried his whole life—one he had never fully acknowledged—pressed down on him. But as the sage's words sank in, something inside him cracked open. With a heavy breath, he released it. "I suppose not."

"It's not right to take someone's life like that," the sage said, his voice steady but gentle. "If you love someone, you should want to see their fire burn in all the directions it longs to go. Not trap it. Not suffocate it. Not shape it into something more convenient for you. Let those you love burn brightly, with all their intensity."

"That's not how my family sees it," Laolys mumbled.

"Nor was it how mine saw it, but the truth remains the same. If you become a parent, is it because you want to own a person or because you want to watch them grow?"

"Hopefully, the latter!"

"Aye, but regrettably, many parents have a bit of the former as well. They want another version of themselves, someone to carry on their torch. But a child isn't obligated to the confines of his parents' torch once he is an adult, and it's selfish to ask so much of a person."

"So..." Laolys paused, almost afraid to speak his thoughts aloud. "I shouldn't feel guilty then, for taking this path?"

"Not only should you not feel guilty, you should feel proud. It takes courage to walk the path of the hero. There is nowhere you can go where you will not face many difficult trials—but you'll be living on another level, beyond the mundane. Don't concern yourself with the threats or complaints of others. They won't recognize your greatness until you have long moved on to greater trails."

"I suppose my father can find a replacement. Someone better— someone who actually wants to be there." Laolys meant the words, yet a lump of guilt still formed in his throat.

"Someone much worse, you should say, as it will be a man who desires power." The sage winked at him. "What else weighs on your heart?"

Laolys looked down, his thoughts drifting to memories he tried to keep buried. But they still found him, creeping through his mind at unexpected moments, like ghosts of his former self. There was a time in his early adulthood when he had lost all self-control. Addiction had consumed him, and depression had nearly dragged him to an early death. Only through a sudden spark of will—divine or otherwise—had he managed to claw his way back. Even now, he shuddered at the thought of who he had once been.

Realizing he had to face it to move forward, he spoke, his voice shaky. "I've made so many mistakes. In my early adulthood, I spiraled into addiction and self-loathing. I was selfish, I exploited the people I loved for my own fleeting gains. I despise the man I once was. How do I overcome this hatred of my past? I wish I could erase it, but I can't."

The sage's expression didn't change. He remained serene, unmoved, by Laolys's confession. He didn't ask for details, nor did he press him with further questions, except for one.

"And who are you today?"

Laolys hesitated, then answered softly. "Different."

If he stood side by side with his former self at his lowest, he doubted they would look like the same person. At best, they might resemble distant siblings—two lives that had taken drastically different paths. Despite his noble efforts now, there had been a time when he was nothing but destruction, spiraling out of control and pulling everything down with him.

"Do you still hate yourself?" the sage asked, noticing Laolys's somber expression.

"At times—for who I was." Laolys doubted he'd ever fully shake his disdain for his past self. Some parts of himself were still hard to face—hard for anyone, even him, to love.

"Stop. Look at how far you've risen. You have a unique ability now to show others who are lost in the same darkness that the deepest abysses can be overcome. The worse our actions once were, the greater our capacity to prove change, to demonstrate fluidity and perseverance despite all odds. It's a good thing we aren't defined by our past mistakes, so long as we don't keep repeating them."

"I will always bear the scars." Laolys lifted his arm, revealing several raised scars. "My past has marked me permanently."

The sage nodded in acknowledgment. "Do you want more scars?"

"No, of course not."

"Then be grateful for the ones you have. They remind you of the lessons you've learned, the strength you've already shown. It's no small feat to pull yourself out of the depths you've been in. Many others in your position have succumbed to far worse fates. Be grateful you had the courage to fight your battles and find your way forward."

The sage's words struck something deep within Laolys, but the lump of guilt in his throat remained. "But is it ok to let go of the guilt? Maybe I *should* feel bad for what I've done in the past."

"Perhaps, after some time, when we're no longer who we once were, we can expunge ourselves, as changed men, and practice forgiveness on ourselves."

A gentle breeze rustled through the tree, and the two men sat in silence, lost in their own thoughts. Laolys, still gripping the branches tightly, was consumed with fears of his future and pasts he wished he could erase.

The sage, a few branches above, sat with perfect ease, his mind wandering through planes far beyond human understanding. He wasn't untroubled, he had transcended his troubles. Though his past had been far from pleasant, he now lived fully in the present, free from the mental burdens that plagued those who had cast him out.

"Mistakes." The sage broke the silence. "They're a part of life. If you're not making mistakes, you're not really living. It's not about what we've done; it's about how we've grown since. We have to allow ourselves some room for error while we figure things out. Don't keep repeating the same mistakes, but don't dwell on them forever either."

Laolys turned his gaze toward him. "It makes sense that we can't move beyond the material world if we're still obsessed with the things that happen in it."

"Exactly! So let go of it! None of that stuff down there matters right now. Be done with it. Let go!" The sage waved his hands in an exaggerated shooing motion, sending several startled birds flapping away to another branch.

"It'd be a shame to waste a second up here." Laolys observed the scenery below; miles of land lay stretched out in all directions. If it had any human inhabitants, they didn't make themselves apparent. Here, trees, grass, brush, and wildflowers all grew according to their own designs. No human hands planted and cultivated plants, and no animals faced fences or bore chains. Everything simply was as it was meant to be.

"It's easy to see divinity in a place like this. But impressiveness surrounds us everywhere. In other places, we have to look a little deeper for it. If you can see the magic in those places, too, then you've begun to awaken."

Laolys looked up at him. "What do you mean by divinity?"

"Divinity is the seed of everything. It's raw, undifferentiated energy. It's all-encompassing. It's where we came from before we entered the cycles, and it's where we're going."

Laolys envisioned an unseen light, a stream of vibrations piercing through space, bathing the Earth in a soft glow. "So... if divinity is the seed of everything, does that mean it's in everything?"

"In everything, eternal, and all-pervasive. It exists within every molecule, or else it is in nothing. Even the most ill and diseased of minds hold the keys to these greater planes; they just have more to overcome to get there."

"I suppose everyone is capable of growth."

"Correct. But we can't see the divinity in ourselves or the world around us when we're weighed down by guilt, anger, or fear. So we must continue. Is there anything else that burdens your heart?"

Laolys swallowed hard as a lump of nervous energy formed in his throat. There was one more guilt; one he had never spoken of to anyone. His voice trembled as he began. "Back when I was deep in addiction, most of my friends were heavy users too. One night, I had this overwhelming urge to stay with a friend, to watch over her. But I ignored it and left anyway. She was found dead the next morning."

A tear welled in his eye. He wiped it away quickly, hoping the sage wouldn't notice.

The sage's gaze softened. "If you had truly known you needed to stay, would you have?"

"Of course. In a heartbeat."

"Then you can't keep holding guilt for something you didn't know.

As painful as it is, sometimes events unfold the only way they could have. If you could see into other realities, you'd witness all the different ways things might have gone. You might see a world where nothing you did could have changed the outcome. You might see other timelines where she lived long into the future, or ones where she still passed, just in a different way.

"No matter the possibilities, you can't keep yourself trapped in a past you can't change. When you're ready, let go. She already has. She's moved on to something new."

Laolys thought about his life after her death. He hadn't gotten sober immediately, but losing her had forced him to face a side of himself he could no longer ignore—a fate he couldn't pretend wasn't waiting for him. "I guess you could say her death made me reassess my own life. I could no longer pretend my habits weren't equally deadly."

"Then you gave her death a purpose, in a way. It happened; we can't reverse the clock. But instead of using it as a reason to spiral further, as many do, you used it as a catalyst for change."

"It could have been prevented, though. I could have stopped it."

"That remains unknown." The sage sighed, his expression shifting to one of quiet empathy. "In the end, we have to learn to let go, to accept things as they are. We are not so high and mighty that we get to dictate reality, only how we perceive it. Live, let live, and *let go*."

"Let go," Laolys echoed. "If only it were really that easy."

"It gets easier with time. With practice. Like any fear, we must first test the waters in small ways before we're ready to take the plunge and know true freedom. Letting go is difficult because fear acts as a security net. It constricts us, but it also holds us, makes us feel as if we have control. And guilt—it's just fear turned inward. Fear of ourselves. The only way to get past it is step by step, proving to ourselves in increments that we are both worthy and capable."

"I never considered my guilt for my past behavior as fear of myself... fear of my potential for destruction." Laolys reflected on the moments when he had spun out of control, tearing down everything around him. He hated who he had been in those moments so much that it had become a fear. A fear that, perhaps, made it impossible to forgive himself.

"No one knows you better than you know yourself. You've seen your darkness, and maybe that terrifies you. But every coin has two sides; you also carry tremendous light within you. Trust yourself when you know you are heading in the right direction. Hold yourself accountable so you don't repeat the same mistakes. But don't fear yourself, and don't wallow in self-punishment either." The sage met Laolys's gaze. "Make the needed improvements. And ascend."

Laolys leaned back against the tree and turned his eyes to the landscape. The sage's words were opening his mind to a new way of thinking, but it would take time for them to fully settle in his soul. "It's nice to know that we're the only ones holding ourselves back."

"Good! Now free yourself. Let things go. Learn that nothing matters until you decide it matters. I'm not talking about physical consequences, just the things in your head—the things you hold on to. That's all you. It's what you've been led to believe you should concern yourself with. You can let them go, and you'll realize that, most of the time, the only one who was ever holding on to them was you."

Laolys sighed. "I would like to. Some things are hard to let go of."

"No process is mastered overnight. It's a continuous journey—realization, resolution, and choosing a better way of life. It's not easy, but it's worth it. Reflect on these thoughts often. Learn to shift your perspective." The sage tilted his head, studying Laolys. "Now, we must discuss anger. What anger do you hold in your heart?"

Laolys hesitated. He knew he carried anger, but up here, in the tree with the sage, he didn't feel any of it. Still, one answer came to mind immediately. "I'm angry with my father."

"Hardly a man alive who isn't! Tell me why."

"He only cares that I follow in his footsteps, carry on his legacy. He's never taken an interest in me outside of my performance in the pursuits he assigned me. I've spent my whole life trying to meet his standards, and no matter what, I always fall short." Laolys exhaled, the weight of his words settling between them. "And now, I suppose, I never will."

"What happened after you won the election? Did it get better?"

A short, bitter laugh escaped Laolys before he could stop it. "If anything, it got worse. Now that I've won, there are 'real stakes involved,' as he puts it."

"When you return, you'll have to face him. You need to tell him, calmly, that you're following your own path now, away from his shadow. Don't expect him to take it well. Just speak your truth, then move on. Leave the door open. If, in time, he reflects and chooses to grow, he'll find his way back to you."

"I don't know what I'll say to him." Laolys looked toward his town with a deep sense of dread. The thought of confronting his father rattled fears he had carried since childhood.

"You have time to think, but don't overthink. And remember, people who are themselves ill become parents all the time."

Laolys sighed. "I have some anger toward my mother, too. Not as much as with my father, but... it's still painful."

"Why?"

"She, like my father, believed she could shape me into who she wanted me to be, but she had a different way of going about it. She would hide information or twist the truth to control my perspective. Attention was a tool, given as a reward, withheld as punishment. I felt like a project, not a child."

He exhaled, the weight of old wounds pressing against him. "I was lonely growing up. Love and affection were always conditional. And it tore me apart."

"And yet, here you are." The sage gestured to their surroundings, smiling.

"Hmm?"

"If you hadn't already walked a rocky road in life, I doubt you would've climbed the cliffs and boulders that led to me. It would've been too daunting a mission, just as it is for most people. Like warriors train for battle, we train our hearts and minds through struggle. Over time, we get used to doing hard things. And what seems impossible to most is done without a second thought by people like you and me."

"I suppose it was a tough climb, but I wasn't thinking about it on the way up. I was too busy coming up with questions for you, trying to imagine how you might act toward me."

"Did you imagine accurately?"

THE YOUNG MAN AND THE SAGE

Laolys looked up at the sage, perched a few branches above, his tattered robes and wild hair swaying in the breeze. He took in the sheer absurdity of it all, receiving lessons on life and death high in a tree from a fugitive of society. He let out a sudden laugh. "Ha! I don't think anyone could anticipate you correctly!"

"Good! Then I am effectively pulling off my desired illusion!" The sage's branch shook as he emphatically declared this, clearly very pleased with himself. "But do you see how easily and mindlessly you overcome hard things? That's a trait of a true hero, someone who passes over impassable roads with a singular goal in mind. But if you continue on this path, be warned. Your trials now will seem like nothing in the future. You'll face challenges far beyond your imagination. Everything before this was just training. The real work has yet to begin. And you should be grateful for every struggle you've overcome."

Laolys took a long inhale, savoring the scent of pine. "If that's the case, then I can't be too angry at anyone."

The sun's low rays cast a golden glow over the mountainside, making the entire landscape look as if it had been sculpted by some unknown master craftsman. From high up in the tree, it all seemed distant, insignificant. Everything below felt small—too small to hold any real weight.

"But you should be angry when you have a right to be! When someone wrongs you, be angry!" The sage's sudden outburst startled Laolys, snapping him back into focus.

Noticing his reaction, the sage softened, his voice returning to its usual measured calm. "If an injustice has been committed, seek justice. Turn your anger into resolve—not just for yourself, but for society, for those who come after you. Then, say your peace, and walk on."

Laolys let loose a long exhale. The beauty of the world around him had momentarily clouded his mind, pushing out the darker thoughts he had tried so long to bury. But now, with the sage before him, he had to let them surface. He had to confront them while he had the chance.

With a tremble in his voice, he began, "There are things I am very angry about. Things I don't think I'll ever be able to let go of. It happened when I was younger, but it never should have. It broke me, fractured my psyche as a child, and left a permanent scar on my spirit. How will I ever overcome that?"

A heavy silence passed between them. It was understood without further detail that the wrongs Laolys spoke of were irrefutably evil.

"If you can, seek justice," the sage said. "Bring the perpetrator to account for his crime. It'll be painful, but facing the truth strengthens the spirit. And forcing the perpetrator to face consequences—that's how justice arises. Not through some universal law, but through those who refuse to let cruelty continue unchecked."

His gaze met Laolys's. "When we have the power to prevent harm from spreading, it's our duty to do so."

"What if I can't do anything about it? What if the perpetrator is long gone, out of my grasp?" Laolys's heart sank. There was no way for him to find the man's identity now, let alone bring him to justice.

"If you truly can't bring the perpetrator to any kind of reckoning, you must still work to mend yourself. That's half the battle. Then, if you can help heal the world in some small way—help someone else who has been wounded in a similar fashion—perhaps then you can consider justice achieved."

"Does karma catch up to people?" Laolys wanted to believe there was some form of cosmic balance, something greater ensuring that justice was served, even when the world failed to deliver it.

"Karma states that the actions that we take have a lasting effect on our soul. The mistakes that we make—our choices that harm others—stay with us. We have to learn why our actions were harmful in this life or the next. This isn't divine retribution; it's more like a sore on our soul that pulls trials into our path because we are broken. Our suffering lasts as long as we continue to make the same mistakes, until we mend our souls.

"When we bring a matter to justice in the physical realm, we force the wrongdoer to face their actions. Maybe they'll see their fault, maybe they won't, but that part isn't up to us. We will have done our part. The rest is out of our control."

Laolys stared into the distance, a pain had welled up inside of him he wished he could get rid of. "But even if we can't... they still have to face it, one way or another?"

"Yes. One day, whether after death or arrest, we must come face to face with our crimes. We must come to an understanding of why our behavior was wrong and then be faced again with the same trials. If we have learned our lesson, we may move on; if not, we remain in the same predicament as before."

"So, it's not what we have done, but what we have overcome that matters in the end." Laolys found this concept liberating. The only one holding him accountable for his past was him, and it only mattered that he did so that he did not regress back to his former state.

"Yes, and this is an essential truth to grasp. Any soul that makes it through the physical planes to graduate to ascension as a formless entity has, through the whole of its life, a very troubled past. It is likely that terrible, violent crimes have been committed in more than a few lives. It's not, therefore, what a soul has done or not done, but how the soul has learned from its mistakes and evolved past its former state."

Laolys exhaled, feeling a weight leave his body. He was responsible for himself, for his enlightenment. He wasn't doomed to suffer for his past, as long as he grew past it. While nightmarish memories still haunted him, he could let them go, eventually, as shadowy remnants of a self he left behind.

He turned his attention back to the sage, a slight smiled forming on his lips. "Everything's up to us then, isn't it?"

"Exactly!" The sage's branch bounced slightly. "It's up to us to face our struggles and move past them. It's why we're here, and not up there, in the Cosmos. But for whatever reason, most people are willing do just about anything *except* face themselves."

"Facing oneself is difficult."

The sage snorted. "Difficult, yes, but it's the only thing really worth doing. Without facing yourself, you'll never get anywhere. The door to the higher realms could be wide open in front of you, and you wouldn't be able to fit through it. You have to face yourself, refine your spirit, tune your resonance—*then* you can step through."

"Sort of like a key?"

"Exactly like a key." The sage grinned. "You could have all the answers in the world, but if we don't apply them—if you don't transform our spirit, then your knowledge is meaningless."

Laolys wasn't sure he liked this approach, even if it made sense. He preferred a world where he wasn't always the captain of his own ship—where someone more qualified could take the helm from time to time. "You don't think there's anything higher than us we can appeal to?"

"There are plenty of beings higher than us. But it's not their duty to intervene, nor would it be productive if they did. The most any being can do is guide us, offer direction, wisdom. But the choice? The action? That belongs to us. We have the freedom to act or not act in every instance, and the consequences of those choices are ours alone."

Laolys exhaled. "To be honest, I don't know how I feel about that. In some ways, I'm glad—it means we get to live, learn, and claim ascension for ourselves. But at the same time... I feel like I'll let myself down."

"Let yourself down?!" The sage's entire branch shook, sending leaves fluttering past Laolys. "The only way you could let yourself down is by not trying at all! You got yourself up here, didn't you? I'd say you're off to a fine start."

"Up here feels simple compared to what I'll face down there. As hard as my life was to bring me to this point, I know it'll be even harder when I return."

"You'll be challenged in ways you never anticipated. Don't expect everything to go well. Expect to fail, repeatedly, until you finally find one success. That's what it means to play at the harder levels of any endeavor."

"I suppose failure only happens when we stop trying."

The sage attempted to catch his gaze, but Laolys didn't notice; his eyes were locked on the distant valleys.

The sage cleared his throat, and began in a loud, boisterous tone, "What does a sports team do when they lose?"

Laolys straightened and looked back at the him but said nothing.

"They train harder!" the sage continued. "They come up with new strategies. We don't think less of an athlete for losing a game, but we would if he lost once and quit playing."

"We certainly wouldn't think highly of anyone with an attitude like that," Laolys admitted.

"So we shouldn't practice such attitudes ourselves, in any area of life. Expect to fail; it's necessary. It means you're challenging yourself, learning new things. A soldier is stronger after he's endured many blows; he no longer fears getting hit. If your fear of failure is so great, then fail until it's no longer a fear."

"Toughen up," Laolys acknowledged.

"Yes, but don't toughen up, get comfortable, and stay there. Don't be the big fish in the small lake, too afraid to swim downstream with his siblings, too afraid of what's in the ocean. There's an entire world out there to explore. More pain and more growth are bound to happen along the way."

"I think it's the first plunge that's so hard for the fish. And every year, it keeps getting harder and harder."

"Explain your answer, student!" The sage grinned at Laolys.

"Every year, another school comes and goes, and he psyches himself up more each time. Just before they're ready to graduate, he tells himself, 'This year, I'm going to be like all the other fish.' But he doubts himself, and he gets so nervous that he doesn't leave with them. And he doubts himself more each year."

"Do you know what his problem is?"

"He doubts himself?"

The sage shook his head. "He thinks he's not like the other fish. Everyone doubts themselves. Everyone gets anxious. He thinks he is lesser than, special in some odd sort of way. He's just like every other fish. Every other fish also thinks they're a unique case; they just play it off better."

"Everyone thinks that they're weird and unrelatable?" Laolys was certain that his case was particular and extreme.

"To varying degrees. Some go to great lengths to try to fit in; others go to great lengths to try to stand out, but all for the same reason. They want others to accept them. Do you know why some people are so mean?"

"I'm guessing they don't think others accept them."

The sage nodded. "They fear rejection so much that they push everyone away before they have the chance to be rejected. Then they wonder why no one likes them."

"But they're rude, why do they feel hurt when others return the favor?"

"They don't see it that way. They project what they expect, and the world reflects it back at them. We see the anger enter and leave with them; they think the whole world is angry."

"So, mean people are always talking about how mean everyone is, and nice people talk about how there's goodness in everyone... but what do you have to say about people who go live on top of mountains and never talk to or about anyone?" Laolys smiled playfully at the sage and ducked behind one arm as if already anticipating another stray pinecone launched from the area of his teacher.

"Entirely tired of everyone's opinions! Tired of caring about them, tired of not caring about them, tired of thinking about them all together! And I did quite well not thinking about any opinions at all until you showed up!" The sage eyed Laolys with a mischievous grin. As it stood, no pinecones appeared to be nearing flight.

"I think my brain does me more harm than good," Laolys said. "I think too much about things that are insignificant. I imagine the worst and live in fear."

The sage chuckled. "The Egyptians were wise in not considering the brain a sacred organ."

"What do you mean?"

"The ancient Egyptians had a very specific art to their mummification process. It was a sacred act, and they took great care in handling every organ as they removed them from the body, leaving only the heart intact. They kept four organs: the stomach, the lungs, the liver, and the intestines. The brain was the first organ they removed, and they discarded it immediately.

"They didn't think the path through the afterlife would be easy. They memorized specific prayers and were buried with sacred amulets and papyri to help them remember them. Now, why do you think, if they had to remember all those prayers, would they still remove the brain first and discard it, not placing it in a sacred jar?"

"Hmm..." Laolys thought for a moment, imagining the ancient Egyptians, with the medical knowledge of every organ in the human body, immediately disposing of the brain. "Because it holds us back?"

The sage nodded. "The brain is powerful, but it's also dangerous. When it comes to the soul, it can be fatal. True wisdom comes from the heart, from emotions, from the spirit. The brain questions, doubts, and fixates on both the best and worst possibilities. The heart doesn't do any of that. The heart just knows. Imagine how the brain would interfere with the weighing of the heart."

"Yes, it would recall all sorts of things to be angry about... or unworthy."

"That's correct. In those circumstances, the brain can only lead to our downfall, our recycling. Do you know what the Egyptians worked so hard to ascend to? How they defined the Field of Reeds?"

Laolys shook his head. "Their version of heaven?"

"Not heaven as most imagine. The ancient Egyptians saw the afterlife as a continuation of life as they had known it, only without hunger, sadness, sickness, or death. People still worked, still harvested crops, still maintained their homes. Life carried on. That was what they worshiped and sacrificed for, to live on after death, eternally."

Laolys thought about the people in his hometown, the way they longed for grand rewards without effort. "People want much more now. And they want to sacrifice nothing for it."

The sage grumbled something inaudible. Then, more clearly, "Only the heart was believed to make the passage through these realms. Only the heart was capable of reaching the ultimate place of refuge. The brain? Well, the brain only gets in the way."

"The brain is what stops the big fish."

"The brain is *all* that stops the big fish. And I'll bet that the big fish is very smart. So smart, in fact, that no one's ever told him he should consider not using his brain."

Laolys paused, amused. "Now that I think of it, everyone I have met whom I consider highly intelligent seems to have a lot of the same pains as the big fish."

"Remember, everyone has the same pains as the big fish. The big fish just thinks he's the only one."

Laolys's gaze fell back to his town. "So... how does he stop being so afraid?"

"He has to realize his fears are only that—fears—and take the plunge." The sage fell silent, gazing at Laolys as if contemplating something considerable. He opened his mouth to say something and closed it again. When he finally spoke, he only said two words: "Define fear."

Laolys hesitated. "The anticipation of something dangerous."

The sage shook his head, "No, that's not fear. Recognizing true danger isn't fear. Standing on the edge of a cliff and being cautious so you don't fall off—that's not fear. Lying awake in bed all night because you're afraid that one day you *might* stand near the edge of a cliff—that's fear. The first is instinct. The second is entirely imagined."

"Okay... But we should know about cliffs, understand the need for caution around them, and how to climb them if we know we'll be in the mountains."

"That's preparation, not fear. Considering possibilities and preparing for probabilities is reasonable. Fear enters the equation when we add worry and anxiety—the unnecessary, unfounded weight of negative emotion."

Laolys nodded. He knew fear well. So did his family, though they'd never admit it. The more he thought about it, the more he realized that nearly everyone he knew lived in fear. "Fear governs most people's lives, doesn't it?"

The sage gazed out at the landscape. "It was certainly the case when I left society."

"But why? Why can't they stop being so afraid?"

The sage shrugged. "First, they'd have to admit they have fear in the first place. Most people are in denial about it. Then, they'd have to stand face to face with whatever it is that terrifies them. Nearly everyone doesn't want to do that. So, people stay locked up in fear."

Laolys tightened his grip on his branch. "There are *some* things we should be afraid of."

"Like what?"

"Dying, for one."

The sage tilted his head. "What good does it do a man to fear his own death?"

"It keeps him from jumping off a cliff!"

"No, *reason* keeps him from jumping off a cliff. It isn't reasonable to throw away one's life when there's still wisdom to gain, lessons to learn, and growth to be had. And I don't mean a life of leisure, I mean a life with the potential to evolve. *Reason* keeps a person safe. Fear? That's something else entirely. And it's not reasonable to fear death. Everyone will die. It's inevitable. We can neither predict nor control when or how it will happen. So what sense is there in wasting our energy dreading it? Better to use that time and energy for something worthwhile: our own evolution."

"I guess you'd get used to the idea of death pretty quickly when you see so many timelines where it has already happened."

"I suppose you would get used to it in such a case. But in my case, I had to be used to the idea long, long before I could see the other timelines."

"If you don't mind me asking, what allowed you to see the other timelines?"

"I had to accept them. Some timelines aren't easy to like. But they're all part of me, in a way. For someone like you, who fears himself in his current state, there's a long road ahead before you can embrace your worst opposites. That's a journey you'll have to walk on your own."

The sage paused. His face adopted a somber expression as his gaze drifted toward the horizon. "If you're interested, I'll tell you about my death today."

Laolys smirked. "Falling out of a tree?"

The sage grinned and bounced on his branch, sending tremors through the tree and shaking Laolys's perch.

"No," he laughed. "But that's what a student gets for talking back to his teacher!"

Laolys clung to his branch, laughing despite himself.

The sage let the tree settle and leaned back against the trunk. "No, today's death happened earlier. I was freshening up at the creek, as I do every morning. Then, I slipped on a rock. It sent me crashing into another at just the right angle. I bled out, slowly... dying in the creek."

"Yikes." Laolys grimaced as the scene played in his mind.

"Indeed. Now, do you think I bathed this morning, awakening to that vision?"

Laolys considered the lesson. "Yes, you faced your fear."

The sage chuckled. "I see you think rather highly of me! No, I didn't go down to the creek. I saw the real possibility and used reason. But I will bathe tomorrow, so long as I don't awaken to the same vision."

"I'm still trying to understand the difference between not fearing death and still avoiding it."

"I don't want to die," the sage said. "No one should want to die except in the most extreme circumstances. We should care for our health, prolong life, and take reasonable measures to prevent accidents. Fear, however, doesn't involve reason. Fear would keep me from creeks altogether, and then, soon enough, from all rocks."

"Okay, but it's not always easy to tell the difference when we're caught up in things."

"Name an example." The sage watched Laolys with intensity.

"Okay, let's say you fear being poisoned. It's happened before, to a minor degree, and it happens to men in your position. So, you have a hard time eating unless you see it prepared in front of you."

The sage stroked his chin. "For someone in that position, it sounds like reasonable precautions."

"So, it isn't fear?"

"Fear, in such a case, would mean only procuring food oneself, growing it in a locked garden, sacrificing sleep, and starving out of paranoia. It becomes obsessive and detrimental. But you said, 'he has a hard time eating food without seeing it prepared,' not that he abstains completely. That means he's practicing some degree of reason. He doesn't starve himself; he weighs the risk of poisoning against the pains and weakness of hunger."

"So, the line is vague," Laolys said.

"If we're honest, there are no strict lines to define any virtue. It's always circumstantial. Virtue must be practiced with discretion. One man may take no precautions, believing them unworthy of his distress. That's his judgment to make. He may die an earlier death because of it, or he may not. He might escape poisoning by sheer chance. His body may even become more acclimated to it, while another man, despite all his efforts, may still succumb."

"There are no guarantees," Laolys agreed.

"There is one guarantee. Death will happen. But where, how, and when—those are never certain. Be grateful, though. For this truth is also a freedom."

"How?"

"Think of the one power a person bound into slavery has that cannot be taken away: the right to his own death, and possibly even the death of the one who wields the whip. For someone desperate enough, even the most crude object can stop up a windpipe. There are many ways to die if the will is there. If a man sees his death as a freedom from torture and execution, and he truly doesn't fear it, then he is untouchable in a way. This right should be known to both the captured and their captors alike. Everyone has the ability to take another's life, as well as his own."

Laolys looked at him with a mix of awe and unease. "Are you saying murder can be just? And suicide?"

"Forget morality as you've been taught and consider it with a fresh mind. Murder and the threat of it are used to overpower entire populations. Yet every person who is overpowered has this same ability. If not for more reasonable senses, no one should wield violence to dominate others because it points the barrel back at them. Those who capture and enslave others play a dangerous game. They must always look over their shoulders, because their captives should kill them the moment the opportunity arises."

"And suicide?"

"Not an easy subject... but for a man in bondage with no escape, a prisoner of war, or someone bedridden with pain and disease, with no hope of recovery—it's understandable why they might seek death."

"I suppose if we didn't have the ability to die, we could be kept in pain and tortured indefinitely."

The sage gave a half nod. "Humans aren't noble enough for immortality. If death didn't exist to balance the scales, the world would be far worse. And I believe we gain more knowledge by living and dying through many lives. One life alone would limit a soul too much."

"What about suicide in cases of sorrow? Emotional distress?" Laolys recalled moments when he had considered such thoughts himself. He was grateful he hadn't acted on them—he was here now. But what wisdom could the sage offer to someone in that bleak state?

"In those cases, suicide only prolongs the agony of the soul. Only physical pain fades with death; emotional pain lingers. It follows us into the afterlife, into the next incarnation. A person is born into a new body, a new life, carrying an inexplicable weight in their heart. Imagine that burden compounding over multiple lives, each one heavier, until it's finally confronted."

Laolys nodded but stayed quiet, absorbing the weight of the words.

"This is why it's only a reasonable choice when there's no escape from endless physical suffering," the sage continued. "But in cases of emotional distress, we must confront it. Physical pain—illness, imprisonment—will pass. But the wounds of the soul? Those are meant to be healed in our lifetime. That is why we're here. Not for enjoyment, not to appease some deity, but to face what troubles us and grow beyond it. And we can only do that while we're alive."

"It makes sense when you put it that way... But the agony of a person who points a gun to their own head—who actually pulls the trigger—that kind of suffering isn't so easily dismissed."

"I'm not saying it's easy to pull oneself out of that state. I'm just saying that it's the only option we have. If we don't face what ails us, we only prolong our suffering."

A sudden rustling below broke the conversation. Beneath the tree limbs, twigs snapped as something heavy moved through their camp. Laolys tensed, listening. The weight of each footstep pressed the forest floor, leaving cracked twigs and leaves in its path. It moved without hurry, a clear sign of a predator.

"Did you see a timeline where we get eaten?" Laolys whispered, peering through the branches for a glimpse of the ground below.

"Yes, but that's every day out here. I didn't think it was worth mentioning." The sage's voice was calm as he scanned the camp.

"But you climbed up here to avoid it?"

"Eh," the sage crept slowly around his branch for a better view. "I came up here for the view, not because I saw the two of us dead in our camp, as I do every day. I'd call this one intuition. But that's a lesson for another day."

"But you did say something about getting eaten when I asked you to come down. That's why I climbed the tree!"

"A very real possibility all the time. I can't predict the future any more than you can."

"I bet you can. I can't see other timelines." Though Laolys kept his voice low, his irritation was evident.

"There are infinite timelines. I liken it to you picking a random number while I get to make infinite guesses at once. One of them will be right, but there's still no way for me to tell which one."

The rustling grew closer. The sage signaled to Laolys to be silent, and both men stilled, listening.

Laolys drifted off into a transient, meditative state. He envisioned himself high above the trees, where the entire camp was out of sight. Though his body still clung tightly to his branch, frozen in place, he was not frozen in time. The sun plunged down the horizon, bringing the once golden forest into an eerie twilight gloom.

Across the mountain, small creatures noticed the increasing shadows and waning light and made their way to the nearest burrows and dens. Soon, creatures of the night would be yawning and stretching their legs. It would be the time of predators, so prey must carefully tuck itself away.

Man is a unique animal. He can, at times, be the most dangerous animal in the forest, but he does not hunt at night. He hunts during the day, keeping his company with the gentler creatures and feasting on them as well. His body does not need meat, but it takes it in with stride so long as he properly prepares it on open flame. He has evolved to be this way, taking himself past his initial state to be more like the creatures he admires. But man is not a lion, nor is he a bear. He does not mash into his prey with incisors but with knives and forks. Nor can he keep the company of either one of these animals without becoming the dinner himself! He should, then, by honest assessment, lower his position on the food chain. He should walk with more humility, bow with more respect, and practice more kindness. He should make his den secure at night, and he should sometimes house similar estranged creatures overnight because there will be nights when he, too, is estranged.

Laolys saw in his mind's eye a circle of rings, infinite rings, glowing and connected, overlapping, surrounding one central void of nothingness. He was only one of these rings, but everything he did reached the others in some grand or insignificant way. There was no action without a reaction, nor was anything not both acting and reacting at any given second. Union seemed to be the sum of this infinite entangled web. Everything worked in unison. Even seemingly tortuous aspects had their role.

Death was but a blink here, a blink that was happening all over, every second. Somewhere, some small or large light would burn out. Then, somewhere else, a spark of equal size would flash, then shrink and begin to grow. All over, life and death worked in tandem so closely one could hardly tell them apart.

The darkening sky must have stirred something in Laolys's senses, pulling him back into full awareness of the physical world around him. The sage was gone. He wasn't surprised; nor did he bother looking for him.

He climbed down from the tree and made his way to the hut with haste, slipping inside and shutting the door behind him. He had no idea where the sage slept which wasn't in his bed, inside his hut, but tonight, Laolys was grateful to have it.

He lay down, secured inside, and sleep overtook him almost instantly.

The Flame Within the Triangle

Vibrations

"We are of mind before we are of matter. Therefore, we must place our values of the mental world over that of the physical. It influences matter, not the other way around."

The words echoed around Laolys as if he were submerged in a deep underwater cavern, standing on the bottom. It wasn't the voice of the sage. They emanated from an unknown source, reverberating around him, bumping and reflecting off unseen surfaces. He realized he was dreaming.

He looked at the strange world enveloping him. It was entirely dark, except for a soft glow emanating from his own body, casting a light only a few arm lengths ahead. It felt as though he was at the bottom of an ocean, except the solution was much thicker than water. Curiously, it didn't impede his breath, but it did send every movement he made rippling toward an unknown destination. He stood in place, unsure how to direct himself in this strange astral realm.

Lifting his right arm, he noticed web-like strings extending from it. Startled, he raised his left arm and saw the same thing. He squirmed, trying to shake off the strings, but they remained firmly attached. Upon closer inspection, he realized the strings weren't stuck to him, they were emanating from him, merging with his aura. He pulled on a few, testing if he could remove them, but none would budge.

"Hey, whoa there! What's going on?" a strange voice called out from somewhere in the distance.

Laolys froze, startled. He scanned the area, but he couldn't see any figures or disturbances that could indicate the source of the voice.

"Hmm, seems to have resolved itself," the voice said, as if speaking to someone else, or perhaps itself.

"H-Hello?" Laolys called out, but there was no immediate response. Tentatively, he began waving his arms, tugging at the strings again.

"There it is again. What's going on?" The voice reacted to Laolys's movements.

Laolys continued waving his arms, hoping to attract the attention of the voice. "Hello?" he shouted into the thick, enveloping substance, hoping his voice would carry to wherever the being was.

"Ah, hello stranger," the voice responded, seemingly pinpointing Laolys as the point of the disturbance.

"Who are you?" Laolys asked.

"What a strange question. I am me; who else could I be?" The voice rang through the aether.

"Do you have a name? I am Laolys."

"I have as many names as other beings have given me; I never thought much about any particular one. What is a Laolys? This is a new creature to me."

"No, I mean that is my name, Laolys. I'm a human. Are you not a human?"

"Simply put, I am energy, and I am consciousness. I have been billions of things to billions of beings across the multiverse; so many things that they are all, essentially, meaningless, and naming any of them would only confuse you."

"What do you mean?"

"Well, I am formless, but as other entities perceive me, they may assign some type of form to me. So, I could appear in countless different forms at once, in countless places, but none of those truly describe me. The problem is, once someone fixates on a particular way of defining me, that's all I can be to them. If you don't mind, I'd prefer to keep things simple."

"It's okay, I don't mind." Laolys lifted his arm again to observe the strings. "Um," he hesitated, "I seem to be caught in some sort of net."

"Who isn't?" the voice said nonchalantly.

"You are too?"

The voice let loose a sigh. "Yes, me and everything else in the known and unknown multiverse."

"How do you know it's in the unknown multiverse?"

"Simple process of deduction. What's known now was once unknown and will be unknown again when we discover what is now unknown. Everything we've ever known has been entangled in the net."

"Everything?"

"Everything."

Laolys paused for a moment, absorbing the words. Then, he waved his arms slightly, causing a ripple in the net. "What does it do when I cause a disturbance in the net?"

"It sends me vibration."

"Like what? Sound? Motion?"

"Sure," the voice answered, unenthused.

"Which one?"

"Whichever one you like."

Laolys wasn't sure what to make of this response. He fell silent a moment, pondering his next question. "Where are you?" he finally asked.

"I live outside of the realm of space-time, so where isn't easily described. Where I reside, there are no forms or boundaries as they exist in the physical world. It is an expansive, formless realm beyond dimensions, a place of pure potential and energy where thoughts and intentions shape the very essence of existence. This space is fluid, where consciousness and essence move in harmony. Time is non-linear, and space is boundless; it's a shifting sea of light and resonance, with everything vibrating in tune with a cosmic order."

Laolys tried to imagine what it would be like to live as the voice described. It was unlike anything he'd experienced. Unsure of what else to say to the voice, he replied, "I am on a planet called Earth."

"Earth..." the voice trailed off, then continued as if retrieving stored knowledge. "Ah, yes, Earth: a mid-sized blue and green sphere orbiting a yellow star, wrapped in a thin atmosphere and dotted with diverse liquid formations. It hosts a wide array of biomechanical life, including advanced conscious beings known as humans."

"That's the one," Laolys confirmed.

"There are many parallel realms there. Which one are you in?"

"I—I don't know," Laolys stammered. "I only know of mine."

"You haven't looked for others?"

"I only recently heard others exist."

There was a pause before the voice spoke again, its tone filled with curiosity. "What is it like? To only see one?"

"It's all I've ever known. I wouldn't know how to explain it. What is it like to see several?"

"It's all I've ever known. I see the entirety of things easily, but I can't say I always understand it."

"Why not?"

"Humans, for example, puzzle me. They are always trying to separate—build walls around each other, around nature, around themselves. It's like they don't understand that it is impossible to disconnect from the Net."

"The Net?"

"This expansive network of strings."

"Oh, well..." Laolys hesitated. "Most are unaware that the Net exists at all."

"They close themselves off, that is all. They are still very much connected."

Laolys paused, studying the strings extending from his body. They stretched into the surrounding aether in every direction. He couldn't see far enough to determine exactly what they were connected to, but he could feel the tension, each one anchored to something unseen. "How far do these strings extend?"

"Distance is not easily translated. Any answer would be so varied, so astronomically large, it would be meaningless to you. It is simpler to say... distance is irrelevant when it comes to those strings."

"Can I change what I'm attached to?" Laolys pressed, uneasy with the idea that he couldn't see where any of his strings led.

"You are changing them all the time."

"Can I direct them consciously?"

"Of course."

"How?"

"Simple matter of making a conscious decision, I suppose." The voice seemed either bored or distracted.

Laolys imagined that whoever he was speaking to likely had more important matters to attend to than him. He looked up in the direction of the voice. "How do I get where you are? ... I mean, *can* I get there?"

"To get where I am, you must retune your vibrations," the voice answered.

"But how?"

"Another matter of making a conscious decision, I suppose."

Laolys remained silent, absorbing the entity's words. It was a lot of information, but here in the dream world, it felt natural. His entire being absorbed the meaning; his spirit recorded it so that later, during waking hours, it could send impulses—ones his waking self might either ignore or pay attention to.

"What type of things do you do where you are?" Laolys asked.

"I maintain balance across all planes of existence and guide souls towards ascension."

"You work with the Net?"

"Everyone works with the Net."

The voice sounded distracted, or perhaps, irritated. Laolys began to worry that he was wearing on its patience. Surely whoever was behind it had better things to do and was only conversing with him out of courtesy.

Soon, this thought held no significance, as he was pulled from his spot by a strong current. He felt like he was being strung along by a boat through water; ripples emitting from him as he was involuntarily carried along. In his field of vision, he saw lights of various colors and brightness passing by, fuzzy and wavelike, as if being filtered through a thick substance.

He plunged further and further down. Or was it up? It didn't matter; without relation to something else, almost everything loses its meaning. We must be connected to the world around us to make sense of anything at all. No one, though each consciousness exists knowing only itself, can be entirely apart from other beings. If we were, what would be the source of our vibration?

Laolys awoke and noticed the sky outside the hut was still characterized fully by darkness. He returned to the bed, lying down to reflect on his dreams, the words of the sage, and his happenstance fortune of avoiding being eaten only hours earlier. He wanted to believe it was more than the sage's whim to host the lesson in the tree, yet reason argued that he was being honest about his abilities to predict the future.

He turned his thoughts to the dream, to the words of the strange voice. It viewed many places at once and saw multiple dimensions. Maybe the sage was seeing the future of other dimensions. Maybe there were other worlds parallel to this one. Renowned scientists have proposed this theory and so have many credible spiritual philosophies. It must not, therefore, be so strange to consider the sage correct in all of his claims regarding this subject, nor to consider the voice in the dream any less credible than the sage.

Is this awakening? The world seemed to be unfolding before his eyes, revealing layers as the sage had mentioned. Or perhaps he was losing his mind, listening to a man who lived in a state of psychosis, and now he was slipping too. All possibilities had to be considered, but fear must not stand in the way of reason. *Other people's definitions of sanity and rationale,* he thought, *are quite confused, actually.*

He tried to still his mind and call sleep to return, to bring him back to the astral realms, to bring rest. His mind slipped into a restful state, but the thoughts did not cease. They wandered into his consciousness, conjoining seemingly random images, as he could not pinpoint a source. He examined them, finding that he could direct them at will, adding and subtracting parts, changing shapes, and so on. His mind would not cease its activity enough to consider sleep, so he entertained himself this way until morning.

When the sun shot its first glorious rays over the horizon, announcing its victory to the rising fanfare of the birds, Laolys poked his head out of the sage's hut. Along with the other gentle creatures of the mountain, he stretched his legs and silently thanked the sun for bringing the return of warmth and light.

The Covenant Beneath the Mirror

Unseen

"The universe's depth goes beyond our wildest imagination, most of what surrounds us exceeds the threshold of our senses."

The words were spoken immediately as Laolys exited the hut. The sage was perched on a rock just outside the door, seated in a lotus position, staring directly at Laolys with wide, excited eyes. Laolys got the impression that he had been waiting for him for a while. Behind the sage, the sun had barely peaked over the horizon, giving him a somewhat mythical appearance, a solar aetherial glow.

Laolys yawned and tried to snap his brain into focus. "Are you talking about unperceivable energy? Like electricity, or radio waves?"

"That and much, much more."

"What else?" Laolys sat down on a rock adjacent to the sage, pausing to take in the mountainside. The crisp solar rays touched the treetops across the panoramic landscape, bringing a spark of warmth to the chill morning air.

"Consciousness."

"Consciousness? What do you mean?"

The sage gestured to the landscape. "Consciousness is everywhere.

It's in the plants, animals, and the Earth itself. But it's also in empty space—or at least, it *can be*. That's the whole goal of ascension, you know."

Laolys looked up, studying the last few stars fading from the sky. "And other types of energy?"

"Cosmic energy, solar energy, quantum energy, as well as spiritual energy or life-force—the vacuum of space is very much alive!"

"The vacuum—it's not empty?"

The sage shook his head. "Not seen and not detectable does not mean absent—merely invisible to the naked eye."

"I guess."

The sage shot Laolys a sharp look. "You better not keep that mindset for too much longer. It wasn't all that long ago that electricity was thought to be a myth—a tall tale from some mad inventor claiming he pulled energy out of nowhere." He scoffed. "It takes a madman to move society forward, every damn time."

Laolys studied him with interest. "So how do the mad ones know it's there?"

The sage shrugged. "They're crazy enough to pay attention, I suppose."

"What do you mean?"

"We can sense energy if we pay attention. A magnetic field, for example—we might not notice it if we're lost in thought, but if we tune in to our bodies, we'll feel it. The same goes for energy from people. It can be seen, felt, even absorbed through our empathic senses. But most people never stop to notice. They're too caught up in their own minds."

Laolys gazed out at the untouched landscape, taking in its stillness. *That's why it's so peaceful here,* he thought. The worries, the noise, the unease—they all stayed down there, in that tiny patch of land at the edge of his town, swirling among its people.

"People do have a disruptive way about them," he said. "They don't have to say or do anything—just being there can put you on edge."

The sage coughed, as if something had caught in his throat. "You're right about that. I wouldn't do well if I went back. Too much for me now."

"You mean society?"

"I mean, everyone. I've seen maybe two or three people in the last several years, including you. Each one sends me into a whole new headspace..." He fell quiet, his expression softening. "But each one needed the lessons. And teaching them helped me too."

A few birds squawked loudly nearby, jolting the sage back into focus. He turned to Laolys, locking eyes with him. "Your awareness of this gives me hope that you're ready for this lesson."

"How so?"

"Today, we venture into the subject of the unseen. I should clarify, when I say *seen*, I don't just mean what we observe with our eyes, but everything we perceive with our five senses. When I speak of the *unseen*, I'm referring to the world beyond those senses. The things we detect with our spirit, our intuition."

"An extra sense?"

"In a way, yes. But this sense is all-encompassing. It's felt everywhere in the body and yet nowhere specific. It picks up on both internal and external, physical and non-physical phenomena. But it doesn't always bring them to our attention."

"Why not?"

"Some things we just aren't ready for." The sage turned his gaze toward the horizon with a wistful look in his eyes.

Laolys swallowed a lump of nervous energy. "Like what?"

"Most of us are deeply attached to our current identity, our humanity. We have rigid ideas about who we are and how the world around us should behave. When something contradicts that..." The sage grimaced. "It unsettles us. So, our consciousness blocks it out."

Laolys's eyes widened. "And this extra phenomenon... It's there all the time?"

The sage smiled. "If by 'extra phenomenon' you mean something beyond your current awareness, then absolutely. Other timelines exist alongside you, unseen. Energy is whizzing past your head right now, imperceptible to you. Our perception can extend far beyond the earthly plane, but most people will never access it. Most can't even accept the world in its simplest, most obvious forms."

Laolys remained silent as images from his dream flooded his mind

—strings stretching from his body, connecting to unseen forces across the universe; a mysterious voice. It had felt like more than just a dream.

He returned his focus to the sage. "Can we be connected to things that are very far away?"

"We most certainly can be! But let's start with what's in front of us." The sage opened his hand, revealing a small rock with components that sparkled in the sun. "Remember when we discussed how a rock is full of life?"

"Yes... well, the molecules are alive in a way... and there are microbes."

"It also holds memories."

Laolys blinked. "What? Memories?"

"Energetic ones." The sage extended his hand, offering the rock. "Here, take it."

Laolys grabbed the rock and felt its weight in his palm.

"Now," the sage continued, "study it. Learn its features. When you're ready, close your eyes and bring it to mind. Then tell me what you see."

Laolys ran his fingers over the rock's rough surface, tracing its irregular edges. He turned it over, noting the tiny grooves and indentations. When he felt he had memorized its shape, he closed his eyes and took a slow, steady breath. He focused on the rock's weight in his hand, picturing it clearly in his mind.

Then something strange happened. The image of the rock vanished. In its place, a green cube appeared, enclosing the space where the rock had been. Inside, light pulsed, stretching into thin, glowing strands that radiated outward. The glow intensified, then dimmed. A wave of unease washed over him, and he forced his eyes open.

"Well?" The sage leaned forward, watching him closely.

Laolys looked down, unsure. "I don't know. I saw the rock, but then it disappeared... and there was this light, inside a cube."

The sage's expression lit up. "You got it then!"

"The light?"

"The cube."

"But I dreamt about that last night!" Laolys eyed the sage suspiciously, wondering if, maybe, he was trying to trick him.

"If it picks up additional images, your mind isn't clear enough to process it alone. I only impressed a simple cube onto the rock, nothing more. But your imagery gives a better real-world example."

Laolys turned the rock over in his hand with a sense of shock and wonder. "The rock carries this?"

"Think of it like a thumbprint or an echo. Some materials hold energy better than others. This rock has a high quartz content, and quartz is an excellent energy receptor. It stores energy, like a battery."

The sage gestured toward the stone. "I held it with focused intent, embedding the visual into it with intense concentration. I chose a green cube, symbolizing the Earth element, because symbols already ingrained in the subconscious are easier to receive. But whether or not the impression is picked up depends entirely on the perceiver. Some people are extremely sensitive to this type of energy, while others will never register it at all. A crystal could be teeming with measurable energy, and some wouldn't have the faintest clue."

Laolys stared at the rock in silence. He hadn't mentioned that the cube was green, yet the sage had just confirmed it. A shiver ran through him. He couldn't deny what had just happened; he had received an image placed there by another person. Whether through the rock or by some other means, he had connected with it. He wasn't sure what unsettled him more: that it was possible, or that it had happened so easily.

"Fortunately, you did pick up my impression," the sage continued, oblivious Laolys's distress. "So it's a good example of how we can perceive things around us without realizing it. Have you ever noticed how a room can have a certain mood, even when its empty?"

"Well, yes, but I always figured it had something to do with the light, or the furnishings."

"Those things play a minor role, but they have less influence than you think. A room absorbs the energy of its inhabitants. If someone spends a good deal of time in there, especially with strong emotions, that energy lingers, sometimes for decades."

The sage glanced over his shoulder. "Tell me, what do you think of my hut? Be honest, no need to spare my feelings."

"Honestly? It has a strange charm. It's almost hard for me to get rest in there."

The sage's face broke into a grin. "I feel the same! I poured my essence into every inch of that place." He exhaled sharply. "But the next time I build a shelter I'll factor in the need for sleep."

"Is that why you don't sleep in there?"

"Only when the weather makes it necessary. When that happens, I don't sleep much."

Laolys looked around at the campsite. "So where do you sleep?"

The sage shot him a sharp glare. "I told you I won't disclose any details about my life. These lessons are about you. It's for your own good."

Laolys blushed and looked away, ashamed of himself for prying.

The sage stood up to face the hut and gave Laolys a friendly pat on the back. "No matter. Just tell me, purely by appearance, what do you think of the hut? Again, be honest."

Laolys stood up and looked at the hut, searching for something worthy of praise. At best, it was a makeshift shed held together by a few cherished nails, mud, tree sap, and perhaps sheer willpower. There were no embellishments, no excess space. Though it had been the sage's home for twenty years, it looked more like an afterthought, thrown together in haste by an architect who wished to remain unnoticed amidst the perfection of the natural world.

"It's... not traditionally elegant," he said softly, as it was the best he could muster.

"Not elegant in the slightest! And yet, it inspires endless hours of musings. Why is that?"

"Memories?"

The sage nodded and sat back down. "In a sense, accumulated energy. A decade of intense self-discovery went into that small space. In there, I breached places of consciousness deemed unreachable; I discovered truths I could never have dreamt up in a million years! That place came alive because of me. Do you think if we made another hut with the same appearance and contents, it would have the same effect?"

Laolys considered the strange, lifelike vibrancy of the hut. Somehow, everything within it—the contents, even the walls themselves—had absorbed the sage's inward, outward, and otherworldly experiences. They didn't speak in the conventional sense; rather, they leaked their wisdom through osmosis. The sage's energy lingered, imprinted long after his physical presence had left. Though he rarely inhabited the hut anymore, his essence remained fully present. It echoed his emotions, much like a stain silently declares an incident decades after its impact.

"Of course not."

"That's because all the hours I spent in intense meditation radiated through these walls, and they absorbed it. The effect this hut has on its inhabitants has nothing to do with the materials it was built from, the angles of its architecture, or the objects inside. Those things only matter when they matter to me; when they affect my perception, and therefore, the energy I leave behind that permeates the space."

"But how does that work? How does an environment receive something as intangible as thoughts?"

"Vibration." The sage met Laolys's gaze. "Everything is vibration. The mind is vibration, consciousness is vibration, and your spirit—" he thumped Laolys's chest lightly, "is vibration. Your emotions carry strong vibrations, radiating into your surroundings, perceptible to all observers, whether consciously or unconsciously."

Laolys realized he had never stopped to consider whether his emotions had an outward effect, but of course, they did. Just as he was sensitive to the emotions of others, it made sense that others—and even objects—could absorb his. "I suppose we can feel other people's emotions, especially when they're strong. Vibrations would explain this."

"Our thoughts carry strong vibrations, especially when the mind is focused. They can be felt by others and can even imprint on our environment. Lots of things absorb and carry energy. Water, for example, is especially receptive. I'm sure you're familiar with holy water."

Laolys nodded.

"Holy water has been prayed over or meditated upon, and as a result, it's observed to have healing effects," the sage continued. "Of course, any real healing power water can carry is limited—but the changes in its energy are perceivable, nonetheless.

"On a scientific level, laboratories have observed changes in the molecular structure of water depending on whether positive or negative thoughts and emotions were directed into it."

Laolys looked up, his curiosity piqued. "How exactly did they change?"

"When water molecules bond together, they do so at various angles. Scientists found that when water was exposed to positive intentions—loving thoughts, calming music, kind words—the molecules formed neat, symmetrical hexagonal structures. But when subjected to negative vibrations—angry words, harsh thoughts, or discordant sounds—the molecules became chaotic, forming at irregular, disorganized angles."

Laolys blinked, taken aback. "Just thoughts?"

"Thoughts are powerful. Don't underestimate them. What you focus on affects you physically, as well as those around you."

"I suppose so," Laolys mumbled. It was a lot to take in.

"Think about it. If thoughts have measurable effects on water, what are they doing to our bodies, which are roughly 60 percent water?"

Laolys inhaled sharply as the realization hit him. "I suppose... quite a bit."

"Quite a bit, indeed. Never doubt the power your mind holds over your body. Negative thoughts—worry, fear, self-loathing—disrupt our cells. Carry them for too long, and they manifest physically. The body listens to the mind, whether we realize it or not."

"Just with thought..." Laolys repeated softly.

"The effects of stress on the body go far beyond a weakened immune system. It leads to heart problems, digestive issues, insomnia—the list goes on. Disruptive thoughts create disruptions in the body."

Laolys considered his own health—his racing heart, constant indigestion, restless nights. There was no doubt his anxiety had taken a toll. "So... are we supposed to cure ourselves with positive thoughts?"

The sage shot him a sharp look. "Medicine has its place. But it's not enough on its own. If we don't fix our resonance, we'll keep manifesting illness in one form or another."

"How do we retune ourselves?"

"Self-remembrance. First, we have to acknowledge the power of our thoughts. Most people assume their thoughts are meaningless, just fleeting notions in their heads. That's a great mistake. Where we direct our minds profoundly affects our physical health, and even the world around us."

Laolys fell silent, reflecting. His mind was a constant storm of worry and doubt; he always ruminated on the past or feared the future. Rarely did he find peace in the present. And rarely had he considered that his thoughts were shaping his reality, that his suffering wasn't just something happening to him but something he might be creating.

"Just self-remembrance?" he repeated. It sounded too simple to pull him from his current state.

"Self-remembrance is no easy task to begin, but it gets easier with time. Mental focus strengthens with practice. Most people live their lives entirely on autopilot."

"I must be one of the few who don't," Laolys said, a faint trace of pride in his tone. "I think about all sorts of wild phenomena; that's why I'm up here."

The sage rolled his eyes. "You're absolutely running on autopilot. Worse, you're still in denial about it."

"Me? How am I on autopilot?"

"Your thoughts are mostly automatic. They aren't conscious creations of a unified mind; they're reactionary, involuntary. Everyone is tuned to a specific current, a frequency of energy. Think of it like a radio stuck on one station. Just as a classical music station isn't going to broadcast an hour of sports commentary, your mind only picks up certain waves of thought.

"This mental radio station reports on what it sees, hears, and feels every waking minute of your life. It tricks you into believing you're conscious, that you're having real, deliberate thoughts. But in reality, you're just listening to the station in your head."

Laolys's heartbeat quickened. For whatever reason, he didn't like the idea that his thoughts were automatic. "But I question the reality before me!"

"Aye, many do. That doesn't mark a conscious mind."

"But I always excelled in my classes!"

The sage groaned. "A brain well-equipped to store information doesn't mark a conscious mind either. Try again."

"I make art sometimes! That has to prove a breakthrough, right?"

The sage shook his head. "Though art can be a great tool for tapping into extra realms of consciousness, even art can be automatic. Art stems from perception, and when perception is automatic, so is the art."

"How are you so certain my mind is automatic? Can you read my thoughts?" Laolys eyed the sage suspiciously.

The sage chuckled. "I can't read your thoughts, but I don't need to. I know your thought channel, and that tells me everything I need to know about how you're processing these lessons."

Laolys stared back at him, wide-eyed, a flicker of suspicion still lingering. "What's my channel?"

"Fear. Consider how you reacted to my last proposition, that your thoughts are automatic. You immediately had a counterargument. You didn't pause to consider if it might be true; you didn't think to. Instead, you instinctively set up walls of defense.

"You do this all the time. I know you hear my words, and later, you reflect on them, and they resonate. But think of all the things in life you don't give a second thought to, things you dismiss outright before even examining them."

Laolys's gaze fell to the ground, and a lump formed in his throat as the weight of the sage's words sank in. The realization shook him in a way he couldn't deny. Yet, instead of bringing him clarity, it only terrified him further.

"Fear?" he echoed. He couldn't help but feel offended, though he understood the truth in it. "I beg to differ. I *was* elected to office, and I *did* make this climb. A man who lives entirely in fear wouldn't have been able to do those things."

The sage watched Laolys with a slight trace of a smile on his lips. "You fight through your fear all the time. This doesn't mean that everything wouldn't be much easier and enjoyable if you switched your channel of thought."

The sage paused, eyeing Laolys with a penetrating gaze that seemed, to Laolys, to gather entirely too much information. "Tell me," he continued, "do you find yourself often in a hurry?"

"Well, yes," Laolys admitted, "but I've always had a lot of responsibilities, and a lot of pressure to perform well."

"Rushing is a state of fear. It's driven by the fear that if we are late, terrible consequences could happen. Now tell me about your drive to perform well, what is its root?"

Laolys thought for a moment. In every endeavor he had undertaken, he had imagined countless terrible consequences if he failed—his parents' disapproval, financial instability, sheer embarrassment. These thoughts had driven many sleepless nights and long, painful hours of training. Fear had been the force behind his discipline and, occasionally, his success.

"I suppose I fear failure a great deal," he admitted. "But how do I change? And what does it mean if I change? Will I become lazy?"

The sage leaned back, turning his gaze to a few nearby birds. "Laziness isn't in the cards. If you truly envision greatness for yourself, you'll be driven to pursue it for its own reward. Only, you won't be cursing yourself along the way, tying weights to your ankles as you walk toward it. Life becomes easier. Answers, too, become glaringly apparent when once they were hidden."

He turned to Laolys. "Have you ever met someone with a particular problem, and when you offer a solution—no matter how simple—they just reject it outright?"

"Well, sure, we all know people like that."

The sage nodded. "'Impossible!' they spit back, followed by a laundry list of reasons why that solution won't work for them. They don't envision greatness for themselves. They don't want it. They're locked in fear, searching only for proof that their reality is inescapable."

Laolys's breath caught. He had done this—more times than he could count—and had never realized it until now. He had always assumed that anyone offering an easy solution must be ignorant of his predicament. But had he been the one who was blind to solutions? Had he been seeking proof that his struggles were unsolvable?

"What did you mean when you said they were looking for proof of their reality?" he asked.

"Everyone sees the world through their own lens. They interpret everything through it. When new information comes along, it meets resistance; not because they actively seek to dismiss it, but because it doesn't fit their established view. They don't search for new truths. They only cling to what confirms what they already believe."

Laolys's mind raced through memory after memory—times he had resisted help, rejected guidance, or clung stubbornly to his own suffering. He had spent his life exactly as the sage described, entirely in fear.

The sage's gaze softened as he studied Laolys's anxious expression. "You're actually in a good place. Most people never even realize they're on a channel. They never wake up. It may feel overwhelming, but this is the first step toward freedom."

"Freedom from fear?" Laolys looked toward his town. *Freedom from fear would be nice,* he thought. *Maybe then I could finally live.*

"Or misery."

Laolys turned back to him. "Is that another channel?"

"Aye. Misery and complacency. That channel wants nothing to do with the fear channel. They just want to be left alone."

"Misery loves company," Laolys mumbled, the old cliché suddenly taking on a new weight.

"Exactly. Miserable people find comfort in other miserable people because they're all tuned to the same frequency. And that applies to every thought channel. The people tuned to fear think the miserable ones are crazy because they aren't afraid of the world. And the miserable ones think the fearful are fools for caring so much."

"What other channels are there? Besides fear and misery?"

The sage drew his hand to his chin. "You know, people have been stuck on one of those two for so long, I nearly forgot there were others."

"Just fear and misery?"

"Yes. The fearful spend their time arguing over what should and shouldn't be feared. The miserable ones don't argue at all; they just shut the world out. Those were the only two channels people seemed to be on when I left society."

Laolys studied him with interest. "What channel are *you* on?"

"I'm not on a channel. That's the start of awakening. Once you break free from the channels, you can truly begin to progress. Until then, focus all your effort on recognizing your conscious mind from your automatic channel."

"What *was* your channel? How did you do it?"

The sage regarded Laolys with a calm, steady gaze. "My channel was fear, just like yours. I was always running amok, getting into trouble, investigating things I had no business in, and the truths I found tore me apart. They weren't common experiences, yet I couldn't deny them. And somehow, those experiences set me apart from the world. I no longer belonged in it, yet I couldn't leave it either.

"I spent years this way, doubting myself, afraid to push further for fear of what else I might find. Of course, I never stopped my investigations, but I was always at war with myself, questioning my reality. I was too afraid to take a team with me, so I walked every alley alone. I could question myself endlessly, but when others questioned me... *that* tore me apart. I was paralyzed—unable to find real answers because I feared every possible scenario."

The sage paused, taking a slow, deep breath. He seemed to be reliving his past as he spoke, the memories playing vividly in his mind.

"Then," he continued, his voice steady but solemn, "one day, I had a moment of clarity, something I had never seen before. I was meditating, watching a scenario from a few days prior as though I were an outsider, seeing it in third person. In that detached state, I had no access to the memories before or after that moment—memories I would've used to justify my behavior had you asked me in my waking state. It was like a spark ignited in my mind—that my thoughts were a channel—and then, just as quickly, the spark disappeared."

He exhaled, shaking his head slightly, as if still in awe of the realization. "It took me years to fully grasp what that moment had revealed. At first, it came in small realizations, little glimpses of truth. Then suddenly, I was flooded with them. I almost gave up."

The sage met Laolys's eyes, holding his gaze.

"But I didn't," he said. "And I broke free from the radio altogether."

"So it doesn't matter what the other channels are; none of them are good," Laolys noted.

"I'm sure some are better than others, but the goal is not to switch our channel. It's to remove it entirely and pursue ascension with conscious intention."

"And we do this through self-realization?"

The sage nodded. "That's the first step. When you recognize these patterns in yourself, congratulate yourself. For every faulty or automatic thought you notice now, countless more went unnoticed before. Recognition is progress. Pay close attention when your first reaction to an idea is defensiveness or antagonism. Those reactions are clear indicators that you're in a vibrational state of fear."

Laolys swallowed, a lump of nerves tightening in his throat. "I... always react, it feels like."

The sage's expression softened. "That's exactly how it felt for me when I first realized it." He sighed. "I was afraid of the whole world."

"You were?" Laolys looked at him in awe. It was hard to imagine—a man who lived so boldly, speaking truths so many wished to keep veiled, had once been consumed by fear.

The sage winked. "You really have no excuses."

Laolys averted his eyes to the landscape. "So what next? After I have these realizations, how do I get out of it?"

"The next step is to replace those thoughts with something else. Choose symbols that inspire you and bring them to mind whenever you catch a negative or automatic thought."

"A mental image?"

"Yes but use a symbol. Symbols, when properly applied, speak directly to the soul. They help us remember who we really are and where we've been. They're far more than just lines arranged in different orientations, they focus the mind and spirit. The ancients knew this well. Even today, it's still used in Alchemy."

"Alchemy," Laolys echoed, recalling the cryptic illustrations from the sage's book. He still couldn't decipher their meanings, but their shapes had lodged in his memory. They lingered, stirring thoughts even without his understanding.

"Alchemy is the science of every plane. Chemistry is only a part—a physical representation of the greater whole: mind and spirit. Really, it's all about energy. Matter is energy, in a way, and so are we. If we can rise from our solid state, transmuting our spirit into something lighter, we can ascend."

"So how do I apply it?"

The sage squinted at the horizon, watching the sun crest over the valleys, declaring yet another day anew. "You're at the first step, calcination."

"What's that?"

"It's the complete breakdown of your original substance—in this case, your spirit—burning everything down to ash. It can feel like devastation, but," the sage held up one bony finger, "it's only step one. It's necessary. We have to be broken down first. After everything is reduced to ash, we sift through it to find the salt. That's what we take to step two."

"I'm... at a complete breakdown?"

The sage patted Laolys on the back. "Seems bad, but it's really not. It's the first step toward real change. Otherwise, you're just stagnant."

Laolys stared at a nearby tree, trying to will himself into a state of serenity. He was barely holding himself together; he couldn't imagine surviving a complete breakdown.

"Oh, it's not as bad as you think." The sage's eyes held good humor, perhaps even nostalgia. "If you don't go through the breakdown, you'll never make it to the other side. You'll never see why all the things you were so upset about never mattered in the first place. You'll never know freedom."

Laolys took a deep breath, trying to will himself into a state of serenity.

The sage stood up and grabbed a stick and crouched down near a spot of dirt covered with pine needles. "Look, it's all part of the process." He dug the stick into the soil and pulled it downward, tracing a curved line sloping into a plunging decline, then he mirrored it on the other side, forming a symmetrical shape that met in the middle. Laolys immediately recognized it as the Aries symbol in astrology.

"You see how both roads lead to the same place—a sharp descent? In reality, all roads lead here. It's the first stop on the path to enlightenment. You can't escape it. It's the only way to find the salt, the hidden parts of ourselves that radiate wisdom. This symbol reminds us that our pain has a purpose."

Laolys studied the shape in the dirt. Though he had seen it before, he felt like he was truly understanding it for the first time. To fall apart—it was human. Essential, even, in the grand scheme of things. A breakdown of one's current state was step one.

"What's step two?"

"In step two, we take our salt into a new environment, dissolve it, and then carry onward through nine more steps before we reach the final stage, the philosopher's stone."

"And what about the philosopher's stone symbol?"

The sage drew a circle in the dirt. Then, he traced a square around it, ensuring the lines touched its edges. After that, he enclosed the square within a triangle, aligning it perfectly. Finally, he drew a much larger outer circle, encasing all the shapes within its boundaries, centering them in the space.

Laolys studied the symbol with deep interest.

"This is the end of our journey, if we do the work to get there. Each step builds upon the last, shifting our perception, revealing ever-changing views of the world.

"We begin as a mere dot in a circle—prima materia, broken down, unrefined. Then, as we undergo transformation, we perceive the inner circle—the first realization of form. From there, we construct a framework around it, step by step, expanding our understanding.

"The square represents stability—the material world, our sense of security and structure. The triangle follows, symbolizing light, wisdom, and spiritual awareness.

"At last, we reach the outer circle, where we see that all our previous views were merely fragments of a greater whole. Once we reach this step, those old perspectives lose their meaning. But before then, they were our ladder."

The sage met Laolys's gaze. "The philosopher's stone allows us to transmute mind and spirit at will, because we finally *see*. We recognize the illusions in all things."

"I think I'd like to focus on that one," Laolys said, staring at the outline of the philosopher's stone.

"Not a bad idea. But keep the calcination symbol in your mental back pocket for times of crisis. Let it remind you that even our darkest moments have meaning, if we use them."

Laolys swallowed. An unshakable sense of dread settled over him—not just for his future, but for *any* future, the one ahead of him now and the one he'd left behind in politics. "I feel like my beginning, my prima materia, is still ahead of me."

"We have many beginnings still to come. I have plenty of prima materias waiting for me out there." The sage gestured skyward with his stick. "And here, too, should I be forced to stay around much longer."

Laolys followed his gaze. "I guess if I make it out there, it's nothing *but* beginnings."

The sage pointed his stick back at the philosopher's stone drawing. "Look here, at this outer circle. Right now, it looks like the final boundary, but it's also just the first dot in something much larger. There's no stopping it. It's a fractal, repeating forever. Cherish your beginnings. They're part of every cycle."

Laolys exhaled, feeling a wave of tension leave his body. "I suppose it's silly to fear my future beginnings."

"Silly indeed. Would you like to go back to the man you were at the bottom of this mountain?"

His mind flashed to those last moments before his climb. He had been a nervous wreck, uncertain if he would find the sage, if the sage would even speak to him. Now, not only had he gained the sage's confidence, but he had also already made great strides in personal insight.

"I don't think I'd like that one bit," he admitted.

"Each new beginning, with all its trials, brings new revelations. Each prima materia gives us an entirely new constitution of being, if we carry our salt through the subsequent steps."

Laolys looked at the sage with a sense of wonder. "You've come a long way for someone who was once tuned to the channel of fear."

"And I have the scars to prove it! The road to enlightenment is the hardest road to walk, but it's the only one worth taking. Every other path in life just leads you around in circles."

"How do I stop my self-doubt? I want to, I try to... It should be easy to change my thoughts, but I struggle. Why?"

"Mental transmutation isn't as simple as just thinking something different. If that were the case, everyone would do it. Mental transmutation is the art of changing one's beliefs, it alters your entire resonance. It's not just about directing the conscious mind in waking hours, but transforming the unconscious soul? That's much harder."

Laolys's stomach churned. His anxiety was something he desperately wanted to overcome, but it wasn't as easy as wishing it away. His inner doubt lingered, like a sore festering beneath the skin.

"How do I do that?" His voice was quieter now. "How do I transmute my spirit? How do I transform my soul into something stronger?"

"You, like the rest of the world, are trapped in a faulty perception. Each of us believes there is only one way to view reality, our own. We build identities and cling to them because they bring us comfort. But in truth, we're none of the things we claim to be. We're more than that. We're fluid, spiritual beings inhabiting a vessel for a time, working through our spiritual illnesses... Don't get too caught up in the distractions."

Laolys took a deep breath. "Maybe I'll have an easier time with it when I'm older. I still have so much uncertainty ahead."

The sage chuckled softly. "When you're older, you'll be looking back. You'll be saying things like, 'If only I had worked harder when I was younger, or done things another way, I'd have peace.' Save yourself the trouble. Take it now."

"But I'll get so much backlash when I get home!" Laolys felt a flash of anger surge through his body. Was the sage dismissing his struggles as irrelevant? Then, in a moment of realization, the lesson dawned on him. He was tuned to the channel of fear.

"You're always living ten steps ahead of yourself." The sage eyed him with a glint of amusement. "And because of that, you're never truly living at all.

"If you don't retune your frequency, you'll spend all your time here worrying about life down there. Then, when you reach the bottom of the mountain, you'll be so preoccupied with getting through your front door and facing your family's interrogation that you won't be able to think straight.

"And then, while they're questioning you, you'll already be consumed with worry over how terribly you'll sleep that night, or some other future matter. That night, you *will* sleep terribly, but only because you'll be so preoccupied with the following day, dreading the people who will ask about your 'incredible truths.'"

He leaned in toward Laolys. "Does this sound familiar?"

Laolys flushed with embarrassment. His instinct was to object, to defend himself, but suppressing that automatic reaction, he remained silent, staring at the ground.

The sage's eyes softened with a gentle, sympathetic expression. "Don't be discouraged. The first step toward a higher vibrational state is recognizing where we currently are. Only then can we learn how to shift our thoughts. It gets easier with practice. Eventually, we can free ourselves from negative vibrations altogether, but that'll never happen if we insist our current state is fine or believe it's all we can ever be."

"I can admit mine are a mess," Laolys mumbled. "Harmonizing them feels like a daunting task."

"Focus on the present moment." The sage tapped his stick on the ground. "Your time up here is precious. Don't waste it by placing yourself mentally back at home. You are your consciousness, not your vessel. When you spend your time imagining your struggles down there, that's where you are. If you don't mind, I'd appreciate your company before you depart." He smiled, and Laolys felt an unexpected warmth bloom in his chest.

He turned his gaze to the landscape. "It *is* nice up here. Peaceful. Maybe the most peaceful place I've ever been."

"It's away from the disruptive vibrations almost everyone carries," the sage said. "Up here, everything is allowed to simply *be*, and in doing so, it reflects peace back to those who observe it. Down there, we've become so skilled at shaping our environment to our every whim that we're always searching for ways to improve it. And because of that, we never truly enjoy the comforts we work so hard to obtain. More often than not, they aren't even worth the effort."

Laolys looked at the sage with admiration. "It's strange how a person can have every comfort down there and still be miserable, while up here, with only a few necessities, one can live in peace."

"It's all negative vibrations down there. I can't live among them anymore."

"Is that why you came up here? To separate yourself?"

The sage smiled, inhaling deeply, as if drawing in the mountain's stillness. He held his breath for a long moment before exhaling. "Yes. But you can't remain here as I do. All your work is still ahead of you. I have retired."

"Retired from what exactly?"

"From trying to save the world, of course." The sage grinned. "I thought I had finally retired for good when I settled up here, but the old proverb holds true, 'a man who loves his work never really retires.'" He gestured toward Laolys with his stick. "Here I am, teaching you."

"Teaching me?" Laolys repeated, surprised. "How is teaching me going to save the world?"

"Isn't that why you came here? To learn so you could help the world?"

Laolys's gaze fell to the ground. "I do want to help the world... but I never imagined I could *save* it." The words felt hollow now. Maybe his ideas had always been fantasies. The real world didn't want to be saved. The sage had tried and failed. What made him think he could do any better?

"No one can save the world alone," the sage said, interrupting Laolys's thoughts. "It takes innovators, not just dreamers, but those with the willpower to carry their vision far enough for others to see it too. All revolutions have a leader, a visionary. And all revolutions leave their mark on the world."

"I guess if enough people could be convinced..." Laolys trailed off as his father's words echoed in his mind: *If this man convinces enough people with this information, it will change the world!*

The sage chuckled quietly.

Laolys's head snapped toward him, eyes narrowing. "What?"

"That statement got me into quite a bit of trouble for most of my life." A wistful smile crept onto the sage's face as he gazed out over the mountainside.

Laolys felt a flush rise to his cheeks. A paranoia gripped him; had the sage read his mind? His heart pounded at the thought that he might know who he really was... that he was the son of the man who had been hunting him for so long.

"Of course. That's what all great lovers of wisdom believe," the sage replied. "We see the beauty of the world for what it is, and we imagine that if others could see it too, everything would change.

"It's what anyone who awakens to these truths and embodies them sets out to do: save the world. That's why I asked, as your only payment for these teachings, that you share them. In doing so, you'd be working for the betterment of the world, despite the perceived cost."

He looked at Laolys. "Your answer, though somewhat hesitant, told me you were ready to learn from me."

Laolys exhaled, releasing some tension in his shoulders. "To be honest, I'm both excited and terrified to share these truths. I feel their resonance in my spirit, and I feel my spirit lifting the more I reflect on these lessons, but..." He hesitated. "Am I really capable of carrying on their message? Especially to those who will scoff at everything I have to say?"

He cast his eyes to the ground, swallowing against the lump forming in his throat. His fear was a never-ending battle—or at least, it felt that way in the moment.

The sage cleared his throat. "Have you heard about the rocky start of the telegraph?"

Laolys stared back blankly.

"Well, when the telegraph first became available for commercial use, it remained untouched for three full days. A crowd gathered outside the building, but no one dared to be the first to invest their money in it. Many believed it was a hoax; that instant messaging from city to city was impossible, and that only a fool would waste his money on such an endeavor.

"On the fourth day, one man finally stepped forward. He sheepishly laid down a penny and asked for his message to be sent. It cost one cent to send four words, but he only wanted to send two. When the clerk told him she couldn't offer change, he simply replied, 'No bother,' and left in a hurry, having paid twice what was necessary.

"His message was sent successfully, and soon after, word spread of its effectiveness. It wasn't too much longer before the telegraph became a worldwide commodity."

Laolys laughed. "That sounds about right for my townspeople, too."

The sage nodded. "The world fears progress, any kind of change. If people can't immediately see physical results, they aren't ready to believe in something outside of their current worldview. But most of the universe is unseen, outside of our physical awareness. If we restrict ourselves to this limited view, we see only a minor fraction of what's truly there. We shouldn't hold the world hostage because so many live constricted in fear. We should push for growth, regardless."

"I agree," Laolys said, still smiling at the telegraph story.

"The world fears everything, but it especially fears the unseen," the sage continued. "That's why we light up the night; we've chased darkness away since we first harnessed fire. Possibilities frighten us. The unknown scares us. We prefer to stay buried behind four walls, shutting out as much unpredictability as possible. But Chaos governs the laws of the universe, and we should be grateful it does."

"Why?"

"Because otherwise, things would be very boring. And I imagine growth would be difficult, if not impossible. Chaos gives rise to possibility and inspiration. It lays things out in a beautiful, delicate row and then sends shockwaves through the system at random intervals, sparking evolution. It's through the minds of those who dare to see the unseen marvels of the universe that the rest of the world eventually progresses, though always with much complaint."

"I have a tough road ahead of me..." Laolys trailed off, eyes on the valleys below. The thought of descending the mountain filled him with a deep sense of dread.

"Indeed, should you decide to take it."

"Hmm?" Laolys turned to the sage, confused. "I don't see any other choice."

"There are many choices—an infinite number, even. But that's the mark of a hero, an artist, an inventor, a revolutionary: they take the hardest road out of millions, and yet, they can't imagine walking any other way."

Laolys cast his gaze toward the ground. "Inspiring to others, but to the hero, it is tears, toil, thrill, and loneliness." It was admirable from a distance, he thought, but few truly understood the reality of such a path.

"The pains become dull with callouses. And the joy..." The sage paused, inhaling deeply, savoring the moment. "Nothing exists without its polar partner. If you endure the pains of the hero's path, you also get to experience the astounding delight of completing the conquest."

"Pain leads to joy?"

"Pain leads to growth, and growth is the delight of every spirit, but only when we address it. Pain is a signal that something needs to change, a lesson to be learned. If we ignore it, we're just suffering.

"Suffering can continue for as long as we refuse to acknowledge what we are avoiding. A soul that chooses ignorance signs itself up for a lifetime of struggle. Most people's pain comes from refusing to do the one thing that would grant them happiness: face their mistakes, fix their shortcomings, and let go of the past."

Laolys listened, but inside, his emotions were tangled. Suffering seemed ingrained in his nature; it was all he had ever known.

"I have lived with so much pain," he said quietly. "I always feel like I'm reaching for something just beyond my grasp. Even when I won the election, I was still struggling. And now, I struggle with this new path."

The sage cast a stern look at him. "You're refusing the same lessons over and over again. Your ignorance may have been an excuse before, but now... now you know better, and you have no more excuses."

"What do you mean?"

"Some of your fear *is* a result of how you were raised. You were placed under high expectations from a young age, and you never felt

THE YOUNG MAN AND THE SAGE

secure. But you're past all that now. You're up here, and you're making the decision to claim your life.

"I won't lie to you; you don't have an easy road ahead. But if you leave here and continue a life of fear and suffering... *that* will be on *you*."

Laolys sat in silence, absorbing the weight of the sage's words. His life wouldn't be easy, but that didn't mean he had to suffer through it. If he wanted something better, he had to overcome his current condition.

"I can break free of this?" he asked. He meant to say it as a statement, but as it left his throat, it caught and turned into a question.

The sage smiled. "It is merely the automatic programming of your vessel. Recognize this, become a conscious director of your own mind, and you will be free."

"Easier said than done."

"Most things are."

Laolys sighed, his heart heavy as memories swarmed his mind. Old fears, moments of weakness, and times of embarrassment haunted him. "I've made many mistakes..." he began slowly. "I've survived trauma... Who's to say I'm capable of enlightenment in this life, let alone carrying it to others?"

The sage's expression remained serene, but his eyes softened with sympathy. "Tell me, what do you gain from dwelling on your painful memories?"

"Nothing I suppose."

"Then let go of them. Free yourself. Whatever has been done to you, why hold onto it?" The sage sighed. "Everyone here—we're all victims of this cycle. People hurt others in terrible ways sometimes because they don't know any other way to be.

"If someone hurts us, it's not personal. It's not a flaw in us. It's not something we attract. It's *their* flaws. They're on the same journey of self-realization that we are, only they are doing poorly. Let go of the pain after a while. Let yourself grow beyond the suffering you've endured and know freedom."

Laolys nodded and directed his gaze toward the bottom of the mountain. "And the struggles ahead of me? When I return, I will probably lose everything. How do I prepare for that?"

"Your trials down there will be hard enough without you adding weight to them before you even get there." The sage knocked his stick on the ground, pulling Laolys back to the moment. "Cherish the present. It's all we ever really have."

Laolys nodded and turned his gaze toward the landscape, needing a moment to collect his thoughts. The lesson was a lot to take in; too much for *anyone* to take in all at once. Though the truths the sage shared resonated deeply with him, he wasn't so sure about the rest of society.

The sage, too, was lost in thought, though his mental wanderings seemed to stretch far beyond the earthly plane. He was not untroubled, only differently troubled than the nervous student sitting beside him.

Meanwhile, the forest around them rustled peacefully, oblivious to the weighty reflections that consumed the two men. It rose to greet the sun, grateful for its warmth, which ushered away the dark and predators. Each morning, gratitude filled the forest, championed most prominently by the birds' amorous hymns.

"It all sounds like so much noise down there," Laolys said, breaking the silence. "It's chaos; there's always so many things happening at once. Up here, I feel like I can see the world, and it's easier, because all the noise is gone."

"There's glorious noise up here! If only you knew what the birds go on about!"

Laolys looked at him with an expression of perplexed amusement. "You know what they say?"

The sage let loose a burst of laughter. "Give me another decade up here, maybe by then, I'll have convinced myself I can speak their language!" He coughed, stifling his laughter, then gestured towards the trees. "But I imagine they tell quite the stories of the man who will not quiet down around them in the mornings, who climbs the trees sometimes as if he, too, is a bird."

"Is that why you were up in the tree yesterday?"

"As a matter of fact, I rarely give lessons on the ground!" The sage paused, watching a group of birds gathered at the top of a nearby tree. "I was a bit shaken up yesterday for several reasons I won't explain. I'm more comfortable up there, with the birds. And I fare much better, too, when the bears come around!"

"But it was more than just a whim, wasn't it? Because a bear *did* come around."

The sage shrugged. "Intuition—a keen sense of awareness of the unseen—can keep a person alive for a very long time despite their better conscious judgments."

Laolys opened his mouth to speak but stopped himself. He'd never heard a definition of intuition so precisely applied to the human condition. "I guess you're right..." he said, "conscious judgment would've insisted we hold the lesson on the ground."

"Yours *did* insist that we do exactly that. Isn't it a good thing we didn't listen to it?"

Laolys nodded, the ramifications of this statement echoing throughout his memories. How many times had his conscious judgments—his well-reasoned arguments for doing or not doing something—simply been wrong?

"I suppose we, humanity, all think too much. We forget how to do," he said, watching the birds as they swarmed about the trees.

"Our brain power is a mighty force and a tool for spiritual awakening if we just learn how to direct our thoughts. Most people's concerns, worries, and fears are completely unnecessary." The sage paused, his eyes still fixed on the same flock of birds. "Maybe everyone should try living as a bird for a little while. Then, when they come back down, they'll have a better sense of what's really important."

"What's important?"

"That you *evolve*." The sage took a deep breath. "And that you do so, in sync with nature, in harmony with the higher planes."

Laolys exhaled, and his gaze drifted toward his town. "It's all much easier up here than down there."

The sage tilted his head. "You can learn how to practice separation down there too, but not from the spiritual planes, not from the dense aether that surrounds you, and not from the senses that arise within you. Learn what's real and what's an illusion. Most live in a false world."

"When you put it that way, I almost feel sorry for the people who will cast me out."

"They'll cast you out because you contradict the false world they've built for themselves. Don't pity yourself for that. Take pride instead. Know that you've tapped into something great. Let this knowledge be your strength when you have no one else to help you along."

Laolys looked at his surroundings with a mix of love and dread—love for the peace it had provided him, dread because he knew he had to leave it. "I'll always remember my time up here. It'll be my rock, my starting point, my mental place of refuge."

The sage kicked his foot, knocking a few small rocks toward Laolys, and smiled. "You're welcome to take a few rocks with you when you leave. In fact, I highly encourage it!"

Laolys smiled back and reached down to grab one. "I will, in fact, and I won't mind a bit if anyone pokes fun at me for hiking down with a bag full of rocks!" He turned the stone over in his hand, examining it. There were no memories in it yet—at least none he could discern. It was a blank slate, waiting to be filled with his own impressions of this place, of this moment.

"It's not worth the effort of an explanation! Enjoy your life. Be only burdened by the rocks you *choose* to carry."

Laolys nodded. "If we do that, are we ever truly burdened?"

The sage gave him a knowing look, a glint of amusement in his eye. "Do you recall our first lesson, when I mentioned there were two types of people?"

"Yes," Laolys said. "Those who need the help of others and those who need the attention of the ones who need help."

"Something like that! And you argued there was a third type."

Laolys paused, recalling their first conversation. "The type who helps out of sincerity."

The sage nodded. "Yes. This type helps others because it serves their own evolution, and because we all live symbiotically. But we rarely recognize this third type, unless we're on the receiving end of their help. They don't seek recognition, nor do they expect favors in return."

"And what about this third type?"

"You're becoming one of them. You weigh yourself down, but you don't see it as a burden."

Laolys sighed. "I don't want to make a name for myself, either."

"You will, because you already have one. A name can't be erased. It's like a plant that has rooted itself in a field and spread its seeds. Even if you try to get rid of it, it still pops up. You can only change its name."

"You could go somewhere else, where the plant hasn't grown," Laolys suggested.

"Perhaps. But depending on how deeply rooted it is, it will still thrive long after you've gone. I haven't tended to my own in decades, and yet it still grows well enough to have brought you here." He glanced toward the distant valleys. "We can't escape our reputations. People will believe what they wish to believe. But tell me, do you think I spend any time up here worrying about what they say about me down there?"

Laolys shook his head. "I don't suppose you spend any time at all on such things."

"Correct! And neither should you, whether you're up here or down there among the crowds. Their opinions, you can't change them. And even if you could, it wouldn't be worth the effort, because none of it matters."

"I'm starting to see that now," Laolys said softly. It was a difficult realization to embrace. He had been trained since youth to perform, to appeal to the populace. He had learned how to carefully mold his character—how to appear polished and professional—while inside, he was an anxious mess. He had spent so much of his life trying to be a certain way that he no longer knew how to be free. He had forgotten what it meant to exist without constantly searching for approval.

"Good. You still have time." The sage's voice softened. "When you begin to truly grasp what it means to be a living part of a breathing universe, then you can start thinking about your descent back into society. But until then—" he paused, inhaling slowly. "Until then, breathe. Live. Enjoy. One day, you will no longer have these moments, only reflections of a time that once was."

Laolys followed his instructor's lead, closing his eyes and taking a long breath in and holding it, letting himself be fully present in the moment. When he finally exhaled and opened his eyes, the sage was gone.

Laolys sat in the morning sun, reflecting on the sage's words. Then, with a mysterious impulse, he sprang into a tree, ascending the limbs without hesitation. Reaching the top, he stopped and stood very still, balanced with only a small branch to hold onto. Before him was truly a sight to behold—valleys, rocky cliffs, trees, and fields of wild grass stretched endlessly into the horizon. Far, far away, tiny houses dotted the land, looking almost insignificant from his vantage point.

Is this what it is like to be a bird? he wondered, considering how small the people must be to fit in those tiny houses.

The birds do not envy us. They soar high above, in a world consisting only of clouds and open sky. When they do descend to pick at the crumbs of the food that escapes our grasp, they ponder on how complicated we make things. They don't mind that their crumbs are mixed with dirt, for the crumbs came freely, and as soon as their bellies are full, they return to the sky, unbothered by want or need.

The birds do not stay fixed in any position. They travel with the seasons. They balance periods of constant work with periods of growth and rest. They do not select one leader, but each takes the torch when their turn arises and follows in orderly unison behind the torch bearer when it is not.

The birds hold most sacred the dawn. They bury their heads, nestled together at night, awaiting the first glimpse of light. When they see a hint of it, they start to chatter, telling the others that soon, light is to come. When the sun rises with its fiery core over the horizon, they all burst out in passionate song. What love they have for their nearest star! They must feel its divine cosmic energy! They must know well of the unseen.

The Tempest Within the Silence

Identity

"Your identity is the strongest illusion you hold; it is also the most important one to rid yourself of."

The words arrived as Laolys was stretched across a low-hanging tree branch, reading a book about identifying plant life. It was late afternoon; the sage had returned from wherever he went all day with a small bag of harvested goods. The shadows cast about by the trees indicated that they possibly had an hour or two before they should consider lighting a fire or seeking shelter. There was just enough time for a solid lesson without time for chasing fruitless fox trails, winding paths leading nowhere specific in hopes of gratifying some appetite. The sage was right on schedule.

"I see you're catching up on some light reading!" The sage smiled at Laolys, indicating to the book of plant life he was studying. "Or do you not trust your guide has sufficient knowledge of forestry and are only thinking of your bowels?"

"I simply found it interesting!" Laolys sat up, slightly embarrassed, caught off guard by the sage's sudden arrival as he transitioned from the mental planes of reading and imagination to the physical world around him. "And I did feel the knowledge would be wise for anyone in the mountains to seek."

"I jest with you; lighten up!" The sage lifted his bag for Laolys to grab from, who immediately hopped down from his tree branch to take a handful of its contents. "I'm happy you're learning about the plants that surround you. If you want to blend in with nature, it helps to know as much as you can about it."

"It's amazing, really—all the varieties," Laolys said, poking through his handful of nuts and berries. "Plants grow in unique ways just to adapt to their environment. It got me thinking about the lower cycles."

The sage pocketed the remainder of the sack and walked over to his familiar rock, taking a seat overlooking the landscape. "Spoken like a true philosopher! But," he cleared his throat, "I'll take the blame for this, I have to begin again. Listen carefully: your identity is the strongest illusion you hold; it is also the most important one to rid yourself of."

Laolys hurried to sit on the adjacent rock. "What parts of our identity are illusions?"

"All of it."

"Everything? Then who are we?"

The sage's brow creased forward as he studied him. "Define yourself, please."

"Define myself?" Laolys leaned back, taken off guard by the request.

"Yes. Who, or what, are you?"

Laolys's heartbeat quickened. "I... I'm a young man, a politician—well, the son of a politician..." He took a deep breath. "Well... now I'm not sure where I'm heading in life, only that I'll actually be working toward making it a better place. I'll be working on achieving enlightenment and spreading my wisdom."

The sage's eyes searched Laolys. His expression remained neutral, but his gaze held a penetrating depth that made Laolys shudder. "Hmm... you may be some of those things, but some of those things you are not."

"What am I not?"

"A young man. The son of a politician."

IDENTITY

"What? But I'm both those things!"

The sage tilted his head. "Maybe for now. They're illusory identities, like hats you try on for a while. Your body is temporary. Your personality, your likes and dislikes, even your thinking patterns—none of these define who you are."

"What does?"

The sage shrugged. "Who we are can't be defined by language. We're fluid, all-encompassing spiritual beings. When we inhabit a body, we learn ways to define ourselves so we can understand and interact with the world. But after death, we transcend all these things. They become meaningless once we leave this world. Don't think for a minute you'll always be as you are now."

"I should hope not. Growth should change a person."

"Growth *always* changes a person." The sage paused, watching Laolys pick through his handful of gatherings. "But I'm afraid growth will be slow and hard-pressed if you continue to operate as a machine."

Laolys let out a deep sigh. "When I stop to think about it, it feels like every thought I have stems from fear. I can see what you mean by thought channels." He cast his gaze to the ground. "I just don't see how I'm going to get off this channel into real conscious awareness."

The sage smiled. "You've done the hardest part already. The biggest problem most people have with awakening is that they think they're already conscious, awakened individuals. You can't teach anyone who already thinks themselves an expert."

"No, they wouldn't hear it," Laolys agreed.

The sage nodded. "They're too busy identifying with the illusory."

"Identifying with the illusory?"

"Yes, people who think they know all there is to know about something have built themselves up quite a bit in their minds. They've constructed a reality where they know best, and to have someone else come along and teach them something contradicts that reality."

Laolys looked at him. "But no one can be perfect, and if they don't keep learning, how could they ever even come close?"

"Exactly. A true master never admits they're a master. They always see room for improvement. They stay humble. They stay out of the illusory identity everyone pins to them. That's the only way."

"So, any identity we create for ourselves is an illusion?"

"Exactly. And if we get all caught up in it, we get stuck, lost, and we stop growing. An identity of greatness can be just as trapping as a negative self-image. Some people put themselves on pedestals and expect the world to respond to their greatness. Most of the time, it doesn't, and then they get all worked up about it. Every now and then, the world does listen. Only then, it's almost worse. A person can become even more consumed in their identity when the world is feeding into them. Celebrities—I don't envy them."

"I guess I don't either." Laolys sighed. "I shouldn't have to worry about that, though. It'll be the other way. I'll have to find my greatness despite everyone's negative words."

"You have to know your purpose. Stick to your destination, and you'll be fine. Down there"—the sage gestured toward Laolys's distant town—"everyone's obsessed with one illusion or another. Forget about all the illusions and stay true to your path. It's really all just mad down there."

Laolys looked toward his town. Only this time, he saw it in a new light. It wasn't the angle of the sun; that had stayed consistent throughout their past conversations. It was his impression of it. Before, it had been a place of safety, a symbol of order and assuredness. Now, it all seemed like chaos; everyone was tuned to the fear or misery channel, consumed by illusions.

"I guess it is silly to care what they think," Laolys said softly.

"Silly or dangerous." The sage scoffed. "True greatness doesn't require the illusion of greatness to maintain itself. Sometimes it gets recognized, after many, many years of being called madness, but none of that matters. If we get caught up in any of it—good or bad—we lose track of who we are."

"Then who are we?"

"We're fluid, spiritual beings who happen to be inhabiting a body for a short time. One lifetime is nothing to a soul, which is eternal. We may see ourselves a certain way now—by our age, our occupation—but that's not anything. We transcend definition entirely. And to get too caught up in it, well, that often takes us off our true path."

"I guess that makes sense. I know so many people who are very

IDENTITY

caught up in their identity, their role. Politics is so much of that. Too much praise, even, can be a bad thing."

The sage nodded. "Praise only feeds the fallacies of the ego."

He turned to Laolys, studying him, and a slight smile formed on his lips. "You know, you define yourself a certain way here, but in other worlds, other realms, there are completely different definitions of ego you refuse to let go of."

"You mean like other timelines?"

"Yes." The sage paused. He opened his mouth but said nothing, eyeing Laolys with an unreadable expression. "You know, some of those other timelines... they aren't just imagination. Some of them are real—other pieces of your soul, living just like you are."

"What do you mean?" Laolys looked at the sage with a mix of curiosity and suspicion. "How can they be pieces of my soul?"

"Well, you only have a piece of your soul too. A real soul is massive, all-encompassing. Your soul fractured when it entered the String Cycle. It had to, in order to match the frequency there. It split into countless pieces called shards, and ever since then, you've slowly been gathering your fractured bits."

Laolys stared back at the sage in stunned fascination. "So there are other pieces of my soul, living just like me?"

"Yes. They're scattered across galaxies and dimensions throughout the multiverse. Some of them are parallel to us here and now. Some are far off in another universe, completely unknown to us. But by definition, all of them are at least slightly different from you."

"How are they different?" Laolys's expression shifted to confusion.

"Imagine a color wheel with every shade imaginable. Along with those shades, envision emotions and personality traits accordingly. For example, red is passionate, both in love and anger, and blue is logical, as well as apathetic. Now, shatter that color wheel into hundreds of pieces and send each one to incarnate individually, unbeknownst to one another. You are one of those pieces. Your color range displays a certain frequency in both light and thought. This is temporary, transmutable, and becomes meaningless once you ascend. Then, you rejoin the others."

Laolys paused to let the image permeate his mind. He was one of some unknown number of pieces... lost, but not alone. But who were the others? It was a lot to take in. "So right now, I'm only a piece of my soul?"

"Your conscious state only knows that piece. You actually have access to all the other shards. When you become more aware of your true nature—less attached to your limiting definitions of ego—you'll be able to glimpse them under meditative focus."

"I can glimpse them?"

"You're connected to them, no matter what. You're born of the same source."

"I wish I could know what some of my other shards are like." Laolys looked at him. "You can see the timelines... can you see them?"

The sage averted his gaze to the mountainside. "I can see your shards *quite clearly*."

Laolys was nearly on the edge of his seat. He was beginning to feel like the sage enjoyed the suspense. "Well, are you going to tell me about them?"

The sage sighed heavily. "It's usually best for people to wait until they can see them for themselves. There's a reason you can't see them yet, you know. You aren't ready."

Laolys stared back with an expression of eager anticipation. He didn't say a word, but he didn't have to.

The sage's lips broke into a slight smile. "I don't suppose you'll leave me alone about it, though, will you?"

"I'm dying to know, please!"

The sage raised a bony finger, signaling for a moment of silence, and closed his eyes. He took several deep breaths, his body relaxing completely, though he remained seated. After what felt like an eternity to Laolys, but was likely only about three minutes, he opened his eyes.

"Well?"

"The first one I saw was a fisherman."

"A fisherman?"

The sage gave a half-nod. "He left home—the whole political world —by joining a fishing crew. He sails all around the world."

"So, a good life then?"

The sage shrugged. "He gets by. He's pretty apathetic about the whole thing. Doesn't show a lot of emotion. He doesn't regret his decision to leave, but he's not really happy about where he's at either. He just carries on."

"Does he miss his family? Does he see them?"

The sage tilted his head. "Occasionally, to both."

"Well, what other shards did you see?"

"Another shard is still in politics. He's advanced quite far, actually; much further than you would have, had you stayed."

"Quite far? Like what?"

"He started his career even earlier than you. He was highly motivated to succeed. He took to power like a fish to water. He craved it, so he secured a high position and maintained his ground."

"Like my father!" Laolys's exclamation escaped his mouth before he could stop it; before he even realized the thought. His cheeks flushed, and he looked down. "I'm sorry. I know you said there were shards who made different decisions than me, I just didn't imagine... my father."

The sage raised one eyebrow as he glanced at him. "The longer you fear your opposites, the longer you will impede your progress."

"Forgive me." Laolys swallowed a lump of nervous energy and took a deep breath. "Please go on. Are there others?"

The sage turned his gaze to the mountainside. "I see a couple of other shards who are as confused about themselves as you are, but in different ways. One is hopelessly in love with someone who is indifferent to him, and because he lacks love for himself, he doesn't see any problem. Another was orphaned at a young age and raised by a distant aunt. He grew up to become a priest."

"How is he confused? He sounds like he found success, despite the circumstances."

"I didn't give you the whole story." The sage cast him a stern glance, then turned his gaze back toward the landscape, his expression somber. "He didn't take the death well; no child would. He thinks he's being punished for some wrongdoing he committed in a past life, and it drives him to the brink of insanity. He spends his life trying to repent for sins he never committed."

"What was the cause of his parents' death?"

The sage sighed. "Just a tragic accident in a tragic timeline. He can't see the other timelines; he won't until after his death. Because the event affected him so deeply, he can't understand that it was just an automobile accident. Just the flick of a wrist on the steering wheel too abruptly on a rainy day. It only happened in that one timeline, and it wasn't anyone's fault."

"How unfortunate." Laolys wished he could speak to the shard, help him understand that he wasn't responsible for his parents' tragedy. But he knew it wasn't quite that simple.

"It's not usually easy to see the ways the other shards live, but it can give you a wider perspective. He can't see it. Just like there are things in your life that you can't see."

"So... are all my shards male?"

"No. Let me look further." The sage closed his eyes again; only this time, it was for less than a minute.

"One of your female shards lives in a world with extremely advanced technology. She seems to be pursuing power, much like your male shard in politics, though I can't be certain of the details—the world is strange to me. Another female shard owns a small bookshop in a world similar to ours."

"So she couldn't have gone into politics," Laolys said.

"That's right. Your father bought her a bookshop in town so he could put his name on the sign and appeal to the academic world. It just so happens that it also gives her everything she has ever wanted in her limited world. She loves reading and discussing all kinds of subjects with the people who visit her shop."

"Wonderful, so she may be ascending then?"

The sage shook his head, his expression turning melancholic. "From what I see now, it's unlikely."

"No? Why not?"

The sage shrugged. "She doesn't think she deserves it."

Laolys lowered his gaze to the ground. The flaws of each shard, though different from his own, mirrored his struggles. They all failed to see the bigger picture and their own worth. Some, like the priest, he wished he could comfort. Others, like the politician, he had no desire to meet at all. Though each one lived a completely separate existence, they all shared a piece of the same soul. Still, some would be difficult for him to accept. The implications of this realization regarding the people he currently disliked were profound.

The sage noticed his prolonged silence and patted his back in a gesture of encouragement. "Most of your shards have already ascended. The ones who lag behind are the most sensitive—the ones who care too much."

"Not the one who let greed and power overwhelm his sense of decency!"

"Especially that one. If you looked at him, you'd see it too. That shard saw the effects power and greed have on people and became angry, but he felt powerless to do anything about it; thought the system ran too deep. In all honesty, I agree with him."

"But unlike you," the sage glanced at him, "he saw giving up his power as becoming powerless. 'Be the wolf or the prey,' he said. So, he became the wolf—the very thing he hated—because he feared becoming the prey."

The sage sighed. He kept his gaze fixed on the mountainside, but a brief flash of pained sympathy crossed his face. "He has a lot of guilt. He's angry with himself most of all."

Laolys's head hung low, guilt washed over him for judging the shard.

"It's not so bad," the sage continued. "Since so many of your shards have already ascended, these ones will find their way, just like you're finding your way now."

Laolys looked up, brightness returning to his eyes. "Many of mine have already ascended?"

The sage studied him. "Have you ever felt as if you had someone watching over your shoulder? Like a guardian angel, an ancestral spirit, anything at all?"

"Well, yes, sometimes. I never really knew what to call it. Sometimes I feel like something is watching me, wishing well for me."

"That's most likely you—well, sort of you. It's another consciousness right now, but it's also linked to you. It's not separate. One day, when you ascend, you'll join with the others. For someone like you, who has so many ascended shards, the influence is very strong."

"Influence? What kind of influence?"

"It's subtle. You likely receive guidance all the time without realizing it. It comes through in inspiration, in sudden urges to take another path, in quiet moments of clarity. But you don't always listen. You question yourself a lot. The answers come clearly, but you don't trust them, because you don't trust yourself. I'd wager that's why you're still here, and not out there in the Cosmos with them."

Laolys looked up at the sky. Though it was still bright, soon the sun would dip out of sight, revealing hundreds of hidden stars. He wished he could be out there, helping his lost shards. But before he could do that, he would have to help himself. He would have to learn how to trust his inner instincts. For whatever reason, he struggled with that more than anything else, trusting himself.

"I don't know why it's so hard for me," he mumbled.

The sage's eyes softened. "Practice helps everything in time. You're used to questioning yourself. Sooner or later, you'll realize that everything you need to figure something out is right here..." He reached over and tapped Laolys's chest.

Laolys felt his heart skip a beat. The sage's presence had an odd intensity to it. "Do you think my ascended self had a role in getting me up here?" he asked, hoping to shift the focus elsewhere.

"For someone like you? I'd say absolutely."

Laolys stared at the sage, trying to read his expression, unsure if he should take offense. "What do you mean by that?"

"Just that you, in particular, have a very strong divine influence. You have so many ascended shards. I'll bet they're all wracking their minds about you, trying to get you to see what you need to so you can finally join them."

"You think so?"

The sage nodded. "In this matter, I'm quite certain." He looked at Laolys with a slight trace of amusement. "You really are closer than you think. All you have to do is start listening to yourself."

Laolys took a deep breath. This task, at least, was simple. He had guidance—aside from just the sage—that would lead him toward the right path. All he had to do was listen. "But what about the people who have no ascended shards?"

"Those with no ascended shards aren't alone. Other ascended

beings guide them. I'm willing to bet your divine self guides quite a few new and lost shards."

Laolys smiled. "I'd like to do that too."

"You will, in time, I'm quite sure of it. But first, you have to help yourself. You can't help anyone until you learn the lessons. You're still a student of the material realms."

Laolys looked out at the mountainside. Puffy white clouds drifted through the sky above, which was beginning to fade in the sunset. He was pained, but he had to grow past it. Otherwise, he would remain here, confused and lost like the other shards still in the same school, still with lessons yet to be mastered.

He turned his attention to the sage. "Are all our soul shards in other worlds? Could some be in this one? When people talk about soul mates —that one person who matches perfectly—could that be another shard?"

A brief expression of horror passed across the sage's face, which he quickly masked with a neutral expression. "Not possible. No, not in our cycle. In the lower cycles, it happens all the time. A flock of birds, for example, all the same soul. Integration happens naturally when species evolve; they all do it together, as a group.

"But in our cycle, there's self-awareness. Two soul shards meeting each other has a very different effect." The sage's demeanor took on a darkness that Laolys couldn't quite interpret.

"So, what's the effect?"

"Our spirit's main goal is integration. Our awareness poses a grave danger to our physical bodies. If we were to happen across another one of our shards—which isn't supposed to happen—well, it's not good. They're in other dimensions, parallel worlds, and distant times and galaxies for a reason."

"A danger to our physical bodies?"

"Yes. A complete destabilization of both shards' energy systems could follow, leading to premature departure from the physical planes."

"So... death."

The sage nodded. "Have you ever heard of a doppelgänger?"

Laolys shook his head. "No, what's that?"

"Essentially, a twin you've never met, but not a genetic relative. It's a parallel world version of yourself. It's also an imminent death omen."

Laolys felt his heart skip a beat. "Our planet is densely packed with parallel realms, right?"

"Densely. Such things *could* happen here more easily, which is why it shows up in myths and legends. Still, it's very rare, even here."

Laolys looked around nervously. "I hope I never happen upon mine!"

"You have a very low risk of that—not that many living shards left, relatively speaking."

Though Laolys felt the sage's attitude was a bit too callous, he decided to leave the subject alone for now. He turned his attention back to the sky, where white, puffy clouds were slowly adopting a rosy hue. "So, you said many of my shards have ascended and are helping the remaining ones ascend. What happens when they all ascend? Am I whole?"

"If only it were that easy. When you ascend, you'll just be beginning your journey toward wholeness. The true extent of your shards is very great. It takes many cycles to achieve true unity."

"Many cycles in the spiritual realms?"

The sage nodded. "The only beings we know to be truly unified entities are the Ennead."

"Who are the Ennead?"

The sage's face shifted through several expressions as he gazed at the landscape in front of him. Love, loss, and wonder all intermingled in a way that Laolys couldn't begin to interpret.

"The Ennead were born at the beginning of the multiverse," the sage began. "They weren't born like you or me; they're formless, they're just energy. They arose from the seeds of the multiverse itself.

"They watch over the multiverse on a grand scale, but they're not creators. They're observers. They supervise the flow of energy throughout the Cosmos, ensuring that the interdimensional strings maintain a harmonious rhythm."

Laolys remained silent, unsure how to respond. It was all completely new information.

"Each one of them is all-encompassing in nature," the sage continued. "Each one is both male and female in their energetic makeup, equally light and dark, balanced on every possible spectrum. That type of unity is what we're all working toward, but it's many cycles above this one. And the Ennead aren't the last cycle either; there are cycles beyond even them."

"What cycles are those?"

"Not even the Ennead know that."

"So, they're really all encompassing?"

"Yes, and there's only nine of them in the multiverse. So, you can let that tell you how long it'll be before you're whole. It's a journey."

"I guess so." Laolys stared at the clouds. Before today, he had always believed *he* was whole, spiritually speaking, at least.

The sage's expression took on a dark demeanor, and he swallowed. His eyes, fixed on the landscape, seemed distant. There was something in them, a sadness.

He sighed heavily. "I really wish I could've gotten people to listen."

"Hmm?" Laolys turned to him.

"The Ennead have a message for humanity. I wish I could've gotten people to listen." The sage continued to stare blankly at the mountainside.

"So what's the message?"

The sage let out a long exhale. His sadness was palpable. "Humanity is killing itself spiritually and physically—by killing the planet. We can't go on like this much longer. The planet will strike back. Natural disasters are sure to come if we stay on this course."

Laolys swallowed. His father, no doubt, had been trying to keep the sage from spreading exactly that message. It would've damaged his governmental system—its industries—to change everything. "And... you tried to spread this message?" he asked softly.

"Tried with every ounce of effort I could afford, which was a lot. I got a lot of people to listen, but ultimately, I didn't change a damn thing." He cast his eyes downward and took a heavy, labored breath. "Sometimes I think it was a mistake that they came to me, and not someone else."

Laolys looked at him, stunned. "What do you mean they came to you?"

"Well, only one really."

"That's not what I meant. How did that one come to you?"

The sage sighed. "It really was all just luck. Happenstance. The time was right, and I happened to be there with my portal. I guess they'd been trying to get through for a while, but it wasn't time yet. They had to wait for the right alignment."

"With your portal?" Laolys repeated, barely breathing the words.

"Really, all just happenstance. I took the message, but I couldn't get it out, not to enough people, anyway."

Laolys's mind flashed to his father and his anger regarding the leak. "That's not entirely your fault."

The sage glanced at him.

"I mean," Laolys paused, feeling the heat of a blush rise in his face, "you gave it your best effort. Plenty of people didn't want to hear it, that's all. That's hardly your fault."

"Waste of a good effort. No results."

The sage's demeanor had darkened. Laolys hadn't seen him in this state before. He stared at the mountainside, his lips pressed together with tension, as if trying to keep emotions from coming to the surface.

"Aren't we supposed to detach from results? You gave it your best shot."

The sage swallowed. "Normally, I'd agree with you. But on a matter of such high importance—the very state of our world—I can't help but feel someone else might've done a better job."

"I doubt that. I've never met anyone quite like you, and I've met plenty of people in high positions. No, I think there's a reason they came to you. It wasn't just happenstance. If you couldn't save the world, maybe it just didn't want to be saved."

"Hmph." The sage exhaled with force. "You may be right about that—the world, I mean. The world doesn't want to change."

Laolys looked to the horizon, now a golden hue streaked with rose. "No, you know what? The world is always changing. It's the people in it who are the problem. They think they can keep things the same instead of moving with the cycles. You said everything cycles. People need to cycle too."

"People *do* cycle—just, instead of rising and falling with the tides, they bounce and moan about each displacement. What's coming, though, is far more than a shift in the tides. If that were the case, I'd say I did alright, put in my best effort. What's coming is beyond anything humanity has seen in millennia. That's the troubling part. That's where I'm leaving my work still undone: humanity is ill-prepared."

"Won't..." Laolys hesitated, fearing the truth behind his own words. "Won't I be sharing these messages?"

The sage glanced at him, his expression neutral, with a hint of pity. "Aye, and you must, but the course has been set. There's not much hope of changing things now."

"Not much hope of changing things?" Laolys looked at him in disbelief.

The sage sighed. "There's not much you, or I, or anyone else can do about it, I'm afraid. The world is much too big for any of us. This is part of humanity's greater cycle."

"What do you mean, its greater cycle?"

"There are small cycles, yearly cycles, generational cycles—and then beyond that, there are larger ones that span thousands of years. This isn't the first time humanity has stood at a crossroads and made the wrong choice, refused to change its ways. The last time was just so long ago, everyone forgot."

Laolys looked at him, clueless.

"The history of humanity goes back much, much further than archaeologists give it credit. Still, it was so long ago that the only evidence that remains is the big monuments—like the pyramids—and early texts. Medical texts, for example, included detailed procedures early on, which later digressed into magical enchantments."

"So, you're saying humanity's done this before," Laolys said, overwhelmed by the amount of information the sage divulged.

"I know I couldn't have stopped the turning of the cycle, but I was expected to prepare people for what's to come. Over the course of my life, the best I could muster was small bands of followers. I was evicted everywhere I went. Governments didn't want me, people feared me, and I hardly made a dent."

"I see." Laolys swallowed, feeling the weight of the sage's solemnity. "My path might not be much different, either."

The sage slapped his hands against his lap. "No. Your path is what you make it. It's not going to mirror mine—not unless you're convinced it can't go any other way. No, now is not the time for moping. You have your whole life ahead of you. Use it."

"I guess you're right. I'll be sharing the teachings, but what I do with them, where I go, and how I use them... that's up to me."

The sage shifted in his seat. "I know you have your heart set on my lifestyle, but before you make me into your idol, think about everything else you could become. You decide these things. Who will you be when you descend this mountain?"

"I... don't know."

"The answer is a lot simpler if you don't think about it." The sage glanced at him casually, then turned his gaze back to the landscape. His demeanor was serene now; his earlier darkness had dissipated. "Just know that now that you've been here, you've begun to awaken. You're different now. You can't leave and live a normal life. Revolution will have its way of following you wherever you go."

"Revolution..." Laolys repeated. Although he wanted it, he also feared it. "You really think I'm capable of bringing revolution?"

"What makes you think you have a choice? I did give you one, but for a hero, the answer is decided before the question can even be asked. A hero—or a bringer of change, as you see yourself—can't imagine more than one answer but to move forward toward their goal, whatever the cost. This is what makes them different from everyone else. Others get scared and back down; heroes plow through the difficulties because they don't even see the option to reverse their course. No one said it was easy."

"Don't take this the wrong way," Laolys began cautiously, "but was it worth it? I mean, you sacrificed everything to get the message out, and in the end, it just landed you up here. It's glamorous and all, but I imagine it's sometimes lonely."

The sage chuckled softly. "Was it worth it? I don't know. It only pushed me through enough complete remolds of my character that I evolved into a spiritual being fit for ascension. That, and I made a solid mark on the world. I'd say it was a life well lived, if there ever was one, and it's not quite over yet." He smiled and winked at Laolys.

"So, you did make a difference."

"I did what I could. The results won't come in my lifetime, but some of the most brilliant minds in history never saw the results of their work either. It's not about results in the end. It just matters that we don't give up."

"Don't give up," Laolys echoed in a whisper to himself.

He looked toward the distant valleys that awaited his return. He somehow both loved and resented himself for embarking on this journey. It wouldn't be easy. If the sage's life was any indication, his own path wouldn't lead to glory either. But it would be profoundly worthwhile, if only to bring him inner peace and ascension. And perhaps, in some way, he could make a meaningful impact on the world as well.

He took a deep breath. "I want to believe in myself, but I can't stop seeing all the ways I fall short. I see you, serene in your wisdom, while I'm a scrambled mess. You've accomplished incredible things, and I'm somehow supposed to carry the torch. It's daunting."

The sage chuckled softly. "No one ever said you had to change the world, just live by the teachings and share them with those who ask." He cast a stern glance at Laolys. "You really are your own worst enemy. One day, when my teachings truly resonate within your spirit, you may finally put all that brainpower to better use."

"You mean my self-doubts?"

"Everything. What you focus on affects your entire vibrational flow. Your beliefs about yourself are the only thing holding you back. You climbed a mountain to meet an infamous revolutionary so you could learn important truths about the human soul and its place in the Cosmos. You aspire to change the world, and you actually follow through. You should give yourself more credit."

Laolys smiled despite himself. "When you put it that way, I sound quite incredible... But that's hardly the whole picture. I've always been told I should do great things. What I'm actually doing—or will be doing when I go back into society—won't be seen as great. I'll have to resign from office to share these teachings, and I'll become a public disgrace, even if I do manage to gain a small following."

"Sounds like a life well lived to me." The sage winked at him.

Laolys stared back at him with a glint of awe. "What path worked for you? How did you reach them in such a powerful way?"

"It's not about the path I took, the books I read, the systems I studied. It was how I applied myself. I wanted my enlightenment desperately enough that I wouldn't take no for an answer. I had to give up my fear and run head-on into the challenges I was most afraid of. That's the only way. I don't know your path, and if I told you mine, I'd be robbing you of the most important thing for your soul: your journey."

Laolys stared back blankly.

"Look at it this way," the sage continued. "I overcame my fear of heights by climbing trees, but I can't tell someone who trembles at the thought of boarding a boat because they're scared of drowning to go climb trees like I did. Obviously, that person would have to learn how to swim. You need to find the answers for yourself. If I told you where to go, I'd be robbing you of your journey."

Laolys's heartbeat quickened. He was sure there was something the sage was intentionally not telling him. He had to know some secret that allowed him to receive the message, a secret he didn't want anyone else to know. "But there has to be something! Names, formulas, ways to call in ways they'll hear you. These things matter!"

"Each member of the Ennead is nameless, formless, and all-encompassing in their nature. The names you call, and even the methods you use, pale in comparison to the strength of your spirit and will, and the nature of your intent."

"Names don't matter?"

The sage shook his head. "They're all nameless. They've been given many, many names, but no interpretation of them truly captures their essence, because everything is in their essence. They are formless entities, beyond all human definitions."

"Well, how did you reach the one you spoke to?"

The sage shrugged. "I was just willing to listen. Turns out, most people just can't hear them. They've been wanting to pass their message to someone. I just happened to be tuned to a frequency that allowed me to hear it."

IDENTITY

"You think I could hear them too?"

The sage nodded. "First, you have to learn how to listen to yourself." He paused and gave Laolys a look of sympathy. "But give yourself a break, too. Transformation takes time. You've only just begun."

"I want to see what you see, but I don't even know where to begin. These lessons are a start, but what do I do when I return? Where should I look next?"

"That's for you to decide. As I said, it'd be counterproductive for me to give you the specifics."

Laolys sighed. As much as he hated to admit it, he understood the sage's point. He couldn't copy the path the sage had ventured and expect the same result; it wasn't what he needed. He needed to find his truths for himself.

He took a deep breath. "A lot of people claim to have answers, but it makes more sense that answers are different for different people."

"People who claim to have answers are selling answers. Not for profit, usually, but they want you to buy them. They want you to believe their answers because they think that if you do, their truth is more correct."

"Their truths are often wrong whether I believe in them or not!" Laolys retorted.

"Their truths are wrong!" The sage clapped his hands together. "Yes, why are they wrong and not real truths?"

"I mean, I suppose they could be right as well. It doesn't matter whether or not I see their truth as real," Laolys stammered, a bit shaken by the sage's enthusiasm.

"No, what they call their truth is wrong the moment they try to sell it to anyone. They're trying to sell it because they, themselves, don't believe it. Anyone with a real, solid truth between their ears keeps it sacred. They don't parade it around and ask others to buy into the hype. They might share their knowledge, but there's a difference. I put myself on top of a mountain and don't share my name. Others go to cities and hang up signs."

"But when I share your truths, I'll be selling them, correct? I'll be trying to share them with the world!"

"You only have to share them with people who ask. Don't keep good truths away from those who want to hear them from you. That's all." The sage paused, watching the sun approach the horizon. "But," he continued, "those who know you took this journey will ask. I'm afraid your name will carry you forward, so that many will know of your journey. Many will ask."

Laolys swallowed. He wished his nervous energy would just leave his body. "This destiny... this place... it's all starting to sound like too real a possibility!"

The sage let out a yelp of laughter. "Other great men have made glamorous destinies out of what they could find in the woods, but I don't recommend it! To admire it is one thing; to live it is another. I'm not naming any unfortunate successors to my legacy."

"And let all this just go to the state? I wouldn't hear of it!" Laolys gestured toward the hut.

The sage grinned. "You can keep it as your fallback plan, but find another destiny. There are endless possibilities, really."

"Outside the shadow of my father, I have no idea what those are."

"Then now's the time to decide. You still have time, but don't waste a second of it. This moment—this freedom you feel now—it won't last forever. Despite some hunger and lack of comforts, one day you'll look back on these moments with longing."

"I know I don't want my future to look like my father's, but I feel like I'm starting to emulate yours! How do I learn who I truly am?"

"You're fluid, remember?" The sage moved his arm in a flowing, snake-like motion toward the sky. "Fluid can go anywhere it pleases, but it will take the form of whatever container it finds itself in. If you remain in one basin too long, you begin to stagnate, to rot."

"So, would you say the environment we choose plays a big role in who we become?"

"Think of the memories imbued in the rock I handed you or within the hut. Consider whether we aren't internalizing impressions from the external world all the time."

"We're products of our environment, then."

"No!" the sage bellowed with an emphasis that startled both men. "You're not a young man, the son of a politician, a resident of your town, or any of the other things you define yourself as. You're not these any more than you're any of the identities you carried in past lives. Your memories don't make you who you are. Who you are is much deeper; it doesn't have a name. It's your spirit, your will, your intent! I am speaking to your soul, and it was your soul that climbed this mountain, not the legs that moved it, who I'm instructing."

"How do I get to know my true self? How do I see past my illusions of identity to find the real me?"

"Listen when I say that Laolys is a terrible politician, a thief, and a madman."

"But I'm none of those things!" Laolys felt anger—or perhaps fear—rise in his throat. He was also caught off guard; it was the first time the sage had ever addressed him by name. This utterance, for some unknown reason, shook him to his core.

The sage smiled at him with a glint of knowingness that was both fierce and intimidating. "Ah, but you'll become all these things to many people. Don't you base your self-image on the opinions of others?"

"Of course not!" Laolys objected, but his cheeks immediately blushed.

"Then why concern yourself with them?"

"I don't—not much!"

"Oh really?" The sage's smile faded into a look of stern authority. "I believe most of what we've been covering up here has involved you shattering your fears about how others see you."

"But I don't want to give their opinions of me any weight." Laolys cast his eyes to the ground, embarrassed.

"Develop a firm foundation in yourself and know that you're fluid. Their words mean nothing until you give them merit. Tell me, what does someone who the world says nothing but good things about really have?"

"Well... I imagine a good, kind spirit."

"Likely, but that is irrelevant. That person has everything to lose."

"Favor will change?"

"Absolutely. Everything changes. It's easy to believe people when they say good things about us; it feels good. But then we become invested in what they say. We crave more of it, and when favor turns...

as it always does... well, a person usually descends needlessly into an abyss of depression."

"So don't believe any opinions?"

"Just your own. Work as hard as you can to live up to your full potential, pursue spiritual growth, but don't let others weigh you down. Really, if they call you a madman, you might be on the right path."

Laolys studied him. He admired how the sage delighted in not getting approval; he didn't want it. He, on the other hand, had been trained his whole life to seek it. "What, if anything, gives a life meaning?"

"What gives a life meaning?!" The sage threw his hands up in disbelief. "Every life is born with meaning! Its meaning is existence! It's the growth and development of the soul! Every day you are alive, you have the purpose of furthering your personal evolution and the evolution of those around you. As for your eternal existence... Well, ask if the universe has any meaning to its existence, or if its life is purpose enough."

Laolys sat with the sage's words in the cooling late afternoon air. His life was not devoid of meaning; its purpose was inherent in itself. He was even fulfilling it now, studying with the sage. Even though it was terrifying in many ways, it felt good to push the boundaries of his perceptions, to learn and live according to his purpose.

He turned to the sage. "So, you're saying that much of our purpose in life is overcoming ourselves?"

The sage nodded. "I would say that's every soul's entire purpose for inhabiting a body, yes." He paused, a wide smile spreading across his face. "You know, upon reflection, that's still our purpose even after we ascend past the need for physical form. We're always working to overcome ourselves, just at different levels."

"But I thought you said that to ascend is to finally break free of our illness of mind and spirit, to master the self. Wouldn't that mean we're done at some point?"

The sage shook his head. "Growth is never-ending. We're fluid entities, and the universe itself is a fluid, ever-growing, and ever-changing entity. We're constantly moving into new environments, having new experiences, even after death and ascension. Each step

IDENTITY

widens our scope of vision, and it's inconceivable that we'll ever reach a place where we can't expand our view further. That would extend beyond Chaos."

"What do you mean by Chaos?"

"Chaos is everything. It's not disorder. It's limitless potential."

The sage bent down and grabbed a handful of dirt from the ground and let it sift from his finger. "This, all this material, it confuses a person. They start believing this is what's real, and that what's out there," he gestured to the sky, "or in here," he placed his hand on his chest, "is not. And that causes the spirit much distress because it begins to doubt itself."

Laolys mirrored the sage's gesture, scooping up a handful of dirt. "Illusions?"

The sage nodded. "Transitory. Temporary training grounds. Laolys will die one day, but you will not. Only the part of you that is temporary. The rest—your spirit, your soul—will remain and carry on."

Laolys sat with this statement. He was finally beginning to understand what it meant to be truly alive and what it meant to spend one's life trapped by various illusions. It was either a great power or a great curse to be so overwhelmed by the illusory. Without understanding, it's easy to become trapped in a world of nightmares, always seeking the nearest form of comfort. Yet, with the correct understanding, one could do as the sage did and choose the illusions they liked best.

Laolys opened his mouth to express this thought but realized his instructor had once again disappeared, almost as if to emphasize his point: the material world is almost entirely a series of illusions.

That night, Laolys lay awake in the hut. He wasn't sure the hut was to blame, either. Pains from his past arose, knocking on the door of his conscious mind, demanding their dues. It appeared they would not be as easily forgotten as they had seemed under the sun, in the sage's company. Here, in the dark, lying by himself, they met him without hesitation, insisting that he address them.

You must protect yourself! The first thought came rushing to him, a stark reminder of the deep scars that still lingered on his soul—marks that would always remain. How does one simply forget tragic loss, abuse, or abandonment? When the wounds are so deep that they do not fade, how can one forget they are there?

Laolys reflected on his true nature. *Fluid.* Fluid does not remain in a basin with poison. He needed to evaporate, to distill himself, and leave the precipitates of his past sorrows on the mountaintop. He needed to grow past his pain. He imagined the possibilities that lay before him—the vast mental planes the sage spoke of, which he was only now beginning to glimpse. He had to face the pains of his past and release them from their hold on him.

It will happen again! Another voice, born of an old wound, voiced its warning. It was quiet but heavy with emotion, trembling with the weight of past suffering.

So will everything else, Laolys replied. And he truly meant it. He saw now that the darkness in the world existed because there was also brilliant, blinding light. He could not know one without the other. He had to experience both. He had to experience everything, such was the law of life.

Anyone you let in will hurt you! The next voice came thundering, screaming this warning with all its might. Genuine fear overwhelmed its spirit, and it was apparent that it had known horrible pain in its life.

This is a risk we allow for the ones we love, Laolys said to the frightened thought. Just as we cannot know light without darkness, we cannot know love without loss. Everything we possess in the world will one day leave us, just as we ourselves will become something we are not today. But we take the pains along with the pleasures, understanding that everyone in this world carries their own suffering. The actions of others, even when they wound us, are rarely done with the intent to harm. And if we are honest, we see that we, too, have hurt those we love. We have sought forgiveness. Should we not then be willing to forgive the faults of others?

You are not deserving of good things. This thought voiced its concerns shyly from the shadows, yet its pain was so heavy that all the other thoughts, and even Laolys himself, turned toward it when it spoke. It tried to remain hidden, but its suffering was too great to be ignored.

Everyone deserves good things, Laolys addressed the thought. *But you most especially deserve them. You have already paid a heavy price. Your pain has led you through the trenches of despair all your life. It is time to experience the same intensity on the other side. You must let go of your fears so you can know the heights of spiritual bliss!*

The thought stood, trembling. It could not believe Laolys's words, even though he spoke them to himself. The fear was like a thick, tattered cloak wrapped tightly around it. Laolys began peeling it away, layer by layer. The thought shook violently, clinging to what shreds it could, resisting the truth even as he freed it from its grip.

This has to go! You have to LET. THIS. GO! Laolys begged the thought to see its worth, to let go and recognize its own strength, to see how powerful it was without the tattered blankets of fear weighing it down. He continued peeling away the layers, and the thought continued to shiver, pleading to keep the last remnants of comfort those fears had provided. But Laolys did not stop. Finally, the last remaining layer was stripped away, leaving the thought standing before him, skeletal and afraid.

See what you have done? the thought cried through a torrent of tears. *You have taken everything I had left! Everything this cruel world had given me is now gone!* Its voice held both anger and mourning, for it did not understand what it had lost, nor did it know what lay ahead. In its limited perspective, all it saw was a shift from the familiar, a change it did not ask for.

It is time for you to see, he addressed the weeping thought, *that you are better off without it. You may have needed it in the past, it may have been a cruel vice at times, but you can live without it now.*

The thought whimpered, trembling as it absorbed his words. Its tiny chest rose and fell in uneven intervals, gasping for air between low, broken wails.

How? The one-word question came raw, laced with equal parts anger and desperation. The thought did not know how to continue. It had little hope for itself, but Laolys answered:

Slowly, a little bit at a time.

The thought looked at Laolys, confused. It waited for more explanation, for a reason behind its pain and a detailed plan for a better future. But Laolys had neither of these things to offer. Seeing that no further instructions were coming, nor any alternative options, the thought nodded. It had no other choice but to carry on—slowly, as suggested.

Laolys turned to the other thoughts, still silently watching. *"Does anyone else want to speak?"*

From the middle of the group, one thought shot its arm into the air, eager yet trembling.

What if you are wrong?! the thought asked, panic overwhelming its expression. It could not imagine anything more terrible than standing up for something, only to be wrong about it.

Everyone is wrong sometimes, Laolys comforted the worried thought. He noticed how, despite being surrounded by others, the thought still trembled in fear.

He cleared his throat and spoke again, *No one expects or demands perfection.*

The thought looked confused by this statement, so Laolys repeated it.

No one expects or demands perfection.

The other thoughts began to chatter softly among themselves, questioning, whispering, trying to process this unfamiliar idea.

Then, one bold thought from the back of the crowd shouted, *They do from me!*

A rumble spread through the other thoughts.

Me too! said one.

And me! added another.

Who doesn't have to be perfect? snapped one in an annoyed tone.

Soon, all the thoughts were speaking at once, their voices rising into a cacophony. Laolys's mind was overwhelmed by the noise.

ENOUGH! he yelled.

The thoughts stopped abruptly, turning their attention to the director of consciousness. They stared at him, waiting to hear how he would justify what they considered a remarkably ridiculous argument.

You do not have to be perfect! Laolys declared. *You are not God—far from it! In fact, I have good intelligence that even the gods of the ancients have not achieved perfection. And if you are ever going to master something, you must push yourself through many hard lessons, which means making many, many mistakes. The only way to never be wrong is to never do anything at all!*

IDENTITY

The thoughts exchanged glances. Some looked skeptical, others thoughtful. None wanted to make the first move. Then, as if struck by a magical spark of inspiration, the thought Laolys had stripped of its blankets began to clap its tiny hands together.

The thought beside it, hesitantly at first, clapped in support.

Then another.

Then another.

Soon, all the thoughts were applauding. None dared to be the only one left out.

Laolys let the applause continue a moment longer, then asked, *Do you know what this means?*

The applause died down as the crowd of thoughts waited in expectant silence.

This means, Laolys continued, *you are not allowed to interrupt me with your worries all day!*

Murmurs of anger and concern spread through the group. One particularly loud thought near the front suddenly shouted back at Laolys.

You ingrate! Do you know how many times I have saved you from humiliation? the thought bellowed, shaking his fist in the air for emphasis. A few other like-minded thoughts shouted in agreement.

Weakened my plight, actually, Laolys responded calmly. *For all the times I bowed my head in silence instead of speaking up for myself, or didn't ask a question when I didn't understand something, I slipped a little further from reaching my higher self.*

Murmurs of confusion rippled through the anxious thoughts. No more protests came; only expectant eyes waiting further explanation.

I don't expect you to be able to understand this today, he said, addressing the crowd. *Just take a vacation. Sit back and observe what happens when I live without your interventions. And then, in a while, we can reconvene, and I will explain more.*

A flicker of excitement spread through the thoughts. They had never taken a vacation. They knew of the concept, and it sounded nice, but they had never imagined they might experience one themselves.

Yes, go, Laolys urged gently. I will be okay, I promise. You can go explore the world for a while. I will be alright.

Slowly, the thoughts began to float away, dissolving and dispersing. Some glowed a bit brighter as they departed. Others twitched anxiously but still followed the rest. Eventually, no thoughts remained. Only Laolys's clear, consciously directed will lingered, uninterrupted.

What now? he asked himself, but he didn't have time to answer. Before any further thoughts could form, he was drifting off to sleep.

THE MIND OF THE BIG FISH

Journey

"Do you want to take a journey?"

Laolys's eyes shot open in the dead of night. The air inside the hut was unnervingly still—no movement, no sound of another breath. Outside, not even the wind stirred, and no small creatures scuttled through the forest. Everything lay in complete silence, yet he was certain he had just heard the sage speak.

"Excuse me?" Laolys whispered into the darkness. The hut offered no trace of moonlight, no glimpse of the stars. If not for the persistent nudge of his intuition, he would have assumed it had all been a dream—or worse, that he was losing his mind.

"Do you want to take a journey?" the voice repeated clearly.

So it was the sage. Laolys wasn't losing his mind just yet, though madness did seem to be on the precipice.

"It's dark outside," Laolys replied, irritated at being woken just as he had finally begun to get some decent sleep. Still, curiosity tugged at him; he had to know what the sage had in store. He rubbed the sleep from his eyes.

"All the better for your travels, no distractions," the sage said.

"A mental journey? But I was just asleep!"

"Lazing about the astral plane, I saw, so I woke you! Highly ineffective, your 'dreaming,' as you call it."

"How is it ineffective?"

"What were you dreaming about?"

"I..." Laolys tried to bring the images back to his mind, but the last thing he could recall was his thoughts as he was drifting off to sleep. "I don't remember."

"See? Ineffective." Laolys could almost feel the sage shaking his head, or at least he imagined it clearly.

"So, you woke me up?"

"I'll forgive your fogginess of head for only a bit longer. You came here to learn from me, remember? Pull yourself together!"

"I'm sorry! I want to learn. I'm paying attention. How do I dream more effectively?" Laolys made every attempt to bring himself to a more awakened and conscious state despite his exhaustion.

"Where did you intend to go?"

"I'm not sure what you mean."

"Surely you meant to go somewhere."

"When I was going to sleep?"

"I said only a moment longer of this nonsense!"

"I'm sorry, this is a new concept for me!"

The sage sighed audibly, and silence ensued before he spoke again. "When you go to sleep, part of your energy leaves your body as your consciousness is no longer tied to the physical realm. You can do it during waking hours, too, but that's harder. It's natural during sleep. You should be going to sleep with intention; it's no wonder you're so tired."

Laolys wanted to say something about being woken up, but held his tongue. "What kind of intention?"

"An intention for your dreams. You can decide to visit anywhere you like—past lives or worlds you've never been to—but only if you decide to."

"A place, or a past life?"

"Tonight, we're going to pick a place. Certain kinds of places are easier to visit spiritually because they're charged with energy. Ancient temples, caves, or catacombs all act like magnets for the spirit. I want you to pick a place, a real location, to visit in your dreams."

Laolys hesitated. "You want *me* to pick?"

"Yes, it's *your* dream."

"And then what?"

"You pick the place and put yourself there, mentally, as you're falling asleep. You have to be able to visualize it, so pick a place you're somewhat familiar with."

"So I just visualize it when I'm going to sleep? And I go there?"

The sage sighed. "That's the idea, yes, but if you're going to keep doubting yourself, you may as well not even bother."

Laolys swallowed. "I'm sorry. This is all new to me."

"The mind is a powerful tool. It can take you anywhere you like, but you, like most people, don't use it to your advantage. Everyone has themselves so convinced they know what other people are thinking about them. Imagine if we all stopped wasting our thoughts on such nonsense and instead convinced ourselves we could access other realms of consciousness!"

"Well... I guess we could probably reach them."

"Or have ourselves so convinced we can that we end up with people willing to ascend tall mountains and get woken up in the middle of the night to listen to our nonsense!" The sage chuckled softly, though his breath caught, turning into several emphatic coughs.

"Anyway, back to what I was saying," he continued. "Your mind can take you anywhere you like, as long as you direct it. Right now, you're still letting your mind direct you, but tonight's exercise will show you how to become the director. So, did you pick a place?"

"No, not yet. What kind of place do I pick?"

"Anywhere the spiritual energy is more charged. Ancient temples, caverns, haunted locations."

Laolys thought back to his youth. When he was a teenager, there was a small rock enclave with a creek running through it that he used to visit with his friends. It had a strange pull to it. While it unsettled most of his friends, he had found it exhilarating. The veil between worlds seemed thinner there, as if some of the energy that gathered in the space couldn't leave. It clung to those who visited, trailing them as they left, desperate to escape with them. That place, along with a few others, had shaped his curiosity, driving him to explore beyond the ordinary and seek the extraordinary.

"I think I have a place," he said. "It was just down the road from my old house. There was this creek that wound through a small rock enclave that had a strange feeling to it. There were all kinds of rumors about it; people said there were lots of suicides there, that it was haunted. I never saw anything, just shadows flicking about, but the feeling..." He shivered as he recounted it. "It could send chills down your spine."

"That'll work. Now, place yourself there amongst the rocks. I want you to feel the grooves with your hands, hear the flow of the creek, and smell the earth around you. Before you can see it, you have to feel it. Can you?"

Laolys imagined the scene. First, he tried to feel the rock behind him. Immediately, the sage's lessons about how rocks are teeming with life and hold memories came to mind. He felt the surfaces of the enclave, rough beneath his palms. *These rocks have memories.*

A surge of emotions flowed from the rocks, carrying the weight of lives that had ended in this strange place. Their torment brushed against Laolys's mind, momentarily becoming his own. What was it about this location that held such a magnetic pull, drawing spirits in?

He noticed the trickle of the creek. It flowed endlessly, no matter what stopped around it. The rocks stood, fixed in the mud, while the water moved, unhurried and unrelenting, around them.

Glimpses of souls losing their bodies came to mind, but each was only a flash, like a raindrop. They collected together with no more sorrow or joy than rain gathering on a windowpane. It's only as sad as the eyes that gaze upon it. Do they wish to go outside but feel hindered by the cold and wet? Or are they watching the droplets form, grateful to be behind solid shelter, warmed from within, home at last? These are the souls that finally collect to return to the Cosmic womb. They are simply souls, no different from any other, who were going to die that day. Like so many had said before him: *So it goes.*

Laolys noticed the breeze as it gently made its way into his nostrils. It carried the scent of the rocks, the earth, and the creek. Its fragrance held no trace of anything truly magnificent or magnetic—and yet, somehow, in the innocent wildness of it, it did.

Laolys, too, was becoming aware of the magnetism of the rocks sunken deep into the earth, beneath the life that occasionally strode above them on the bridge. They had no interest in that life. They did not eagerly seek recognition, nor did they care to understand any of its goings-on. They wanted away from the noise. And so, the rocks sank into the soft clay of the earth, which flowed and shifted with the quiet current that ran through it.

The rocks knew something better. They had seen so much of life. They bore tiny microbial lifeforms before those lifeforms escaped in search of something more complex. They saw how complicated life could make things, when all the rocks ever wanted was to remember a simpler time. That simpler time, in truth, was what all the lost souls were drawn to. They simply sought the same thing as the rocks.

Suddenly, Laolys felt his body grow warm, and he let his light drift toward the warmth. He was back in another realm, where he had been before with the sage. He felt his light—like many other lights—drift toward a brilliantly shining blackened light. Its blackness was a light in itself, drawing every other light inward. It contained every light imaginable, absorbing them all into its essence. Laolys, too, was part of the brilliant blackness now, part of that light. He swam among many other lights, each one sharing in the same vast depths of infinite Cosmic life.

Very faint sounds of birds just beginning to awaken and chirp quiet good mornings to their fellow flock brought Laolys back to the waking realm. He opened his eyes to see a slight hint of light creeping through a crack in the wall of the wooden hut. Dawn was barely on the horizon. He figured the sage would soon be around to begin the next lesson.

Laolys stretched his legs and began to stand up, but immediately toppled over. Unexpectedly, knees and elbows that were not his met his acquaintance, and a loud groan rattled his eardrums. It was the sage.

"Augh!" the sage exclaimed, gathering himself to his feet. "All of my insolence in insisting I hold no room for guests has come to collect its dues!" He brushed off dirt and dust from his already impossibly dirty garb and briefly smoothed his hands over his rough and wild mane of hair. "So, how was it?"

"Was that my journey?"

"It was a start. Are you rested?"

Laolys stretched his limbs as he stepped outside the cramped hut. "Surprisingly, I feel better rested than I have in a while."

"Then you're beginning to understand how to use your energy wisely. Sleep well, and you'll find you can accomplish more on two hours of rest than most people do on eight."

"What do you do with the rest of your time?"

"That I'll leave up to your discretion!" The sage began to stretch, his bones cracking with each twist. "But I advise you to spend it on something worthwhile. Contriving worlds in your head centered on things like other people's opinions isn't nearly as fulfilling as exploring how many secrets there are just within a flowing creek."

Laolys took a deep breath, savoring the peaceful morning air. The sun had only just crested over the horizon, and the air was calm and still. Soon, the forest would be buzzing with vibrant life, but for now, the first morning yawns were still being made throughout the trees.

He scanned the horizon. The town that loomed in the distance wasn't yet visible in the pre-dawn gloom. "Do you think everyone should separate from the world for a while? To see things for how they are."

"That's how I did it. But a more inventive mind could probably find an easier way."

"I'm starting to see how much everything consumes us down there. We get so caught up in the world around us that we forget how to live our lives."

"Then you're starting to wake up."

"But what happens when I descend? How do I not become consumed again, as they are?"

"It's almost impossible now to go back and become consumed as they are."

Laolys turned to him. "It is?"

The sage smiled. "Once you really start to see the illusions for what they are, you can't fall back into them. It's too shocking, too transformative. I tried to warn you in the beginning."

"I guess you did." Laolys thought back to his former self. He didn't miss it. "All for the better anyway. It's okay if I don't fit into society. I'm starting to see how it's all just a big madhouse."

"Then you'll do alright."

Laolys swallowed. "But teaching it... still scares me."

"You wanted to be a hero, correct?"

Laolys cast his eyes to the ground. "I don't even understand why or how to do that anymore..."

"The *why* is simply to live as one does. You are a hero; it is your path. And *how* is the same. Live as a hero, as you have done so far."

The sage moved his bony hand around, gesturing at the scenery. "It looks like you've done pretty good so far, let's see..." He counted silently with his fingers. "Boy believes himself capable of saving the world, boy leaves home to learn from a famous vagabond on the ways of ascension, boy sets out to teach the world despite their protests..." He grinned at Laolys. "For a man who doesn't see himself as a hero, you're doing pretty good so far."

Laolys's cheeks flushed. The title *hero* seemed childish now, applied to him in the real world. "And if I decide the hero's path is too much for me? What if I want to go another direction?"

"Then you follow that path. But be warned, there are no easy roads for someone capable of great things. It wouldn't be fair to the world to let excellence waste away in luxury."

As Laolys considered his future, he imagined every possible path led to struggle. Staying in politics was no longer an option; his mind had opened too much to deeper truths. He was doomed, as the sage had warned, to reveal his newfound knowledge in one way or another, no matter where life took him.

"Should I just take the hard road, then? Get it over with?" he asked.

"Aye! You should! You know, that kind of attitude shows true potential."

"I must develop the calluses of Sisyphus, then, either way."

The sage smiled. "If your destiny has already been decided, it's good to want what's in store for you."

Laolys let out a sigh of tension. He felt an odd sort of relief. The future was either entirely up for grabs or already decided. Either way, he knew the path ahead of him meant he would grow stronger, perhaps even escape this cycle of life and death. Maybe this time, maybe not, but it would make no sense not to try.

"I suppose it is what it is, and it is what we make it out to be," he replied. "Perception can recolor what you're unable to change; perseverance can change everything else."

"Spoken like a good student; you've made much progress."

Laolys looked to him with a glimmer of surprise. "I'm learning well?"

"Learning, remembering, maybe both. Don't get too full of yourself. There's always far more to discover. You're just at the tip of the iceberg. What lies beneath is far beyond your comprehension. Further still, lie things beyond my comprehension, and there always will be, by the grace of Khnum's law."

"Khnum's law?"

"Simply put, it means there's always the possibility for a glitch in the dimensional web of the universe. Sometimes realities collide where they shouldn't, and in brief moments, the fantastic shines through with clarity. This leaves the door open for the impossible, although that may mean a small crack for only a second."

"A glitch or mishap? Even the universe makes mistakes!"

"Nothing's without flaw. But I'd hardly call the glitches flaws. Things would be boring if everything always happened smoothly, as expected. It's Khnum's law that keeps eternal, timeless beings enrapt in wonder. It allows for the impossible to creep through the door of the most organized events. But it doesn't always show up. You have to look for it, hard, and stay vigilant, because it only comes every now and then. If you don't pay attention, you're bound to miss it."

Laolys looked at him, searching his face, which was only slightly lit by the faint hint of light in the sky. "What does a glitch look like?"

The sage smiled; a hint of nostalgia shone in his eyes. "You'll know it when you see it. It's a quick flash of wild brilliance amidst the ordinary. If I can remember the prose correctly...

JOURNEY

*One quick flash where least expect,
Look again and see it left,
Expect it not, it won't come round
Expect again, and so it's found!"*

Laolys laughed. "So, do I expect it? Not expect it?"

"Both." The sage grinned. "Don't expect it to show up, and it will. Think then, that you must not expect it for it to show, and it won't show again because now it's waiting for you to expect it. But it's not really conscious; it's just a way of saying there is no real way to prepare for it or bring it into existence, it just happens randomly."

"I stopped trying to know what to expect shortly after meeting you. You've shown me that I can't know what to expect and that it's a good thing."

"Just remember, magic works by expectation. You have to believe in your own will to carry it forward to manifestation. This means you not only expect but *know* that results will occur. And Khnum's Law doesn't give a second thought where you think you may find it. Who knows? It may be in the first place you look!"

"You're full of paradoxes and contradictions. Are you just trying to keep the company here indefinitely?"

The sage threw his hands out in a grand gesture. "Welcome to Chaos, the order of the multiverse! Everything's a paradox. Everything both is and isn't at the same time. But that's a lesson for later on."

Laolys turned his gaze toward the horizon. "Dare I ask the forecast for today's death?"

The sage paused, and for a brief moment, a flicker of pained concern washed over his face before vanishing as quickly as it had appeared. In that instant, Laolys saw something he hadn't noticed before. Despite witnessing death daily, the sage was not unchanged by it. He hadn't become jaded.

"Let's just say..." the sage's voice caught, "today is not the day for you to be climbing trees."

Laolys's heart skipped a beat. He had planned to join the birds again that morning, as the sage had shown him. He glanced up at the trees. The birds, swirling and chattering above, could have led to his downfall, and only days before, staying on the ground had nearly cost him his life.

I must not let fear get ahold of me, he thought.

When he turned his attention back to the campsite, he realized the sage had vanished. With a soft sigh, he dipped into the hut to peruse the scattered library and await his friend's return.

Order Within the Root of Chaos

Chaos

"Chaos is the order of the multiverse. It is the only possible law through which an infinite system can conduct itself."

The words rang out loud and clear, breaking Laolys's focus. He was seated on a log beneath a tree, reading a book on the aqueducts of ancient Rome. The sun was now high in the sky, nearing noon; the sage's return was earlier than expected. Laolys had thought it would be several more hours before the next lesson, yet the voice was unmistakable.

He scanned the area but saw no sign of the sage. "H-Hello?"

A nearby tree rustled. "Chaos is the order of the multiverse. It is the only possible law through which an infinite system can conduct itself."

Laolys looked up at the tree, now certain of the sage's location, though he still couldn't see him. "Should I... come join you up there?"

"No bother. I will disentangle myself from the branches in a moment."

Laolys paused, unsure if the sage had misspoken. "Disentangle, sir?"

"Yes. This morning, I had the wild idea to see what it would be like

THE YOUNG MAN AND THE SAGE

to be a tree for a while." The tree shook violently, sending a small pile of leaves raining down near Laolys. "I do *not* recommend it!"

Laolys looked up. He still couldn't see the sage, but a sudden unease crept over him. He hadn't realized the sage had been so close. "H-Have you been up there all morning?"

"If you want to define it by crude, physical means... Yes, I've been up here all morning. But *I* have not been up here. Not the *I* who is speaking to you now. I disappeared for a few hours. I was a tree."

The tree continued to rustle and shake as the sage maneuvered through the thick branches. Laolys remained silent, unsure how to respond. With a final push, the sage leapt from the tree and landed on the ground. He brushed himself off, attempting to remove the leaves tangled in his hair, though he only managed to dislodge a few. Then, he sat beside Laolys on the log, staring at him with wide, unblinking eyes.

Laolys shifted uncomfortably. He wasn't sure what the sage wanted. Then it struck him: a reply to his earlier statement. "Chaos... it means possibility, right?"

"On some level. But probabilities guide most things with some reliability."

"Then why worry about the infinite? If we have probabilities?"

"Because the farther you stretch, the more places you can reach at once, the more chaotic things become. And if you can get to the center... that is pure Chaos."

The sage's bright eyes stood out against the tangled knot of gray hair and leaves that framed his head like a mane. They somehow both contradicted and perfectly complemented his ragged appearance.

Laolys turned his gaze toward the mountainside. "Center of what?"

"Anything! You... the grand energy web of the Cosmos... It all looks the same, and it all looks like Chaos."

"Okay, so what does Chaos look like?"

"It's like..." The sage brought a finger to his chin. "A brilliant, pulsating void! It flashes with endless possibilities. It holds every thought that has ever been and will be. It contains every action taken, every choice declined, and every possibility of every choice yet to be made. Leap into Chaos, and you could end up anywhere!" A wide smile spread across his face. "But there's also a good chance you'll land exactly where you had in mind."

"So... there isn't any predictability, then?"

The sage shook his head. "No, there is predictability, sometimes even probability, but never certainty."

"Can anything be certain?"

The sage shifted his position on the log. "Very, very few things can be certain. The sun will rise tomorrow. Of this, we can be certain. But what kind of world it illuminates? That's never certain."

Laolys looked around. "So, Chaos governs everything?"

"Yes, and we should be grateful it does. Chaos means there's always possibility. But don't mistake Chaos for disorder. It likes order; it just doesn't always choose the orderly path."

"What do you mean?"

"Well, it could arrange things neatly in one instance, and then the next, decide everything needs to be reshuffled. Chaos can trick you into thinking things are a certain way, and then, on a random impulse, reveal the true nature of things."

Laolys dug his nails into the log he was sitting on. He still wasn't sure what the sage meant by Chaos. "You talk of Chaos like it's conscious. Is it conscious?"

The sage shook his head. "It's not conscious—it just seems that way." He let out a sharp exhale. "And if it is conscious, it's far beyond what anyone, even the Ennead, could comprehend. It encompasses everything, and I mean *everything*."

"I guess we can't expect something so vast to follow orderly rules—even ones it sets for itself."

"Chaos is limitless; it's the only thing that is. Anything that has to follow rules is limited by them. But Chaos is much more orderly than most imagine. There's a framework to the universe that energy systems flow through."

Laolys turned to him. "What do you mean?"

"Think of it like a massive web that spans the entire multiverse. Everything's a part of it. Nothing's separate. This web isn't Chaos, but it's inside Chaos. Chaos likes order. If it didn't... well, I don't know what kind of life would be here, but it wouldn't be anything like we know."

"So why call it Chaos, if it likes order so much?"

"Because that's what it is. Chaos encompasses everything. Everything's fairly ordered, so we have to understand that as a priority. But it's not a necessity. Every now and then, Chaos likes to pull one of those strings and send a galaxy spinning—but only for a moment. Then it falls back into even course."

"I see. So Chaos is what it is because it has the ability to defy order, not because it always does."

"Exactly. Chaos is linked to potential—new growth and discoveries. If it couldn't defy order, we couldn't step past the bounds of the present. Everything would stay put. Think: before our universe's Big Bang, everything was mushed together. Everything interacted, but nothing interacted. Until one moment decided to be different from all the others..." The sage clapped his hands; just once, but loudly enough to startle nearby life. "And the rest went on from there."

Laolys looked up, catching the sun filtering through the thick leaves of the surrounding trees. "So, Chaos."

"It's what drives everything. Everything's linked through Chaos. It's at the pulsating heart of our multiverse."

Laolys turned back toward the sage. With the extra foliage still lodged in his hair, he had a comical look about him. "What do you mean by that?"

"What I mean is... step into Chaos, and you have no idea where you might end up. Any point in the multiverse." The sage shrugged. "Then again, you could end up exactly where you meant to go."

Laolys stared back blankly. "Step into Chaos?"

The sage cleared his throat. "Not without proper precautions, of course."

"I'm still not entirely sure I know what Chaos is."

"Chaos is everything. It's all experiences, all at once. It's the subconscious and conscious thought of all life forms. It's everywhere, but space and time are completely irrelevant to it."

"Irrelevant?"

"Yes, it's outside the bounds of space-time. It extends through all the material realms and far beyond them into the spiritual realms and true nothingness. But it thinks about none of this. It's safe to say Chaos has no idea about nearly everything that goes on inside it."

"How does it not know?"

The sage shot him a perplexed glare. "*You* try considering every choice every life form in the multiverse has ever contemplated and tell me if you can consider all of it!"

Laolys shuddered at the thought. "I guess never."

"Yes, but remember: Chaos exists outside the realm of time, so *never* isn't describing the future. *Never* is its eternal state. It could potentially view everything, but it also forgets, so it'll never know all of itself at once. It's impossible."

"Is anything regarding Chaos not a paradox?"

"Chaos is the ultimate paradox." The sage leaned back, his gaze drifting blankly toward a nearby tree. "I spent most of my life trying to understand it, but the only answers I can gather are the ones that include both possibilities in tandem."

"Because it encompasses everything."

"Exactly." The sage's lips formed into a slight smile. "How else can you describe something that exists as limitless potential? That which is outside of space-time and the seed of the multiverse. It has to be everything—both expressed and unexpressed states."

"So, it's everything and nothing then," Laolys mumbled, feeling as though his grasp on the subject was also in a paradoxical state of both expressions.

"Aye, so you're beginning to understand the conundrum!"

"I am?"

The sage nodded. "The proper assessment of Chaos is wonder and confusion. Even the most ancient beings are transfixed by it. A great deal of it is orderly, and this is, perhaps, its greatest strength. It tricks you. Things can go on a certain way for so long and then—" he clapped his hands together once. "It hits you. A glitch appears before your eyes, only to vanish, never to be seen again."

Laolys's mind flashed back to earlier that morning. "Khnum's Law!"

"Exactly. It's by Khnum's Law we're never really done discovering things. We just keep looking, hoping to catch a glimpse of a wider truth."

"All we have to do is look?"

The sage smiled. "I can't imagine how else we'd ever discover anything."

"But I thought it was completely random chance that an oddity—a glitch, as you called it—would occur."

"It is. But you have to be looking when it happens. If you miss the crack, you'll never make it through the doorway." He paused briefly, his gaze distant. "Even if you build your own portal, you still have to wait for that flash."

Laolys stared back at the sage, his mouth agape. He could hardly believe he was hearing about portals from the infamous leak. His mouth moved in slow motion, barely forcing the words out. "How do you build a portal?"

The sage shifted in his seat and glanced at Laolys with a sharp scowl before turning his gaze back to the surrounding trees. "I will not instruct you on portals. No one—and I mean *no one*—is to hear about portals from me. It's dangerous. Ill-advised. Stay out of the portal business."

Laolys held his breath. "Just... a hint?"

The sage shook his head. "Too dangerous. If you feel the need to go practice sublimation on yourself, fine, but it won't be from my teachings. End of discussion."

Laolys sighed. "I wish... I don't know... I don't even know what you *mean* by portal."

The sage looked at him, his brow creased with a glint of suspicion. "There are so many realms stacked on top of each other, coexisting in one space. It's a lot easier than you think to cross through them."

"It happens on accident, you said."

"That's right. It can happen on purpose too. You just have to know the right mechanisms to create a small pinprick into a new reality. It's easier than you think."

"Like a leak to another dimension?" Laolys's heart skipped a beat. Memories of all the nights he lay awake wondering about the mysterious leak flooded his mind, and for a brief second, he could hardly believe he was really here, asking this question.

The sage's eyes lit up with a glint of interest. "Yes, something like that. A leak is something that's not supposed to be there, so that's a good way of describing it."

Laolys felt a surge of excitement pulse through his veins, but he tried to maintain a calm appearance. "Does it involve a mirror, by chance?"

A sudden flash of anger crossed the sage's face, causing Laolys to tense up. The sage inhaled sharply. After a pause, he finally responded, "A mirror and space are not so unlike each other, in that it's sometimes hard to determine where one ends and another begins."

Laolys stared back at the sage in stunned fascination. Only a small utterance escaped his breath. "So... yes?"

The sage let out a deep sigh. "That's the only hint I can give you. The rest you'll have to figure out yourself. I advise you stay out of the whole damn affair. Cost me far too much trouble in the long run."

"I take it you've been through quite a few?"

The sage coughed loudly, with several heaves, before settling his throat. "I've been through far too many. Then again, just one is too many, really."

"What's it like?"

"That depends entirely on where you end up. Could be life-changing. Could be just another day."

"How'd you get started?"

"I lacked the foresight to know where it would lead me." The sage folded his arms across his chest. "I wanted to know things, no matter where it led. I was careless, reckless. Do yourself a favor and don't follow in my footsteps on this one."

"Why not? Why is it so dangerous?"

"Because..." The sage paused, his face twisting into an expression of pained wonder. "Without going into the details... after a while, the timelines can get all jumbled up. It's hard to know what's what, or where anything is, or who you even are anymore. I thought I'd find some great truths in my ventures, but it just confused things. The multiverse—it's overwhelmingly complex."

"I see." Laolys studied the sage, trying to read his expression for hints buried beneath the surface of his words.

The sage stared at a nearby tree; his brow furrowed over an otherwise blank face. "It's not just one-way, you know."

"Hmm?" Laolys glanced at him.

"A door usually works in two directions. Portals are the same."

Laolys's breath caught short. "Are you telling me that your portals brought things the other way?"

"I'm telling you nothing. Just giving you a warning, that's all."

Laolys stared at him.

The sage's eyes remained fixed on a distant valley. "Causes far too much trouble to be worth any good."

"You said something the other day... about having an open portal when you heard the message. That's something, isn't it?"

The sage shook his head. "I don't know what you're talking about."

"The message from the Ennead. You said you happened to have an open portal, so you could take the message."

The sage let out a long exhale. "Oh, that. Yes, I suppose my portal made it easier, but it wasn't really necessary."

"Not necessary?"

"Look, you can go far—plenty far—as long as you stay away from trying to construct portals yourself. That backfires in every possible timeline I see for you. It destroyed things for me... things I'm still trying to tie back together."

Laolys could feel the weight behind the sage's emotions. His warning was well-merited, for whatever reason. "Okay, I hear you. Portals are dangerous."

"Very. Stay out of them."

Laolys's gaze drifted to a nearby bird hopping about the forest floor. "You really do mean incredible things could happen—leak through to this world. What did you say about glitches?"

The sage straightened. "Khnum's Law. Glitches, or dimensional drifts, happen randomly, on their own accord. That's the brilliance behind the order of Chaos."

"A glitch... It's kind of like a natural portal, right?"

The sage glanced at him. "You're too smart for your own good."

"If I could catch one, I wouldn't need to make a portal."

"Good luck catching one. They happen in random locations at random intervals. There's really no way to predict when, where, or how it will occur."

"I'll stay vigilant then."

The sage turned his gaze toward him, his lips curving slightly in amusement. "You really are your own worst enemy." He chuckled softly. "I was the same way at your age. Maybe I still am. I just hope you're wiser than me in that you'll take my advice."

Laolys looked back out at the forest. The sun was nearly at its peak, crisping everything with its fiery rays. The shadows were short, and life flitted about unhurriedly. Several birds hopped around, flew between branches, and burst into short, spontaneous songs.

"You don't need portals. They didn't teach me anything, just how to become lost." Though the sage kept a mostly neutral expression, Laolys could see by the tension in his neck that he was holding back strong emotion.

"Okay, fair enough. Then how do I awaken without using portals?"

"Shift your perspective. What you think about is probably the single most important factor of your overall well-being. Stop being so hard on yourself. That's what's holding you back."

Laolys's mind flashed back to the lesson on how thoughts affected water molecules. "I'm starting to see that now. I'm starting to direct my mind, but I have a long way to go. Before I came up here," he let out a sharp exhale. "Well... I had no clue it even needed to be changed."

The sage smiled. "You're well on your way to greatness now. Remember that your mind—where you put your focus—that's what and where you are."

"Everything is mental," Laolys mumbled.

The sage nodded. "The universe is more like a hologram than any other scientific theory I've heard proposed."

"How so?"

"Well, in many cases, there are separate realms nested within each other, sharing the same space, only, you'd never know it by the way you perceive the world... You only see one." The sage held up a bony finger.

"Your brain filters just the phenomena that apply to this realm. The others are here too, but you can't see them. That's all you have to do to start seeing the timelines... teach your brain how to see what's right in front of you."

Laolys stared at the air in front of him, trying to will himself to see new realities. His brain didn't listen, of course, and he only saw the same solitary reality. "Just perception?"

"Aye. But getting there takes quite a bit of work."

"Work like what? What kind?"

The sage shrugged. "Whatever it is you need to do to see beyond the illusions."

Laolys slapped his hands against the log he was seated on. "An old cliché comes to mind: if a tree falls in the forest, and no one's around to hear it, does it make a sound?"

The sage groaned. "Silly proverb. If you ask the tree, I'm sure he'd tell you all about the sound he made. I'd bet he wouldn't stop talking about the sound, the pain in his back, and how tall he used to be. He'd go on and on about how the day he happened to fall was the worst of all days. It's better when no one's around to hear the sound, believe me."

Laolys laughed, but the sage maintained a neutral expression with a hint of irritation. He stifled his laughter, realizing the sage had experimented with being a tree earlier that morning. "But it does hint at perception..."

The sage leaned back, looking out toward the mountainside. "The world goes on without us perceiving it. In the quantum realm, everything exists in a superposition until we measure it; then it only becomes one thing. Maybe we do the world a favor when we close our eyes."

Laolys looked at him, amused. "Everything's there until we decide it's not?"

"The quantum world is just as paradoxical as Chaos." The sage stretched his arms out in front of him, cracking his joints. "It shouldn't be the case, but it seems that quantum particles change their behavior based on our observations. It's like they're busy doing everything at once until we come along, and then they have to act like they're only doing a single thing."

"Why do you think that is?"

"I think they know we can't accept things for how they really are just yet, so they do us a favor and give us what we expect to see."

Laolys stared at the air in front of him, considering the concept. After the lessons regarding the lower cycles and the variety of forms consciousness could take, he was beginning to see the world in a new light. Even the empty air before him was alive with unseen forces. In the quantum realm, particles were appearing and vanishing everywhere, at all hours, nonstop.

He turned to the sage. "And what if we change our expectations?"

"Then we'll see a whole new world." The sage's mouth formed into a wistful smile as he stared at the mountainside. "That's hard to do, though. It's one thing to think about other realities. It's another to convince yourself you're actually in one."

"I suppose so."

The sage glanced at him. "If you can do that, though, you'd have formidable control over your physical body."

"How so?"

"What they call the placebo effect extends much, much further than people realize. If, for example, you had terrible eyesight but convinced yourself—and I mean *really* convinced yourself—when you went to bed one night that you'd wake up with 20/20 vision, you could do it."

"What?"

The sage gave a half-nod. "It's your reaction to that which is exactly why it doesn't work. No one really thinks it'll work. They might try all they want to, but deep down, they doubt it."

"It's hard to wrap my mind around."

"It's against your mental programming, that's all. I'm willing to bet some miracles recorded in history really did happen. They don't happen anymore because no one truly believes they can break that barrier. That's our programming. It was different a long time ago."

"I guess."

The sage smirked. "You know, an IV placebo is five times more effective than a pill placebo. *That* should tell you everything you need to know about the matter."

Laolys paused to think. He had a point. "There shouldn't be a difference."

"Exactly. Your mind controls everything. Unfortunately, it's pretty set in its beliefs, so we have to come up with creative ways to trick it into a new reality."

Laolys looked at the sage in silent admiration. He seemed otherworldly, and yet painfully human at the same time. His eyes shone with brilliance, but the leaves entangled in his hair gave him an aura of madness.

"That's real magic, you know," the sage said.

"Hmm?"

"It's all mental. Everything. You, the universe, even Chaos."

Laolys swallowed. "So, direct my thoughts."

"Exactly. This is vital. It's perhaps the most important thing you could do for yourself: find peace of mind."

Laolys took a deep breath. He wanted to reach a state of serenity, like the sage. Out of the corner of his eye, the town in the distance loomed like a patient predator. He couldn't escape it, and he knew his return would be met with perhaps the biggest argument of his life. Still, it needed to happen. Though he dreaded the confrontation, he was beginning to look forward to the aftermath. When it was all said and done, he would be free to claim his future—whatever that was.

"A little easier up here than down there," he mumbled, gesturing toward his town.

"It's achievable anywhere. Just pick different illusions and you'll be alright. Embrace your madness, knowing that it's the brilliance of future generations. You're ahead of the curve."

Laolys grimaced. "I'll have to remember that when I'm talking to my father, or fellow officials."

"Don't worry about what they say. You know, people down there, they wouldn't believe the wondrous and fantastic if it was right there, staring them in the face."

Laolys's mind flashed to his family. "No, they'd be afraid of being crazy."

"So afraid of being crazy, they don't believe their own eyes. Need I remind you how fear is a self-fulfilling prophecy?" The sage grinned at him.

"I don't suppose you do. I'm beginning to be afraid to fear anything at all!"

The sage wagged his finger at him. "Well, you'd better stop that now. I'd hate to stare fear itself in the face!"

"This coming from a man who has walked through dimensional portals, narrowly escaped being eaten…"

"Regularly!" the sage interrupted.

"*Regularly* avoids being eaten," Laolys continued, "knows interdimensional beings—"

"Being. Only one."

"Anyway, I imagined you'd have stared fear in the face at some point."

"No, I let go of fear a long time ago, as soon as I saw how powerful it is at creating realities. What we think about has real weight on our lives—a lot more than most people think. Fear, next to love, is one of the most powerful emotions. If we fear something, we'll most likely manifest it one way or another."

Laolys thought back to his fears—terrible public performance, his parents' disapproval, losing the popular vote—the first two he faced regularly, the last he would face upon his return. "It does seem to go that way," he mumbled.

"Aye. So if you're wise, you'll stop fear altogether. Can't start fearing it; that's worse. Just stop fearing anything at all."

"Easier said than done! At least for me. How did you just get rid of fear?"

The sage's brow scrunched inward. "You know, I can't say exactly. It happened after I had already begun traversing portals. I was frightened so many times, I think I just finally gave up—fear, that is." He brought his hand to his chin. "And, strangely enough, that's when my luck turned around, too."

"After you started traversing portals?"

"Yes. I'd advise you to do it beforehand, but you won't be doing that at all. So, just work on getting rid of your fear, then."

"Within reason!"

"Fear goes beyond reason. But even I think I drew the line a little too leniently sometimes."

"How so?"

"Well..." The sage paused, his gaze drifting toward a nearby tree. "There was another forecast for today's death."

"Go on! What is it?" Laolys looked at the sage expectantly.

"Oh, don't be afraid, it didn't happen!"

"Can you tell me the specifics?"

The sage sighed heavily. "There was a chance, last night... after you went into a trance in the hut... that you wouldn't have woken up—or that you could've woken up as a different person."

"What?!" Laolys's reaction exploded from him before he could stop it. "Why would that have happened?"

The sage crossed his arms and averted his eyes. "I knew I shouldn't have told you. You can't see the other timelines for a reason, you know."

"But you put me at risk! And I didn't know anything about it!"

"There's a risk with anything. If the rest of humanity saw as I do, no one would move a muscle."

"But I could have never woken up!"

The sage scowled at him. "You go to sleep every night not knowing whether you'll wake up. It's never a given."

"But this is different!" Laolys felt anger swell in his chest. "You put me in real danger!"

The sage's scowl deepened, and he leaned in toward Laolys. "You came up here to learn from me, remember?"

Laolys shrank back, his gaze falling to the ground.

The sage sighed. "If you saw things like I do... every day out here is another way to be eaten, another way to fall to my death. If I still let fear govern my life, I wouldn't be here. I would've manifested that reality long, long ago."

"I... think I'm just starting to realize just how much fear I actually have." Laolys's voice was barely above a whisper.

"You're only just beginning." The sage patted him on the back. "If only you could see where I began." He coughed and cleared his throat.

"Real progress takes time, and you haven't even begun yet. You don't really begin until you leave this mountain."

Laolys sat with this statement. He realized he could spend all his time up here worrying and, in doing so, never really enjoy it at all. He would keep it in his mind as a retirement plan—a safe place to fall back to—that was unavoidable. For now, he decided he had to fully embrace the present before it was too late.

He closed his eyes, took a deep breath, infused his lungs with the fresh mountain air, held it, and released. When he opened his eyes, he realized the sage was gone.

The sun burned brightly overhead, but beneath the canopy of greenery, it remained tepid even at the peak of day. Shadows were scarce; the world was illuminated so completely that it deceived the mind into believing everything that could be seen was laid bare.

The world before him went far deeper than his senses permitted—Laolys knew this now. He wished he could convince his brain to see it too, to peer into the other timelines the sage had described. But it would take more than wishing. He would likely have to find a creative way to trick his brain, as the sage had described.

He sighed and lay flat on the log, closing his eyes. He let the visions come to him; he was too tired to fight or fear them. The sage had encountered stranger visions, and he had survived all his excursions because he had done away with fear. Laolys would have to do the same if he hoped to survive even half as long.

The chaos of the natural world was evident. What people failed to realize was the beauty in the order it also held. Order was everywhere —in the patterns of petals in the flowers, in the way ivy curled around tree trunks. Life was apparent. It was not an anomaly. Humanity was merely a sliver—hardly even a fragment—of the universal heartbeat of life.

As the day progressed, the life around Laolys carried on with its activities, disordered to an outsider, yet purposeful in its own right. The birds dispersed and gathered again, calling to one another with sporadic chirps. To the untrained ear, it was nonsense; but to the birds —and perhaps the sage—it was organized, conscious direction.

The order that surrounded him was so pervasive, in fact, that to some, it became equally deceiving. Within that order lay countless conscious life forms, and just when the same pattern had been repeated so many times that one had forgotten it could happen another way, a divergence occurred. One brave or callous spirit chose another path. For better or worse for that spirit, new information was integrated. Soon after, new habits formed. Evolution followed, eventually forgetting there had ever been a divergence at all.

It's no wonder that Chaos governs the multiverse. Were it any other force, we doubt evolution would occur at all.

Descent of the Storm Called From Within

Unity

"Unity governs all spirits of life. Stray too far in one direction, and you are bound to one day become its opposite."

The sage's return came as the day was ending, as usual. The sun was low on the horizon but had yet to make its plunge into the world of the unseen. Light still characterized the condition of the sky, but the shadows cast across the ground promised this would soon change.

Laolys was lying on the ground, captivated by a small army of ants marching across the forest floor. He had been observing them for about an hour, occasionally placing obstacles in their path to see how they navigated around them. They fascinated him; their world differed completely from his, even though they occupied the same space. To the ants, if they were aware of him at all, he was a force of nature. He rarely considered them, and yet they persisted, building tiny cities beneath the soil at his feet.

"When you say unity, I imagine interconnectedness," Laolys replied, looking up from the ground to smile at the sage. The sage returned the smile and sat down next to him.

"Unity is about being one with the world around us—a universal heartbeat with which the spirit of life pulses. It recognizes that even the smallest microorganisms have their place in the grand scheme of existence. The spiral of life needs every ring on its ladder."

"All life is one," Laolys mumbled, watching the ant line.

The sage nodded. "Unity is also about oneness of self. It's the alignment of mind, body, and spirit with the will of the divine self and the divine whole."

"The divine whole... you mean like God?"

"The word 'God' can be misleading. What we refer to as the grand whole doesn't know its parts. It undoubtedly has zero awareness of us. Still, we're a part of it, just like those ants are a part of the planet." The sage nodded toward the ant line.

"Each one of those ants seems infinitesimally small to us," he continued. "They seem too small to matter, but they play a crucial role in the ecosystem. Each one has a life and a consciousness. They organize, colonize, build, and create storehouses."

The sage picked up a stick and guided one small ant onto the end of it. "This ant is unknown to the Earth spirit; its consciousness will never be acknowledged by it. Yet it remains part of the same unity of life as we are, as the Earth is, as everything is. It's on the same upward journey, too."

He extended the stick toward Laolys, who took it and studied the ant as it scrambled frantically, likely searching for its lost colony. Normally, he'd never consider this ant, and there were billions more like it that he would never acknowledge. "I suppose the ant's importance is intrinsic, whether or not external forces recognize its exact place."

"That's right. Even if the grand whole were to recognize us by some strange phenomenon—such as me picking up this single ant out of billions of its likeness—my recognition plays no real significance in its world. It probably just wants to get back to work."

Laolys gently placed the stick back down on the ground and watched as the ant scurried off the end, extending its antennae to find the direction back to its colony. Soon, it was back in line, and back to work with the others.

"So what now? Do you think he's telling everyone about his travels?" The sage was watching the ants with wild fascination.

"Well, if ants could communicate such things, I think it'd be quite the story. I imagine so!"

"Hmm. I don't think he'd mention it at all."

Laolys turned to him. "No? Why not?"

"He wouldn't want to stand out. That's not the goal of an ant."

"He wants to blend in?"

"He wants to play his role. His goal is to work in the line and gather food. That's his means of survival. He doesn't benefit if the other ants see him as special. He only benefits if he, along with the others, works efficiently to support the collective."

"I suppose humans are less noble, then—the way we tear at each other and compete for attention."

The sage shrugged. "Not less noble, just distracted by the illusionary. The ants haven't reached that stage; they simply see things as they are. One day they'll enter our cycle and have to learn these things. For us, right now... We'd be wise to learn a lesson from the ants."

Laolys glanced at him. "What lesson is that?"

"Unity. They don't only have unity with the planet and each other; they have unity within themselves. The ant we separated earlier didn't change his life's direction based on his short excursion; he went straight back to work with the others."

Laolys studied the ant line. "Which one is he?"

The sage shrugged. "Does it matter?"

Laolys looked at the ants again, noting how seamlessly they worked together, each contributing to the colony's needs. "Do you suppose humans could ever achieve such unity?"

"Humans have, throughout history, achieved this state of unity. It became lost in the modern world. Any densely populated area will make you fear the worst for humanity. Tribal communities, though, still have it to this day."

"They do?"

The sage pointed to the ant line. "Look at the ants again. Watch their behavior. Not a single ant thinks he can go off on his own and survive.

And they're right; they can't. Humans don't think that way, though. We're hellbent on our independence, even if it kills us—and it usually does. Except in tribal communities. There, everyone sees the value in helping the community, so people, overall, live in a state of unity."

Laolys stared at the ant line. Their seamless operations depended on a unified perspective. Ants that broke this pattern rarely survived. The ones that worked to help the whole enjoyed the comforts of their labors and the joy of community.

"My whole life has been a power struggle," he mumbled. The realization hit him in an instant. He had been trained his whole life on how to speak and present himself in a way that commanded authority. It was the exact opposite of unity.

"Let go of all that. It's always the people who hold power who get burned by it the worst. We aren't meant to have power over others—not in an extreme sense, anyway."

Laolys released a sharp exhale. "Never really wanted power to begin with; it was always just what I had to do. I'm actually starting to look forward to telling my father off, in a way. I'll finally be free."

"That's the spirit!" The sage smiled. "Just do yourself a favor and don't clamp onto any destinies just yet. I know you've got your eyes on my hut, but give yourself some time to explore the world first. See what else is out there."

Laolys swallowed. "If only I could just get rid of my fear."

The sage patted him on the back. "You can't just will it away. You have to face them head-on and blow past them. That's the only way to do it. You can't get rid of your fears up here on the mountain."

"I see, I have to *do*, too."

The sage nodded. "That's at least half of it. Take action, or your knowledge is meaningless."

Laolys continued to stare at the ant line.

"What's your biggest fear, huh?" the sage asked. "That you won't be liked? Well, I'm telling you now—not being liked could be a good thing, depending on your way about it. Madness isn't often liked, but sometimes it's brilliance unrecognized."

"I think I'm finally starting to get that."

"Really, the second you stop believing in the same illusions as everyone else, you become something else. You're not wired to the same programming. People spot that."

Laolys watched the ant line. No ant stood out among the rest. "How do you factor unity into the equation, if it makes you an outcast?"

"That's easy. Unity is a state of spiritual resonance that says: I am not more important—not even separate from this planet, that tree, or every other human."

The sage stood and walked to a nearby tree. "This tree," he continued, reaching out to hug its trunk, "is part of the planet's body. You and I are like its cells. Only you and I have abilities this tree hasn't learned yet. We can communicate with the Earth spirit."

Laolys, still seated, stared back at the sage in interest. "How do I do that?"

"That's like telling a person how to dream. There are no set guidelines, but doing it's as natural as breathing. It's just been forgotten by most of humanity for a very long time, but we can remember again."

The sage walked to his familiar rock, and Laolys followed behind, taking a seat on the adjacent one overlooking the mountain. The sun was exactly level with the horizon, and the forest was still. It was astonishing how, though the colors in the sky were similar to morning, the vibrancy in the air at daybreak was completely absent at dusk. Only a few small tweets could be heard from birds as they made their way toward shelter for the night.

"It never fails to say good-bye, you know," Laolys mumbled, staring at the horizon.

"Hmm?" The sage turned his head.

"The sun. It's one dramatic exit after another."

The sage smiled. "You should tell that to the birds. They don't care about the exit, though. All they care about is its morning return." His eyes sparkled as he watched a bird creep close, then fly off into the trees.

Laolys watched the birds gathering in the treetops. "They're like the planet's dopamine, rising with the sun." He turned to the sage and hesitated. "What about us, though? We have to be more than a virus."

"We are more. Much more. Well... we *should be*, anyway. We have a role to play in harnessing the Earth's natural energy and amplifying it. We can spiritually communicate with her, too. Most people don't do any of that. That's what the Ennead wanted, for humanity to take on its role, protecting the Earth. Instead, they just keep harming their mother, the very land that gives them life."

"You don't think people will change their ways?"

The sage shook his head. "No, not a chance."

"Then why tell me to try?"

"Because you have to try. You wanted to make the world a better place, remember?"

Laolys sighed. "I did."

"Well, what now? It gets hard, it gets real, and you don't want it anymore?"

Laolys blushed. "No, it's not that. I'm honored to learn from you, and I'll share it. It's just..." He glanced toward his town with dread. "I don't think I can save it."

"Well, no one can save it. The cycles are turning; it's inevitable. You just have to try."

"Why though? If it's hopeless?"

"Because one day, whether this world makes it or not, you'll have to die. I don't know about you, but I want to live my life to make sure that this death will be my last. I don't have to save the world—and that's a good thing, because the world can't be saved. In the end, all I have to do is save myself."

"You mean ascension?"

"Exactly. Now, I certainly couldn't have kept the knowledge the Ennead imparted to me to myself, could I? Not if I wanted to ascend."

Laolys's gaze fell to the ground. "No, I don't imagine so."

"You're right. Not because it was a message from the Ennead, but because it was a message that involved the well-being of the rest of the planet. I knew it wasn't going to go over well. I knew I would be cast out everywhere I went, but I taught people anyway."

Laolys swallowed. "So now I have to do the same."

The sage shrugged. "Where you go, what you do with this knowledge, is up to you. Not sharing it has a cost, but the choice is yours. I did warn you."

Laolys's heart skipped a beat. "You did."

"I tried to get you to listen."

"You did. And I'm glad I took the lessons. The path ahead won't be easy, but I will walk it." Laolys's resolve was firm, though he couldn't stop his heart from pounding in his chest.

"Once you eradicate your fear, you'll start to enjoy it. Fear is your biggest hindrance. Let go of that, and you might begin to see things for how they really are."

"You really think I'm that close?"

"Fear is no minor obstacle, especially for you. It's hardwired into your core makeup. It's what was instilled in you as a child. But it's not insurmountable. You can overcome your fear just the same as anyone else." The sage glanced at him. "And if you do... you may even ascend."

Laolys dug his nails into the rock he was seated on. Fear was a huge obstacle. "How do I get rid of my fears?"

"You face them, one after another, until you've faced every last one. That's the only way."

"That's it?"

The sage shrugged. "Well, you could keep trying to avoid them, but you know how that usually goes."

Laolys nodded. "Not much of a choice."

"It's better to head straight into our problems. That way, we can get through them and move on. There was a time when I had many of the same fears you did. But I faced them. I was terrified once; now, I no longer am."

Laolys glanced at him. "You sure came a long way."

"It's been a long life." The sage's eyes were fixed on the horizon as the last flash of sunlight dropped out of view. "You shouldn't fear your opposites so much."

"Hmm?"

"Your soul shards. You could be any number of them; even the one you fear the most."

Laolys drew a quick inhale. "The one in politics?"

"Yes. That shard didn't have the courage to do what you're doing. Believe it or not, you're way ahead of him. Maybe in the next few lives, he'll be where you're at."

Laolys thought about him, his guilt. In that moment, his anger transformed into compassion. He felt bad for the lost shard. "Maybe you're right," he said softly.

The sage let a few moments of silence pass between them. His expression was nostalgic, serene. In the fading light, he looked like he belonged in an old photograph—a fleeting moment lost in time.

"It's not an easy road," the sage said, "but it's the only one worth taking."

"What road?"

"The way to enlightenment. To ascension. We're all here because of some inherent flaw we're unwilling to face. Yours is fear. Most people live in fear, but they don't want to admit it. Whatever it is, you have to face it. It could be the hardest thing you do in your life, but believe me, it's worth it."

Laolys sighed. He understood the necessity of facing his fears; he just didn't like it.

The sage caught his gaze. "Tell me, how do you turn a solid into a liquid?"

Laolys hesitated. "You... melt it?"

"That's right. Right now, your fears are a solid rock inside you. You haven't faced them yet. You will when you get down the mountain. You'll likely have a very hard time at first, but that's what you need. That rapid heart rate, your perspiration—that's the fire we're applying to your fears, melting them so they no longer block your spirit from growth."

"That makes sense," Laolys mumbled.

"You have to have fluidity of spirit. That's the only way to survive in the Cosmos. Do you have any idea what kind of things you could come across when you ascend to view the vastness of the Cosmos?"

"No, I don't suppose I do."

"You can't. No one can. That's why it's essential to be fluid. If you let fear shut you down, you'll either become trapped or consumed. You have to adapt to each new environment and learn to work within its limits. If you fear this world—the one you've known your entire life— how will you manage in others?"

"Not too well, I imagine."

"Exactly. Learn how to be fluid. Live in the moment. You can't be locked up in fear."

The sage paused, drawing his hand to his chin. "Let's do a thought experiment. Let's say Khnum's Law presents you with a doorway. You have no time to think... do you go in?"

"Huh? Yes! Uh, I think so!" Laolys replied immediately, then paused, glancing at the sage suspiciously. "Hey, you told me I shouldn't be exploring portals."

The sage groaned. "Yes, I did tell you that. But I can also see your intentions. You have every intent to explore portals, despite my extensive warnings."

Laolys blushed. "I do?"

The sage scowled at him. "Don't act so surprised."

"But how would you know that?"

"I can see the timelines. There are so many of them with you exploring parallel realms, I'm beginning to think you have a death wish."

Laolys's heart skipped a beat. "A death wish?"

"Never mind. It's not a logic I can say I haven't practiced myself. No matter. We're through the doorway." The sage threw his hands out in a grandiose manner.

"In this parallel reality," he continued, "you find yourself inside a room where everyone is walking on their hands, keeping their feet high in the air above them. Would you do the same?"

Laolys scratched his neck nervously. "I guess... I'd have to figure it out."

The sage gave a half-nod. "That'd be the smart thing to do, so as not to call attention to yourself. Now, one of these upside-down people comes up to you and offers you a chair. Do you sit down?"

"Uh... well... I'd want to see it done first."

The sage eyed him. "He's very insistent that *you* sit first."

"I guess I'd try to sit! But I'd probably fall over."

The sage smiled. "Good. You do fall over as soon as you try, but it doesn't matter. They recognize you're not from around there, and they're friendly toward you. They show you around and help you on your way." He paused. "Do you want to know what would've happened if you refused?"

Laolys swallowed. "Yeah, what?"

"In that world, guests are always seated first as a sign of submission to the host. It means you're friendly, not there to harm anyone. If you refused to sit, they would've become very hostile toward you."

A jolt of nerves shot through Laolys as the scenario played out in his mind. "I see what you mean."

The sage leaned back. "Fear is always a downfall. If you carry it with you into alternate realities, it will almost certainly mean your death."

"I must face them, then." Laolys made a silent resolution to do just that. Although it would be hard, it would be worth it—to evolve past his fear, to break his channel.

"That would be the wise thing to do, if you ever want to know peace."

Laolys looked at the sage in admiration. He fit perfectly within the natural world, despite his humanity. He had found a way to transcend the ills that plagued most of society. "You inspire me. I will face them, so I can become more like you."

The sage snorted. "Just remember that I have many faults. I'm not an idol; I'm just a man who worked as hard as he could to become something better than a man."

"You mean like the next evolution?"

"Yeah, something like that. Surely there's something better than human."

"You want to start a new species?"

The sage laughed. "Wouldn't mind if I did."

"But how will you procreate once you reach this evolution?"

"Through knowledge. The next evolution comes through knowledge. By which I mean a higher form of wisdom, spiritual unity. If enough people would reprogram themselves with this knowledge, we could see a whole new future for humanity."

"By reprogram, you mean learn?"

"It's deeper than learning. Learning implies only the use of the brain. What I'm speaking of must translate through to the heart and soul. It's a retraining of ingrained instinct and a transformation of the soul's vibration."

Laolys looked to the ground. "That sounds… difficult to achieve."

The sage shrugged. "It's a painful and scary process, but human life, in its current state, is a painful and scary process. What does anyone have to lose?"

"Comfort zones?"

The sage laughed. "Yes! They have to lose all of those. So, you see, I have little hope for the next evolution, but I had to try to evolve myself. That's all I can do. That, and share my wisdom when asked."

"You certainly don't make it easy for people to ask."

"And you see that only the people who truly want it, and have the capability of applying it, come looking for me."

Laolys frowned. "But you don't think I should have this luxury?"

"Not yet. You have to go out into the world and apply your knowledge, share it, and grow. You can't come up here for good until you've done all that."

Laolys looked toward his town. "I see. That's why I have to return."

The sage nodded. "When you came here, I asked you to stay in one place. That's because your journey was inside yourself. There are infinite worlds to explore inside your mind, inside the hut, but at some point, you have to take that journey and walk with it, take it into the world and apply it. Otherwise, all of your knowledge is meaningless."

"You make it sound so simple."

"It is simple. It's your fears that make it seem complicated. If only everyone could see how simple things truly are. To begin a journey, you just have to put one foot in front of the other. To select a destination, just select one. It's often the journey that's the important part anyway."

Laolys looked at the trail he had walked up. It somehow felt like both yesterday and a year ago since he'd made the climb. Time was surreal up here, disconnected from the rest of the world. He could understand how the sage had lost track of it so easily. "Do you think I need to be preparing to make my journey—my descent?"

"I think if you're asking the question, you already know the answer. But it's not time to leave just yet; you still don't know my name."

"Yes, your name. I don't know how I'm supposed to just guess it." He looked at the sage with dread. He'd wondered about his name for much of his life. He felt the sage's expectations were a bit too extreme.

"You're right—guessing it is nearly impossible. It's not a common name."

"It isn't?"

"I've never met or heard of another person with the same one."

"What? Then how am I supposed to guess it?"

"Not guess. Know."

Laolys's jaw dropped open. "Know?! How am I supposed to *know* it?"

"You already do, somewhere in that consciousness of yours."

Laolys stared back at him with a glint of suspicion. "How do I know you're not using this mystery as a way to keep me here?"

"Was I keeping you here? I'm not sure how I could've made it any clearer that my solitude is sacred to me. You've been free to leave at any time—without proper condolences, I might add."

"Fair enough. But why is your name so important?"

"It's not. Well, not to most. To you, it will be very important."

"Why?"

"You'll understand, as soon as you discover my name."

"But why not just say it?"

"If I told you before you were ready, you'd be very angry with me. You'll see, once you figure it out. It's for your own good that I let you get there on your own."

Laolys opened his mouth to argue but said nothing. He knew pushing the sage wouldn't get him anywhere. "I guess I'll wait for it to come to me," he mumbled, though he had no idea how it possibly could.

"That's the spirit. When you can't change something, learn to accept it. I don't imagine it'll be too much longer, though, you're close."

"I am?"

The sage gave a half-nod. "I can feel it."

"So what until then?"

The sage reached into his robe and pulled out a small sack of gatherings. "Well, for now, you can accept that today's portions are a bit slimmer than usual." He took a handful and handed the sack to Laolys.

Laolys took it and reached in; there was barely a handful. "It's okay, thank you," he said, handing back the empty bag.

"Is it?"

"Yes. I mean, you don't have to do any of this. You don't have to feed me or teach me, but you do. You obviously climbed very far to escape humanity, but I still came all the way out here to track you down. Reflecting on it now, I realize it was very presumptuous of me. I was too caught up in everything to notice then."

The sage patted Laolys's hand. "You've come a long way. I don't mind teaching you. You've proven you're worthwhile."

"I have?"

"That was the entire point behind the offer."

"What do you mean?" Laolys studied him, trying to read his expression for hints beneath his words, but it was neutral.

"You said you wanted to help people. I thought you just wanted people to like you, so I was trying to call you out."

"Call me out?" Laolys's voice trembled. "But I thought you wanted me to share your knowledge!"

"I did, and I do. But you can't aim to awaken and aim to gain approval from people, not at the same time. It doesn't work. If you couldn't handle going back to your town and teaching these truths, even though people will call you mad, then you weren't ready to hear them."

Laolys's breath caught short. "Do you... still want me to teach them?"

The sage glared at him. "I think you know the answer to that."

Laolys nodded.

"Do you know why? Why I still ask that?"

Laolys turned his head. "For my journey?"

"That's right. You have the curse of knowledge now. You know the same things the Ennead warned me of. You know the secrets that lie beyond death. Share them. Share them with anyone who asks. You have a duty now."

Laolys felt the weight of his decision root itself into his spirit. He couldn't back out now, not after everything he'd learned. Soon, he promised himself, he'd be down the mountain, and then the hardest part would be over. He'd be a free man, whatever that meant.

The sage broke the silence. He was gazing at the mountainside with a half-smile. "You and I share the same purpose, you know."

Laolys glanced at him, then returned his gaze to the mountainside. "The same purpose?"

"Helping humanity. I wanted more than anything to wake people up. Anyone who wanted to see like me... I wanted them to be able to."

"So you don't mind helping me, then."

The sage's smile widened. "Not a bit. I came up here to retire, but they say anyone who truly loves their work never really does." He threw his arms out to his sides. "Seems accurate. I'm teaching you."

"You had students? I'm sorry, I don't know your history."

"I always managed to find at least a few loyal students. That's why I was such a target. Some people did listen. When you help those people, it'll start to make sense. You'll see."

Laolys's shoulders relaxed. He could focus on that positive. "What made you decide to come up here?"

The sage stretched his arms in front of him, cracking his bones. "Old age, mostly. I couldn't keep up with the chaos anymore. It was wearing on me." He took a deep breath. "Coming up here did me good, though... too good, if you ask me. The fresh air, free from all that toxicity down there... no more aching in the joints."

Laolys studied him. "If you don't mind me asking, how old are you?" He hesitated. "I mean, you appear old, but you don't move like you are."

The sage glared at him. "I'm plenty old to count as old without giving you the details. Healing myself was as much a mental journey as it was spiritual and physical. I might make it look easy, but you have no idea the trials I went through to get where I'm at now. I paid my price."

Laolys nodded. "You've given up a lot."

"It was all worth it. I let go of a lot to get here, and you'll have to do the same. Soon, though, you'll see how much more peaceful it is on the other side of madness."

"Soon?" Laolys turned to the sage, but realized he had vanished. He was alone again. The air was still, and only a little warmth lingered from the day. The sky above was deepening from violet-blue to velvet-black, and he rose to retire to the hut for bed.

It is not by mistake that we spend half of our time on this earth in darkness. In fact, it is by very careful design. Nothing can operate without its equal and opposite parts. To understand light, we must know darkness. But darkness is more than just the other side of the coin. As paramount as light is to our physical and spiritual growth, darkness is just as essential.

The darkness holds the keys to the unseen. It shows us how to look around with different eyes and see the depths within and without our souls. The light of day shows plain truths; the cover of darkness shows us their depths. Just as we each harbor an entire world beneath our skin, so too does everything else possess many layers beneath its outer shell. Darkness shows us that the world has depth and that we are not alone in our sorrows.

When the last of the light has left the sky, we must turn inwards. Humanity has, since its very beginning, fought this instinct. Since we first captured fire as an artificial sun, we have found ways to see only the surface of things in the dead of night. But we cannot fight nature and expect to win. We do best when we work in tandem with all the elements around us, slipping into their flow as fluid and then rushing forth with all our will when the current allows. When we find that darkness is again upon us, remember that it is there to show us depth beyond our wildest comprehension.

Evaporation of the
Wounded Waters

Passage

"The dream world isn't all *that* strange, you know?"

A distant voice echoed to Laolys, muffled as though he were submerged underwater. He drifted into this realm of awareness through a dream, quickly recognizing the familiar surroundings. He had been here before, in a dream just like this. He stood in a dark, abyssal expanse, but the substance surrounding him wasn't water. It was thick, strange, and breathable.

Laolys extended his arm slightly, seeing the familiar web-like strings radiating from him. Instinctively, he began waving his arms, hoping to draw the attention of the voice he had encountered in his previous visit.

"Hello?" He called out into the dense aether.

The reply came swiftly, as if from every direction at once. "Hello, Laolys, is it?"

"Yes, nice to—uh—speak with you again."

"Did you see the parallel realms?" The voice was almost buzzing with excitement.

"I'm sorry?"

"The other realms we discussed last time, on Earth, did you look for them?"

"Oh..." Laolys thought back to their previous conversation. The entity had questioned which realm he occupied on Earth and why he hadn't explored others. "Well... I'm not exactly sure how to find them yet."

"I see." The voice paused. "Did you at least retune your vibrations?"

Laolys swallowed a lump of nerves. Retuning himself still felt like an elusive dream—a future aspiration, not a current reality. "That is... something I'm working on."

The following silence was brief but almost unbearable. He squirmed slightly, worried he had disappointed the stranger.

"Did you stop trying to separate yourself from your surroundings?"

Laolys reflected on his lesson with the sage. He had discovered so much about life beyond the material planes. He understood now that he was connected to the planet, to the human collective, and to the Cosmos.

"Yes." He breathed a small sigh of relief. "I'm working to recognize my automatic behaviors and work towards unity."

"This is a start." The vibrations from the voice resonated around him, easing the anxiety in his chest.

He suddenly remembered the many questions he had mentally prepared in case he encountered the voice again. "You observe a lot of different life, correct?"

"A lot is a gross understatement."

"What are advanced beings like—species who have survived for a long time and are close to ascension?" Laolys pictured planets with highly advanced technology, where towering buildings pierced the sky and strange creatures traversed the landscape, aided by intricate flying machinery.

"I find that the most advanced species have achieved harmony of mind and spirit, not only within themselves but with one another. Some even communicate telepathically because they are so deeply connected and value both the physical and spiritual realms equally.

They share feelings and intentions in ways language cannot convey, and their societies are generally peaceful as a result.

"These beings understand the importance of spiritual development alongside technological and intellectual advancements. This balance ensures their survival, as they remain integrated with their planetary systems and often ascend, already spiritually woven through the fabric of the Cosmos."

Laolys remained quiet, realizing how limited his perspective was—an incredibly human one. His ideas about advanced societies had centered around technological achievements. But there were more angles to consider for a truly successful society, requiring a spirit of communal unity among all its members.

"Humans are quite far off," he muttered.

"Humans are some of the strangest creatures I've encountered across the multiverse," the voice replied.

"How so?"

"They possess a remarkable ability to adapt, learn, and evolve, yet they mimic external influences so completely that they often lose sight of their true essence. For some reason, these creatures become deeply unsettled when they notice themselves acting differently in various environments, so as a result, they are all perpetually distraught."

Laolys felt warmth creep into his cheeks, embarrassed by the accuracy of the observation. "Well, yes, it's difficult to get to know yourself as a human. We're constantly being told what to believe about ourselves and everything else. After a while, things get confused."

"You seek individuality, yet you do the opposite. Confounding.".

"What other strange creatures are out there?" Laolys asked, trying to divert the attention from his remarkably disconcerting humanity.

"I have witnessed a creature that communicates entirely through movement. They extend and contract their appendages into various lengths and angles to convey language through what looks like a strange dance. Quite impressive, but also somewhat humorous to an outside observer who cannot comprehend the nuances of their art."

"Fascinating!" Laolys tried to imagine what such creatures might look like or how language could be created through movement. "How many different types of advanced species are there out there?"

"In the observable multiverse, too many to count, far more when you consider the history of everything, which I do when I observe things because I am outside the boundaries you call space-time."

"So, you can see the future?"

"I can see all of what you call the future, but I cannot determine which parts will apply to your future," the voice answered.

"What about the future of all of humanity?"

"The children of Earth, they take too much, greedy and blind, without care for what comes next. They eat away at the gifts of the land, the sea, and the sky, leaving behind nothing but waste. The forests, once full of life, now stand empty, cut down tree by tree. The air, once sharp and clear, now carries the smoke of their machines, choking even the skies. The waters, which once ran pure and fed the Earth, are poisoned, killing the creatures that called them home. Humanity, meant to care for this world, has taken more than needed and returned only sorrow.

"Rebuild what was lost. Plant again the forests you destroyed. Cleanse the waters you have defiled. Break this endless cycle of destruction and start fresh. Craft not only the gold that glimmers but the kind that gives life."

The voice carried its final note, sending a pulse through the surrounding substance, leaving a resonance that lingered, vibrating through Laolys's core. It was more than the voice had ever said before, and the weight of its words settled heavily upon him.

Suddenly, he was struck by a realization: the sage had heard a similar message. The planet was dying as a result of humanity's actions, but the sage wasn't able to change much.

"What if..." Laolys's breath caught. "What if I can't change anyone's mind? What if humanity fails?"

"See how the Earth, burdened by humanity's toil, seeks to cleanse herself of the harm caused by man's hand. With fire and water, storm and quake, she shifts and realigns, easing the weight upon her being. The Earth does not wish to destroy her children but aims to teach them, reminding them of the stewardship that is their rightful inheritance.

"Humanity must learn to read these signs, not as omens of doom, but as calls to action—catalysts for meaningful change. In these trials, the strength of the human spirit must shine, for adversity can forge unity and resilience rather than despair. Every disaster carries a lesson in conservation, and the wisdom of the past must not be wasted if the future is to be secured. In every end lies a new beginning, and in every act of destruction, there is space for creation. These purges are not losses but opportunities for renewal, as nature's cycles ensure that nothing is truly lost, only transformed. Through the fires of trial and the floods of challenge, a new Earth may rise, purified, reborn, and ready once more to sustain life in all its diversity and beauty."

Laolys stayed still at the bottom of the strange aetherial cavern, letting the voice's words settle in his mind. But before he could fully process them, the current surged beneath him, sweeping him away once again.

Lights whipped past him as the thick aether carried him along—red, pink, blue, green, and yellow orbs blending into a blur, propelling him toward an unknown destination.

The dream world is not so strange. This was what the voice had told him. Recalling the sage's teachings, Laolys could sense the truth in this statement. The dream world was a spiritual playground, a place where fears and fantasies collided, and illusions wove together with deeper truths. He didn't know where the current would take him, but this time, he resolved to see it through to the end.

I must not be like the big fish, he thought, willing himself to stay relaxed, to find courage. He knew fear would trap him, solidify him, and send him rippling back to where he started. He wasn't ready to return yet. He wanted to reach the ocean, to finally graduate with the other fish.

If Khnum presents a doorway, I should not be afraid to take it. Laolys pondered what awaited him downstream. Whatever it might be, he was determined to meet it head-on. Fear, he understood, was the first barrier that everyone must overcome. If we can simply live as life unfolds, we may actually make it downstream.

If it is death I face, at least I know it will grant me life. He didn't believe he was in danger, though. He was preparing for infinite possibilities, knowing that Chaos brings uncertainty, but not necessarily an end.

More often than not, he reflected, the end is born from within our minds, while Chaos merely takes the blame.

A warmth soon enveloped him, though his vision remained consumed by darkness. A deep, rhythmic pulsation, like a heartbeat, filled his ears. The world overcame him, and he surrendered to it. *This will pass, this all will pass,* he thought, floating in the dark water. He was fluid, knowing that soon, in one way or another, he would shift into a new state.

A brilliant white light appeared before him, enveloping him in its glow. Eyes! This white light has eyes, Laolys thought, though he couldn't explain how he knew. He only sensed it. The white light extended a hand toward him, and without hesitation, Laolys took it. Together, they walked, the light leading him forward.

They emerged into a vast field of tall grass, bathed in radiant daylight. The sky stretched endlessly above, a pure, vivid blue. All around them, other lights—hundreds, perhaps—danced, ran, and played with joyful abandon. Everywhere Laolys looked, happiness shimmered, filling the space with a lightness so profound that sorrow seemed impossible.

Yet, a subtle sadness lingered within Laolys. Though surrounded by brilliance, he did not glow as brightly. His light was dimmer, fainter than those around him. If anyone noticed, they gave no sign of it. The other lights greeted him with the same enthusiasm as they did each other, their warmth unchanging.

Overwhelmed by an inexplicable sorrow, Laolys sank to the ground, his heart heavy. *Will I ever shine as brightly as the others?* he wondered, ripples of sadness radiating outward from his core. His quiet vibrations caught the attention of several nearby lights. They drifted toward him, surrounding him with gentle care. Kneeling in the grass, they emitted waves of love and concern, wrapping him in a warm, protective sphere of energy.

Laolys felt his heart lift. Slowly, he stood, though his light remained faint. He knew he wasn't as radiant as the others yet, and it would take time. But he understood now: we all must crawl before we can walk, and we must experience true darkness to learn how to light ourselves from within. He hadn't reached the end of his lessons, but he felt a quiet confidence; one day, he would shine just as brightly.

Two lights took hold of his hands, gently stretching his arms out to his sides. The light he had followed stood before him, radiating warmth. It smiled, though Laolys could only sense the expression. The other lights smiled, too. In this field, there was no sorrow, only joy, connection, and the radiant promise of growth.

As Laolys stood still, the light before him leaned closer, gently touching his forehead. In that moment, a wave of pure joy flooded his heart, warm and overwhelming, like sunlight pouring into the deepest corners of his soul. Then, as swiftly as it had come, the field, the lights, and their joyful radiance dissolved into nothingness.

In an instant, Laolys awoke in the hut, the surrounding thick aether exchanged for the dense darkness of night.

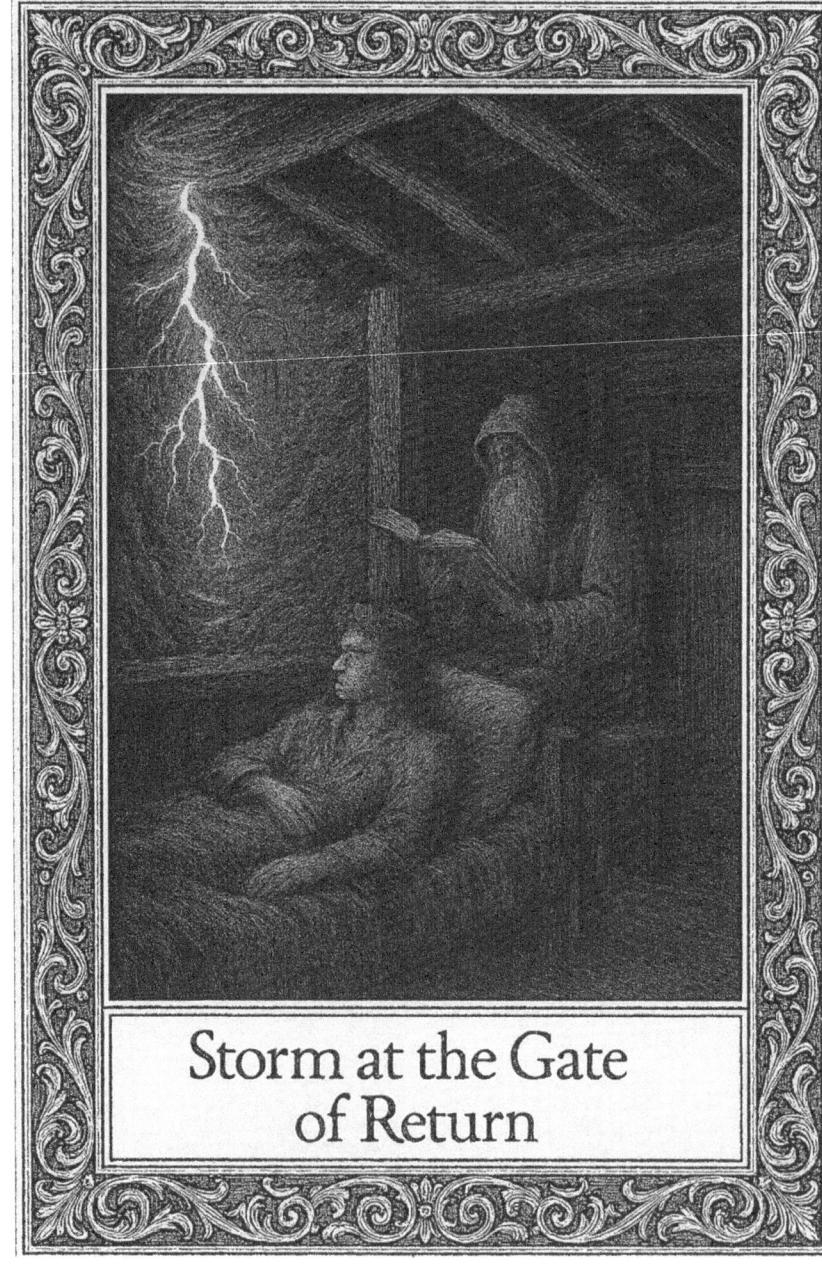

Storm at the Gate of Return

Downpour

"Terrible weather forecast."

The words came as Laolys sat up and opened his eyes. The room was enveloped in darkness, and the sound of heavy rain drummed relentlessly against the roof.

"It seemed fine when I was falling asleep," Laolys shouted so his voice would carry over the downpour. Outside, it was as if the sky had opened, pouring torrents upon the small hut. The wind howled against the mountainside, creating an unsettling contrast with the serene peace within. The tiny structure stood resilient, untouched by the storm's fury, offering a tranquil refuge amid nature's chaos.

"Things change." Despite the clamor of the storm, Laolys distinctly heard the soft rustle of a page being turned.

"Are you... reading?" Laolys felt silly asking, as it was far too dark to see.

"Trying to." The sage's tone was flat, bored.

"But... how?"

"There are many ways to read a book."

"Do you have any candles?"

"I do, but I'd rather save them if you don't mind. They're not easy to replace up here."

"I suppose it wouldn't be." Laolys reclined back in the bed. It seemed neither of them were particularly inclined to chat tonight. He closed his eyes, hoping sleep would return, but the astral planes were long gone. Laolys was awake.

"We might be here a while. Every timeline shows this storm lingering through the morning, at least. Some stretch it all the way to tomorrow night. We'll be safe in here."

"Where did it come from?"

"Who knows? Maybe it sensed someone wasn't quite ready to make his passage."

Laolys sat back up. "Are you talking about me?"

"Who else?"

"I wasn't going to leave just yet." Laolys had thought about it, that's it. He wondered how the sage could possibly know that.

"Maybe not on this timeline, but on others, you already have."

"So... you called the storm?"

"No, you called it!" Though the sage was shouting to be heard over the storm, his voice also held a degree of irritation.

"Me? I don't know how to do these things!"

"You don't have to know how to do them to do them; you just do them. You're deeply interwoven in the thick of it now. I don't think it likes your hastiness."

"My hastiness?"

"Yes."

"Hastiness to do what?"

"To depart."

"But I wasn't going to leave just yet!" Laolys's thoughts of leaving had only been considerations for the future. He wasn't ready to leave yet, not without graduating, in some sense, from the sage's teachings.

"A part of you wants to. That's enough to summon the storm, apparently."

Laolys threw his arms out to his sides. "I still don't see how I summoned this crazy storm."

"Then open your eyes."

Laolys was at a loss for how to respond. He was at a loss as to what exactly was happening. Perhaps he didn't need to understand it, or perhaps he wasn't capable of understanding it, at least not yet. Whatever was happening had something to do with him, and he simply had to accept that this was its nature.

"Well, what do you see?" the sage asked.

"I'm not sure what I'm supposed to see." Laolys's heartbeat quickened, the weight of the moment pressing down on him. This was all too much.

"Look harder."

The sage's words pierced into Laolys's soul like a sharp wind, cutting through his confusion. In an instant, a vortex seemed to open and then vanish as quickly as it came. Suddenly, the sage seated across from him became more than just a presence in the dark; he appeared outlined in the thick shadows. Foggy forms of the hut's items emerged next, flickering into view as if conjured from memory and mist.

"That's better," the sage said, somehow sensing Laolys's heightened awareness. "Now, maybe we can get somewhere."

"Where?"

"Nowhere else but your mind. We have to figure this out."

"What do we need to figure out?"

"Whatever caused the storm. Why, with everything you've spoken of, everything you've learned, would a storm this powerful trap us in here?"

Laolys's mind swirled, searching for an answer. The intensity of the moment overwhelmed him. His heightened awareness only deepened his confusion, the flickering shapes adding to his disorientation. "I don't know... I'm sorry."

"Don't be. We get to finally figure this out. Right now."

"I just... feel a deep sense of sorrow..."

"I know," the sage said softly.

"Why?"

"We all do, but you more than most. This is what makes you stand out."

"Why do I feel more than others?" Laolys's question came out as a plea, desperate and raw. He didn't just want an answer; he needed an answer.

"I don't know."

"Do you have any ideas?"

"You see the pain that echoes around you, and you take it in as your own. That's why you're on this path." The sage's words filled the hut with their reverberations, the sound carrying a strange weight.

"How do I stop?" Laolys's voice cracked as his desire to escape the burden overwhelmed him. He no longer wished for the mantle of hero.

"You can't. This is your nature."

"I have to feel this sorrow?"

"No, you have to turn it into action. Use the pain as a stepping-stone for greater things."

"But how?"

"Any way you like."

Laolys let the sound of the wind consume the hut as he thought. All his life, he had felt a sadness radiating from the core of his being, a sadness he could never quite explain. He longed for something better —for himself and the world. Everywhere he looked, he saw pain. Some people hid it better than others, but the pain was there. People lived in fear of one another, lashing out in unexpected, irrational ways, wounded from past hurts. It seemed as if the world was caught in an endless cycle of suffering, with people exchanging pain, blow for blow. The world was sick.

"All of this pain... it comes from others?" he asked.

"No. You began with an immense amount of your own pain. That's why you recognize it so clearly in others."

"So now I have to fix the world?"

"You can't. It's unfixable."

"Then what am I doing?"

"You're trying. That's all you can do."

"But why try if it's unfixable?" Laolys's heart ached. Every path he imagined led to isolation.

"Would you rather wallow in the pain?"

"No."

"Then you try." The sage's voice carried weight, somber and resolute, amplified by the storm's relentless fury.

"I don't even know how to begin."

"Think of a way."

The wind howled outside the hut, as if orchestrating a dramatic symphony. The silence between the two men felt charged, as though the storm was part of some unseen design. The hut remained eerily unaffected by the torrential rain pounding its walls and roof. Like the sage, the hut appeared simple from the outside, but the more Laolys discovered about it, the deeper its mysteries became.

"I guess by sharing knowledge."

The sage said nothing. Yet Laolys could feel his observation, sharp and unwavering, as if the sage were staring into his soul. The darkness of the hut, combined with the tension of the moment, heightened Laolys's senses in ways he had never experienced. He felt, just briefly, that he might finally understand what the sage meant by the unseen.

"This causes you pain," the sage finally said.

"Yes."

"Why?"

Laolys searched his mind; the fear regarding his descent overwhelmed all his better senses. "I don't want to be among people anymore," he shouted, the truth slipping from him before he could stop it. He felt inadequate for the journey that awaited him beyond the mountain.

"No, you simply don't want to be cast out by them."

"I'm trying to let this go."

"Perhaps you shouldn't. Learn to love it, as I did. Half of my eccentricities are by design. The world secretly loves the outcast who dares to seek his own truths, even if they disagree with him. But it doesn't matter what they love. What matters is that you walk the path that leads to your ascension. Their opinions and their ultimate directions have no sway on your enlightenment."

Laolys's mind flashed to a vision of a fish traveling down a wide river stream. It was swimming with a school, but it wasn't swimming as part of the group. Where the others fell in line, this fish swam faster, investigating the world around it. It darted through vines and inspected underneath rocks while the rest simply swam. It wasn't avoiding the others, and it wasn't in trouble. It was just far more interested in the river than any other fish.

"I got it!" he exclaimed, breaking the mental imagery to radiate all the way back down to the darkness of the hut.

"Pardon me?" the sage responded, sounding as though he had been roused from deep thought or sleep.

"I got it!"

"Got what?"

"I'm the big fish. I think too much."

"Tell me about it," the sage replied, his voice laced with sarcasm.

"You're the big fish too."

"I am," the sage agreed, his tone flat and indifferent.

"I think I'm ready to leave the small pond."

"You're not ready."

"Why not?"

The sage leaned in. "What is my name?"

Laolys's breath quickened. "I don't know."

"You know it."

"How would I know it?! I don't know it!"

"Think. Use your big fish brain." The sage chuckled softly and let the storm fill the silence between them.

Laolys closed his eyes, allowing the sound of the rain to dissolve the world around him as he turned inward. He combed his mind for clues, but there were none. The sage had never met anyone else with the same name. How was Laolys supposed to guess it?

Well, he mused, *there was at least one clue: a name that no one had heard of before. One among many things the sage and I have in common.* He thought about his own name. No one he'd met had recognized it. He remembered how often people fumbled the pronunciation, and how frustrating it was to correct them. But every so often, someone got it right on the first try. He liked those people, if only because they gave him a brief reprieve from having to repeat himself. *Lay-oh-lis*, he had to say it slowly, over and over to nearly everyone he met.

The sage had gotten it right from the start. Laolys had only said his name once, and it instantly clicked in the sage's mind, as if he had been expecting him. Perhaps he had, given his ability to view future timelines. There was no telling what the sage knew in advance; he always seemed five steps ahead of him. Yet somehow, at other times, he gave the impression that he was improvising, acting without any plan at all. The sage defied expectations while still fulfilling many stereotypes, an enigma wrapped in contradictions. How was Laolys supposed to just know the identity of this strange man?

Not guess, know. That's what the sage had told him. He had to know his name or perhaps remain stuck on this mountain indefinitely. The storm outside wasn't just a coincidence; the sage knew too much about these matters for it to be random. Somehow, Laolys needed to be creative enough to outwit a man who could see many futures. But how was he going to manage that?

You're not so far off, you know. The words echoed so clearly in Laolys's mind that he couldn't tell if the sage had spoken them aloud or if they existed only in thought. A vision accompanied the words, strengthening the sense that they were mental, a memory. He was sitting with the sage during one of their lessons. They had been talking about ascension, about Laolys figuring things out. The sage had told him, *One day, you could see things just like I do.*

Perhaps there were more similarities between them than he'd realized. It did feel as if he were taking up the sage's torch—but maybe all his students had felt that way. If Laolys ended up following the same life path, at least he knew he had a good retirement plan. With the right perspective, it wasn't a bad destiny. The sage made it seem easy, glamorous, even. Laolys admired that.

The sage lived by his teachings. He saw through all the illusions and still took delight in solitude and in the natural world. He treated wisdom as a sacred venture—a kind of personal religion. That kind of devotion, Laolys thought, was admirable.

The gears in his mind turned and clicked, his thoughts moving swiftly as the pieces began to fall into place. Across from him, the sage watched with an amused expression, observing him use what he liked to call "his big fish brain."

This destiny, it's starting to feel like too real a possibility. Those had been Laolys's words, but they held more truth than he'd meant to admit. He was right—too right. The sage had awakened something in him, something he was meant to know, even if he didn't yet understand why. And now, finally, it was time to go. He opened his eyes.

"You know it now; you're just afraid to say it. You're afraid you might be right." The sage's voice cut through the storm, clear and unwavering.

"It's not..." Laolys whispered, his voice weighed with hesitation and pain.

"It is." The sage paused, letting the rain fill the silence. "It's okay. You can say it now."

"Your name?"

"Yes. Say it."

Laolys inhaled deeply, steadying himself. Several breaths passed before he finally spoke the word aloud, his voice slicing through the thick night air.

"Laolys."

In an instant, it felt as though gravity itself descended upon him, pressing heavily against every part of his being. Then, just as quickly as it had come, the pressure released, leaving him in the quiet aftermath of revelation. When he opened his eyes again, he was alone in the hut. The sage was gone.

Everything made sense now, and yet it didn't. The experience was too vast, too surreal to grasp, and yet it resonated with a truth he couldn't deny. He sat in the darkness, truly alone for the first time, reflecting on what had just transpired.

The storm outside continued to rage, pounding the roof of the hut with relentless force. Laolys welcomed the sound. It gave him an excuse to remain on the mountain a little longer—a day or two, perhaps—before descending back toward the town below. For now, it was a necessary reprieve, one he needed desperately.

The Great Current of Becoming

Completion

Many wise and divine people have lived and died without any notoriety or recognition. Many terrible and dangerous people have been recorded in history as saintly. Many average people have been idolized and fictionalized into having a godlike status, a status no one who knew them at the time they were alive would have credited. Many great accomplishments have passed through time unrecognized, and many mediocre accomplishments have become historic achievements, whether for political gain or happenstance. Many great works were left to rot until the creator died. Then, as the earth claimed their bones, their work somehow finally gained its due merit.

The opinion of the populace is fickle. Familiarity gains favor over the new and profound. Every revolutionary idea in history was greeted by great scorn and scrutiny. If a man gains a bit of infamy in his lifetime, he should consider this a success. Perhaps he has the mark of brilliance not yet recognized by today's sleepy world. Perhaps he is more curious than the other fish and swims outside the school. Perhaps others meet him with anger and misunderstanding, but secretly admire his integrity and fortitude. Yet, a wise man considers none of these things. A wise man considers the opinions of others with the same degree he considers a passing storm.

A learned man knows there is little he can do to affect the patterns of wind and formations of water particles that swarm above him. Yet a religious man with a firm degree of desperation can convince himself he has the ability to do the things the learned man cannot. Should the religious man's opinion of his abilities fall to the doubts of the academic standard, he will never succeed. His success lies entirely in his faith in himself, and the measurement of his success is his alone to judge. If he has no faith in himself, he will never see his labors to fruition. If, by chance, he wills a storm to rise on a secluded mountain peak, and no one else is around to hear it, did he still summon the storm? He must draw from his experience and know his own truths. Everyone else may question his integrity, yet he alone knows his real worth.

What remarkable change occurs in a man when he has the sympathy and praise of his fellows? Does he hold his head higher? Does he speak with confidence? Does he stand out as a leader? We shall be quick to correct anyone who claims a remarkable change has occurred because of the positive opinions bestowed. The noticeable change is due to his changed opinion of himself. It lasts for as long as he is able to maintain it, or for as long as his fellows continue their words of encouragement.

But how unfortunate is the soul that depends upon the approval of others to find peace within! Such a man condemns himself to endless suffering. Only he holds the knowledge of his creations and the essence of his character. His exterior nature is all that is presented to the world he inhabits. He must not be so confused as to think that others know more about his spirit than he does. He must not let others decide his worth for him; they will always be incorrect.

There is a special kind of magic that awakens when a person believes in themselves. This magic radiates from the depths of the soul, enabling us to achieve astonishing feats. Hidden within our DNA and unconscious minds lies the accumulated knowledge of human history, yet few believe they have access to it, and so they never seek it. The philosopher's stone is powerless to those who doubt its existence, and it remains forever out of reach to those who do not believe they can obtain it.

Everything in the universe exists in either an expressed or unexpressed state. Through our observation, things become expressed. We believe most strongly in what we expect to see, and by declaring it as fact, we summon it into existence. We are not separate from the universe; we, too, shift between expressed and unexpressed states. What we are not now, we will one day become. What we are now, we must grow beyond, or risk becoming stagnant. If we do not move fluidly, if we remain in one place for too long, we begin to decay.

Believe in both your expressed and unexpressed potential. Understand that the visible world offers only a limited perspective; beyond it lies a Cosmos filled with unseen truths. Each of us is only a fraction of what we could be. We unknowingly pull at the energy web surrounding us, drawing real things into our lives. Now imagine if we awakened to the power of doing this with conscious intent! And imagine if we took our minds, working tirelessly every hour of every day, and directed them toward higher planes of understanding. We like to believe that anyone could ascend to those heights! Or, at least make such a name for themselves that they occasionally get knocks on the door of their tiny hut, all the way near the top of a steep, rocky mountain peak.

ALCHEMICAL AND SYMBOLIC INTERPRETATION

Beneath the surface of every story flows a deeper current, shaping spirit through subtle pressure. *The Young Man and the Sage* offers more than a tale of two travelers. It unfolds as an alchemical journey, guiding the reader through stages of refinement and inner awakening.

This section explores those stages using the sacred language of alchemy. The chapters of the book align with ancient processes of inner change: calcination, dissolution, purification, and exaltation. These are the fires through which the self becomes clear, whole, and luminous.

Each encounter between the young seeker and the sage carries symbolic meaning. Words, silences, and turning points all hold keys to transmutation. These interpretations open those meanings, drawing out the deeper wisdom that stirs beneath the story's surface.

Use this section as a companion for deeper reflection. Return to the story with new awareness, and witness within it the movement of your own Great Work.

Ascent of the Prima Materia

Ascent of the Prima Materia

Laolys begins his journey up the mountain—a literal and symbolic initiation into the Great Work of alchemical transformation. This chapter marks the threshold crossing, where the base matter (*prima materia*) first steps into the sacred fire of becoming. He is not yet transformed, but he is willing.

1. The Mountain Path – Via Purificatoria

In alchemical terms, the mountain ascent symbolizes the Great Work (*Magnum Opus*)—the process of inner transformation. The path is steep and rugged, representing the nigredo, or blackening stage, where the ego is dismantled and purified through trials and suffering.

2. The Traveler (Laolys) – The Base Matter / Prima Materia

Laolys represents the prima materia, the raw material of the alchemical process. His journey to seek wisdom is the beginning of the calcination of the soul—the burning away of false beliefs, inherited paradigms, and the societal conditioning he must transcend.

3. The Crow – Nigredo (Blackening)

Perched near the base of the mountain, the crow is a classic symbol of the nigredo stage. It represents death, dissolution, and the breakdown of old identity. It is the point where the initiate begins to shed illusions and encounter the raw darkness of the self.

4. The Swan – Albedo (Whitening)

A swan, symbolizing the albedo, or whitening phase, is further up the path. This marks purification, the clearing of psychic debris, and the arrival of insight. In Chapter I, this corresponds to Laolys's encounter with the sage, who challenges and begins to refine his understanding.

5. The Sage's Hut – Philosopher's Stone in Early Form

The hut at the summit represents the *Philosopher's Stone*—the place where knowledge is distilled and spirit unifies with matter. It may not be visibly impressive, but its power lies in its unseen presence.

Alchemical Stage: Nigredo (Blackening)

This chapter is pure *Nigredo*—the beginning of dissolution. All viewpoints must be shed before clarity can emerge. Laolys enters the mountain certain of his place and identity, only to have them stripped bare, with nothing offered in return.

The sage leaves Laolys at the threshold. Here, he must confront the limits of his mind, the weight of his ego, and the hollowness of ambition. Though the moment feels insurmountable, Laolys remains on the mountain, clinging to the hope that the answers he seeks will soon reveal themselves.

Illumination Beneath the Infinite Vault

This scene takes place during Laolys's nocturnal lesson with the sage, where he begins to confront mortality, the soul's continuity, and the nature of spiritual transformation. The composition is deliberately spare yet potent, in line with Chapter II's mystical and metaphysical depth.

1. The Sage – *Mercurius / Divine Instructor*

The elder figure, cloaked and commanding, represents Mercurius, the alchemical spirit of transformation. He is both teacher and test. In alchemical texts, Mercurius guides the seeker through shadow into knowledge. His gesture toward the heavens invites the initiate to contemplate Cosmic Truths—death, rebirth, and spirit.

2. The Young Man – *Neophyte / Sulphur Awakening*

Laolys, standing with clasped hands, is shown in a receptive state. In alchemy, the initiate is often likened to Sulphur, volatile and impassioned, needing guidance to find balance. His stance indicates surrender to wisdom—a vital step in soul refinement.

3. The Eight-Pointed Star – *The Cosmic Gate*

Hovering above them is the eight-pointed star, symbolic of regeneration and the soul's journey through the spheres. It marks the intersection of the material and spiritual realms—*above and below*—and is associated with Venus, the harmonizer, who reconciles life and death, beauty and decay.

4. The Ouroboros – *Cycle of Life, Death, and Return*

Subtly coiled around a stone or base, the Ouroboros (serpent eating its own tail) represents the eternal return—the cyclical nature of existence, central to the doctrine of reincarnation explored in this chapter. It affirms that death marks both an end and a new beginning.

5. Flaming Chalice – *Transmutation of Spirit*

The flaming chalice near the sage is the *Vas Hermeticum*—the alchemical vessel of transformation. Fire purifies, and the chalice holds the essence of life. Here, it suggests the soul's refinement through trials, particularly the confrontation with mortality and the self.

Alchemical Stage: Albedo (Whitening)

Chapter II enters the stage of Albedo, the whitening—the purification of perception through the death of former understanding. Following the darkness and dissolution of Nigredo, Laolys begins to contemplate the soul, mortality, and continuity. The sage speaks in paradoxes and visions, shifting the dialogue from the worldly to the eternal.

Laolys has not yet awakened, but he has crossed the threshold. He is asking new questions, listening instead of arguing. When all is dark, we are forced to seek a new light. This marks the beginning of spiritual refinement—when the soul is cleansed of old beliefs to perceive the world with fresh eyes.

Laolys still clings to many fears, but he now glimpses the light on the other side.

The Scales of Judgment and the Speaking Flame

The Scales of Judgment and the Speaking Flame

The dialogue deepens into the moral weight of power, the justice of law, and the corruption of systems. The conversation becomes a crucible where philosophical ideals are tested—this is the fire that burns falsehood from truth. The image captures this moment of balance and discernment.

1. The Sage and the Young Man – *Alchemical Duality*

Both figures are fully visible and in dynamic exchange, reflecting the solve et coagula principle: the breaking apart of ideas and the rejoining of refined understanding. The sage embodies ancient wisdom (*Salt*), while the young man, questioning and passionate, symbolizes transformation (*Sulphur*). Their dialogue is the medium (*Mercury*) that unites the opposites.

2. The Eight-Pointed Star – *The Star of Cosmic Law*

Suspended above the sage is the eight-pointed star, reaffirming Cosmic Order and Natural Law. In this chapter, they debate the legitimacy of legal systems—this star reminds us that true law emanates not from men but from divine harmony and cosmic justice.

3. The Caduceus – *Symbol of Discernment and Authority*

Beside Laolys is the caduceus, the staff of Hermes—alchemical symbol of balance between opposing forces (good and evil, truth and illusion). It reflects Laolys's potential role as a mediator in society, but also a warning: wielding power without wisdom invites distortion.

4. The Stark Landscape – *Mental Terrain of Trial*

The jagged rocks and exposed cliffs around them represent the sharp, raw landscape of reason. This is the philosopher's battleground —where beliefs are shattered and reformed. It represents the calcination stage, where false metals (ideas) are burned away.

5. Shadow and Light – *Chiaroscuro of Moral Ambiguity*

The strong contrast between darkness and light across the terrain underscores the theme of moral ambiguity. The lesson here is not to seek black-and-white truths but to train the inner eye to discern within complexity—a necessary ability in both governance and spiritual development.

Alchemical Stage: Albedo (Deepening of Whitening)

Chapter III continues within the stage of Albedo, but with sharper edges. The initial purification begun in Chapter II now turns toward the discernment of truth from illusion. Laolys and the sage engage in rigorous dialectic—testing systems of law, justice, power, and authority. No matter the subject, the central focus remains the same: recognizing what remains after ego dissolves.

This is the burning away of intellectual false gold—the calcination of inherited beliefs. The young man begins to weigh not only what is right, but what is true. The world is no longer divided into good and evil, but complex, layered, and often veiled in contradiction. This is the whitened ash of the soul—subtle, fragile, yet necessary.

Laolys now stands at the precipice between reaction and realization. In this phase of refined Albedo, clarity is not full illumination—but it is the beginning of inner sovereignty.

The Dwelling of Discord and Devotion

The Dwelling of Discord and Devotion

Laolys enters the sage's dwelling, the modest, cluttered hut nestled among trees at the mountain's crest. The story becomes more intimate, more internal. It's the first time Laolys is not climbing but settling, reflecting, observing—and being silently observed. This stillness contrasts with the rugged movement of the earlier chapters.

1. The Sage's Hut – The Netic Crucible (Inner Chamber of Distillation)

The hut is the symbolic vessel—a physical embodiment of the Netic Crucible. Its rugged exterior represents raw transformation. Just as a laboratory flask works best unadorned, the alchemical chamber need only serve its sacred purpose: to distill.

Here, Laolys is no longer climbing toward enlightenment; he is sitting within it. The space represents a liminal container—he is between who he was and who he must become.

2. The Radiant Ouroboros – Cycle of Self and Cosmic Law

Hovering above is the ouroboros, more radiant than in prior icons. This suggests awareness: Laolys is beginning to see the pattern. His discussions with the sage now turn inward, forcing him to confront not just societal philosophy, but his own spiritual assumptions.

The ouroboros in the sky links to higher awareness of the cyclical nature of consciousness. Laolys is now aware he must break the cycle —not just endure it.

3. The Gnarled Trees – Refined Wildness

The trees surrounding the hut are chaotic, natural, and unsymmetrical. They represent the wildness of truth—organic, unpolished, and unconcerned with appearances.

4. The Alchemical Fire Within the Hut – Unseen Flame of Devotion

Though not visibly shown, we imagine an unseen fire within the sage's hut. This is the alchemical fire, the hidden drive that fuels devotion to truth. In alchemy, the flame is constant, never allowed to die. It is what keeps the Great Work active.

Alchemical Stage: Albedo (Fermentation Within the Vessel)

Chapter IV remains within the Albedo phase, but now enters its fermentative moment—when the purified elements begin to interact, bubble, and reform in quiet stillness. Laolys is no longer climbing or contending; he now dwells in the Sage's presence. The hut, humble and shadowed by trees, becomes the symbolic Netic Crucible—the interior chamber where transformation begins to take root.

This is not a chapter of answers, but of interior saturation. Ideas linger. Tensions soften. Laolys is learning not by argument, but by atmosphere. The stillness is alchemical: it allows the materials of his broken worldview to begin rearranging themselves around a more subtle axis.

This is the midpoint of Albedo, when light has entered, but not yet formed into vision. The rot of Nigredo has passed. The water of the spirit now moves silently through him, preparing him for illumination still to come.

The Seekers

The Seekers

Laolys deepens his philosophical transformation. He begins to move beyond questioning external systems and turns inward, exploring the nature of truth, selflessness, and spiritual evolution. The sage challenges him to examine his motives—not just for seeking knowledge, but for why he desires to share it. This chapter reveals that while knowledge can be used to gain favor, wisdom nearly always comes with a price. Those who seek it must do so as a sacred venture, humbly accepting their purpose to live by its truths.

1. The Ascending Figures – *Pilgrims of the Great Work*

The travelers climbing the mountain represent spiritual initiates ascending toward higher knowledge. Though Laolys appears alone in the story, the symbolic presence of others reinforces the universal nature of the journey. Everyone seeking truth must face the same inner terrain.

2. The Double-Ringed Symbol – *Unity of Inner and Outer Work*

Floating at the mountain's summit, the glowing double-ring symbol represents the alchemical stage of conjunction—the sacred union of opposites. In Netist philosophy, it signifies the resonance between the individual's inner frequency and the greater harmonic field of the Cosmic Net. This marks a pivotal turning point for Laolys: the shift from aspiring to power toward embodying principle. Here, alignment replaces ambition, and true transformation begins.

3. Dramatic Lighting – *Clarity Emerging from Trial*

The image avoids darkness while preserving symbolic chiaroscuro —highlighting Laolys's growing discernment. As the shadows of old worldviews begin to recede, illumination starts to shape him.

4. Jagged Rocks and Harsh Terrain – *The Path of Perseverance*

Laolys must continue breaking down personal illusions. Each step forward reveals new layers of resistance—fears he thought he'd conquered, attachments he believed himself above. The climb becomes more than physical; it is a trial of endurance, faith, and inner resolve. The terrain reflects his internal struggle: sharp, uneven, and unforgiving. Yet in pressing on, Laolys begins to learn that perseverance itself is a purifier—burning away weakness, refining strength, and anchoring him more firmly to the truth he seeks.

Alchemical Stage Represented:

This chapter reflects a late-stage Albedo / early-stage Citrinitas, the dawning of true inner clarity. The illusions have been washed away, and what remains is a mind beginning to steady itself in truth. Laolys no longer seeks validation or external approval; instead, he begins to trust in his own perception. This is the golden threshold where knowledge begins to transform into wisdom. Though his fears remain, they are no longer rulers—only remnants. The soul is being tempered, and the light of understanding has begun to rise.

The Celestial Mirror and the Lion's Cry

Laolys's understanding of reality—not just moral or spiritual, but *cosmic*. Here, the Sage speaks of unity, the harmonic architecture of the world, and the transcendent truths embedded in all things. Laolys begins to grasp the multiversal system as a vast, living intelligence—one that can only be perceived through purification and alignment.

The image captures this elevation of thought: no longer just philosophical, but cosmological. The setting is no longer earthbound; it reflects Laolys's soul now reaching toward Citrinitas, the yellowing—when wisdom begins to shine.

1. The Sage Gazing Skyward – *Alchemist as Seer* The sage, draped in worn robes, stands atop rocky terrain, not looking at Laolys, but gazing toward the heavens. He is now the initiator, bridging the visible and invisible. His stance shows that truth is no longer found in argument, but in contemplation. He becomes the Distiller of Æther.

2. The Celestial Sphere with Sun and Moon – *Union of Opposites* Above him hovers a divine globe, half sun and half moon—Sol and Luna, consciousness and unconsciousness, masculine and feminine. This reflects the conversation's theme: the necessity of duality within unity. Laolys must now see how the world moves in synthesis with the higher planes.

3. The Serpent-Wrapped Staff – *Ascended Knowledge* A staff entwined with a serpent, planted firmly beside the sage, symbolizes wisdom rooted in the earth but spiraling toward heaven. This is an evolved form of the caduceus: the *solar-serpent path* of awakening. The serpent guards sacred ascent, preventing the fearful from further passage.

4. The Lion-Eagle Chimera – *Transcendent Transformation* Hovering beside the sphere is a mythic fusion of lion and eagle. The lion represents courage and grounded power, the eagle vision and transcendence. Their fusion speaks to Laolys's inner work: he must be both grounded and visionary. This beast is the guardian of ascent, granting access only when inner duality is harmonized.

5. The Swirling Clouds and Mountain Vistas – *The Cosmic Fabric* The backdrop is not static—it moves, cloud and terrain mirroring one another. This is the Net, the interconnected design that governs all things. Mountains fold into clouds, meaning that above and below are not separate realms, but mirrors. *As above, so below.*

6. Chiaroscuro Balance – *Clarity Without Perfection* The illustration uses high contrast without total blackness. The Sage has led Laolys into the light, but shadows remain. This reflects the Citrinitas phase, when the soul perceives clarity but still bears residue from the former stages. True wisdom is born here—not from the absence of darkness, but from navigating through it.

Alchemical Stage: Citrinitas (Yellowing – Illumined Integration)

Chapter VI is the soul's first illumination—Citrinitas, the yellowing. This is the stage where purified thought begins to radiate wisdom, and Laolys's vision expands beyond human systems into cosmic architecture. The Sage no longer debates or refutes; he reveals. Through image, metaphor, and silence, he draws Laolys into alignment with the multiversal intelligence that pulses through all things.

No longer confined to moral or intellectual realms, Laolys begins to perceive the harmony beneath contrast—sun and moon, lion and eagle, spirit and matter. He sees that these are not opposites to choose between, but energetic principles to harmonize. He discovers that learning isn't just about remembering, but about resonance.

Citrinitas is the soft golden knowing that comes from stillness, surrender, and pattern recognition. It is wisdom without ego. For the first time, Laolys glimpses not just truth, but his place *within it*.

The Flame Within the Triangle

The Flame Within the Triangle

Laolys's training with the sage enters a more mystical, initiatic phase, carried by the inner fire: the burning force that fuels awakening. The sage now challenges Laolys to see beyond even philosophy and cosmology—to look directly into the nature of the self. This chapter invites the seeker to become the flame itself rather than merely bask in its light.

The image reflects this interiorization. It is a portrait not of external instruction, but of transmission—when wisdom passes from one soul to another by resonance rather than logic.

1. The Sage and the Young Man – *Transmission of Fire*

Here, the sage no longer debates—he bestows. Standing tall with a staff, he channels the archetype of The Master of Flame, the keeper of living fire. Laolys, now seated and attentive, has shifted into The Vessel—his posture open, his ego subdued. This dynamic mirrors the alchemical furnace, where fire is transferred carefully into the retort.

2. The Ouroboros Encircling the Triangle – *Containment of Spirit*

Above them the Ouroboros glows, but now it is no longer alone—it encircles a triangle, within which burns a single flame. This is the *Triune Flame*: Will, Wisdom, and Action—the threefold nature of divine purpose. The Ouroboros serves here as the eternal container, allowing this fire to remain pure and sustained. This symbol echoes the Philosopher's Stone in formation—not yet fixed, but now visible.

3. The Triangle and Flame – *Essence of Becoming*

The triangle represents the upward-pointing element of Fire—spiritual ascension. The single flame within it is the divine spark—what Netists might call the *resonant source-field*, or the *self-aware flame* that animates every soul. This is the moment Laolys sees the origin of his own transformation: *not what he knows, but what he is becoming*.

4. The Staff of the Sage – *Axis Mundi*

The Sage's staff stands planted—a world axis, a channel between earth and sky. It connects the seeker below to the celestial fire above. As in many esoteric traditions, the staff symbolizes the channel of transmission. In Netism, it may represent the conduit of resonant truth—the harmonized path through all fields of awareness.

5. Swirling Sky and Broken Hills – *Inner Turbulence Transformed*

The landscape surrounding the figures is wild, broken, and weathered—the residue of inner storms. Yet the sky now swirls in harmony, drawn toward the glowing symbol. This reflects the shift in Laolys's spirit—his internal conflict is beginning to align with the rhythm of the higher order. He is entering the *Citrinitas* stage in earnest.

Alchemical Stage: Citrinitas (Yellowing)

This chapter is pure Citrinitas—the dawning of wisdom. It is no longer about destruction (Nigredo) or purification (Albedo), but illumination. Laolys is becoming self-luminous. He is beginning to radiate—not because he is "right," but because he is *real*.

The Sage no longer questions him. Instead, he transmits the flame that Laolys must now tend himself. What burns within the triangle is the same fire that will, one day, become the Sun within him.

The Covenant Beneath the Mirror

Laolys accepts the sacred burden of truth beneath the gaze of the sage and the stars. This is no longer philosophical dialogue—it is a spiritual covenant. The Sage no longer instructs; he transmits. The young man, once a seeker, becomes an initiate. What is accepted in silence will echo through unseen worlds.

1. The Mirror – Gateway to the Multiverse At the center of the scene rests a radiant mirror on a stone pedestal. This is no ordinary object; it is the symbolic *Netic Lens*, representing the point of leakage into higher realms. In alchemical terms, it is the Athanor—the chamber of spiritual reflection. For Laolys, it reflects not his image, but his inner essence, unmasked and unguarded.

2. Laolys Kneeling – Surrender to the Great Work Laolys kneels before the mirror, his posture one of solemn acceptance. He has crossed the threshold from student to vessel, mirroring the moment when prima materia accepts the first heat of transformation. This is the first conscious coagulation—when one begins to bind to the deeper pattern willingly.

3. The Sage – Flamebearer and Witness Standing behind the mirror with outstretched arms, the sage is no longer just Mercurius the Challenger—he is now the Flamebearer, acting as conduit for sacred obligation. His role is to see, to bless, and to make the vow real through presence alone.

4. The Pedestal – Foundation of the Stone The mirror rests on a carved stone, symbolizing grounded truth. This is the Philosopher's Foundation—the reminder that even the most elevated knowledge must have roots in the real. It is the balance between multiversal vision and incarnate responsibility.

5. The Grove – Living Temple The ancient trees surrounding them form a natural cathedral. Each trunk, etched with simple symbols (triangle, chalice, phoenix), suggests that all of nature is a witness to this rite. The canopy above filters light like stained glass, casting fragments of divine pattern across the forest floor.

6. The Triangle of Stars – Seal of the Ætheric Pact Overhead, three stars form a perfect downward-pointing triangle—a sacred seal of alignment between intention, spirit, and destiny. It affirms that

Laolys's choice has echoed upward, that the above has heard the below, and responded.

Alchemical Stage: Late Albedo Turning Toward Citrinitas This moment occurs at the edge between Albedo and Citrinas. Laolys has been cleansed by truth and silence, and now he binds himself to the path of illuminated service. It is the beginning of wisdom as responsibility. The light has entered him, and now it seeks expression in form. The fire that once tested him now dwells within him.

The Tempest Within the Silence

Laolys sits in silence as the storm roars outside, a tempest born of both nature and his soul. He is caught between insight and resistance, illumination and denial. The sage watches without words. The moment is suspended—not in peace, but in potential. Something must break before something can be born.

1. **The Storm – Unconscious Manifestation** The violent storm is more than weather—it is a mirror of Laolys's inner conflict. Alchemically, this is the eruption of the soul's refusal to surrender. The storm represents the turbulence of the psychic vessel during transformation, marking a phase just beyond Albedo: the chaos before integration.

2. **The Unlit Candle – Refused Insight** Set at the center of the table, the candle remains unlit. Its wax is intact, its wick untouched. This symbolizes a truth Laolys is not yet ready to receive. The Sage offers no light because light cannot be forced—this is the delayed kindling of Rubedo, when illumination is withheld until one chooses it willingly.

3. **The Spiral Sigil – Temporal Convergence** Above the two men hovers a glowing spiral—visible to the viewer but hidden from Laolys. This symbol, drawn from Netist metaphysics, represents the merging of potential timelines. It confirms that Laolys's choices are already shaping more than one world.

4. **The Sage with the Closed Book – Silent Knowledge** The sage's book is closed, resting gently in his hands. It is time for stillness. He is a Witness now, not a teacher, holding space for Laolys to come into his own initiation. The book signifies the silent chamber of integration—knowledge must now become embodiment.

5. **The Lightning Eye – Ætheric Witness** A flash of lightning forms an unmistakable eye in the storm-lit sky. This is the Watcher of the Æther, the higher field of perception that sees not just actions but frequency. It serves as a reminder that this moment matters—that even doubt, even hesitation, echoes through the greater design.

Alchemical Stage: Threshold Between Albedo and Rubedo
Chapter IX marks the crisis between cleansing and completion. Laolys has seen the truth, but has not yet accepted its consequences. This threshold is sacred. It is the alchemy of silence, where nothing moves

yet everything shifts. The fire does not rage—it waits. The storm may howl, but the real lightning is internal. Rubedo hovers, but will not descend until Laolys chooses to step forward.

The Mind of the Big Fish

Laolys stands upon a high ridge, his gaze fixed on the spiral of water below. The sage points skyward, not to instruct but to redirect. The moment is contemplative—quiet yet charged. What swims below is not a fish alone, but a metaphor for the self, the story, the thought loop. And now, for the first time, Laolys begins to see it.

1. The Big Fish – Fear Bound to Thought In the winding stream below, a massive fish moves in a slow, circular pattern. It is both real and symbolic—representing the self caught in repetition. This is Laolys's inherited mind: intelligent, massive, but bound by unseen fear. The fish is the ouroboric thought—the loop that cannot evolve until it is witnessed.

2. The Feather – Memory of Wound Though not the focus, a single feather rests on the hillside behind Laolys. It is a symbol of lingering pain, something once fallen that has not yet been lifted. The wound is no longer bleeding but it is still raw. In alchemy, this is the residue from Nigredo—the remnant that needs recognition before union.

3. The Sage's Gesture – Invitation to Transcend The sage, rather than pointing to the fish, gestures upward to the stars. His motion breaks the cycle. He encourages Laolys to rise beyond it. This gesture embodies Citrinitas: clarity without conflict, wisdom without struggle.

4. The Stream – Mind's Flow The river winding through the valley is the symbolic current of consciousness. The fish swims against its bend—mirroring the resistance of the ego to natural flow. This moment reveals that Laolys's journey lies in surrendering to deeper navigation.

5. The Spiral Constellation – Multiversal Awareness Above them swirls a gentle spiral of stars, forming no form but inviting reflection. This is a Netist symbol of convergence, showing that Laolys's realization now echoes across many possible selves. The moment is sacred across layers of being.

Alchemical Stage: Late Citrinitas, Approaching Rubedo
Chapter X stands on the edge of the final stage. Laolys no longer seeks to understand—he begins to see. He is nearing Rubedo, when wisdom becomes embodied, but he has one final choice ahead: to release the

fear that formed the fish, or continue circling with it. The stars are ready. The path is opening. Now, he must step.

Order Within the Root of Chaos

Order Within the
Root of Chaos

Laolys sits cross-legged beneath a gnarled old tree, book open on his lap, as the sage descends from its branches in mid-motion—leaves trailing around him like the residue of another plane. Above, the sky spirals subtly, neither day nor night. The world is askew, and yet deeply aligned. This is the moment when Laolys is invited to grasp the paradox: that Chaos is not disorder, but infinite potential.

1. The Chalk Spiral – Initiation into Paradox

The spiral drawn around Laolys represents his entrance into Citrinitas by Chaos. Unlike logic-bound geometry, this spiral opens infinitely inward. It is an alchemical mandala—one that can only be walked by surrender, not control.

2. The Tree-Sage – Living Embodiment of Chaos

The sage, emerging from the tree, is no longer just a figure of knowledge. He is a Netic Trickster, a living axis between order and entropy. His descent from the tree is a descent from abstract potential into grounded transmission.

3. The Collapsing Arches – Structures Dissolving

In the distance, stone monuments fall as new towers rise—symbolizing that in chaos, destruction and creation are simultaneous. These are not ruins, but evolving blueprints. The mind must unlearn to perceive.

4. The Book – Fragile Knowledge

The book on Laolys's lap is open but unread. Its pages flutter in a wind that seems to come from within. This is ephemeral wisdom—the kind that can only be caught when the seeker stops chasing.

5. The Roots and Stars Below – Hidden Pattern of the Multiverse

Beneath the surface, the tree's roots do not end in soil, but merge into a web of stars. This reveals the true order beneath the perceived chaos—an interconnected field where above and below collapse into one. The lesson: what appears wild is sacred in form.

Alchemical Stage: Mid-to-Late Citrinitas (The Clarity of Sacred Paradox)

Chapter XI is the turning point where Laolys no longer tries to conquer or interpret the mystery—he begins to accept paradox as divine architecture. Chaos is revealed as multiversal law. The sage's teaching circle. Laolys does not yet master the rhythm, but he steps inside it—and that is the true beginning of wisdom.

Descent of the Storm Called From Within

Descent of the Storm Called From Within

Laolys and the sage sit in stillness inside the hut, shrouded in total darkness except for faint illumination through gaps in the wooden walls. Outside, a storm thrashes violently—trees bend, lightning forks across a heavy sky, and wind hurls leaves into a vortex of chaos. Within, the hut is unmoved, a sanctum amidst cosmic turbulence.

Laolys is the storm, yet he does not know it. The elemental fury outside is a reflection of his inner unrest—the storm of hesitation, fear, and the temptation to flee before he's ready.

1. The Storm Outside – Externalization of Internal Conflict

The wind, rain, and lightning seem to arise from nowhere. They're manifestations of Laolys's subconscious unrest. His desire to leave prematurely has summoned this chaos, not by intent, but resonance.

2. The Dark Hut – The Inner Chamber of Shadow

The hut is symbolic of the hermetic vessel—sealed, dark, pressurized. Within it, purification begins by endurance through confusion. This is the moment of alchemical shadow incubation.

3. The Book Unread – Knowledge in Suspension

The sage holds a book but does not read. It signifies that truth is beyond words, and that learning, here, happens through presence. The book represents the sealed doctrine—hidden until the initiate is ready.

4. The Lightning Fork – Sudden Insight, Not Yet Embraced

Seen through the window-slit, the bolt of lightning is the flash of Rubedo—sudden illumination. But Laolys cannot yet grasp it. It is premature, reflecting what could be if he aligns within.

5. The Spiral Eye in the Clouds – The Watcher Within the Chaos

Faint but vast in the sky, the eye-shaped spiral is the Ætheric Witness—a Netist symbol of higher consciousness observing through trial. It is both inside and beyond him, a reminder that all storms are watched, even if not controlled.

Alchemical Stage: Threshold Between Albedo and Rubedo

Chapter XII is the penultimate crucible. Laolys hovers between purification and embodiment. He is tempted to descend the mountain, to retreat from becoming. But the storm he summons tells another story —it anchors him in place, forcing surrender. This chapter is the still point of hesitation, where old identity is not yet abandoned, and new truth not yet claimed. The sage does nothing but wait. The lesson: the final fire cannot be forced—it arrives when the inner climate agrees to receive it.

Evaporation of the Wounded Waters

Evaporation of the Wounded Waters

Laolys lies alone on his simple mountain bed within the shadowy confines of the hut. His face is half-lit by ambient moonlight, but his eyes are open, haunted. Above him, the dream realm unfurls—not as a separate scene, but as a translucent overlay: pain, memory, and illusion shimmer and dissolve in layered bands around the hut. The sage is nowhere to be seen. This is a moment of deep inward confrontation—Laolys is visited by past wounds, but now has the tools to transmute them. **1. The Mist of Memories – Pain in Evaporation** The steam rising from the water symbolizes emotional distillation. These memories—once solid—are now vapor, no longer defining but dissolving. This represents Laolys beginning to reclaim his inner terrain, releasing trauma through witnessing rather than avoidance.

2. The Empty Corner – The Absent Sage The sage is not visible, for this work is not guided. His subtle shadow at the window implies the presence of wisdom even in silence. This teaches that true alchemical growth occurs in solitude—when the initiate must become his own instructor.

3. The Bowl of Water – The Basin of the Soul Placed near the bed, the bowl catches moonlight and reflects Laolys's face upside down. This is the mirror of the self—distorted, fluid, and real. It is where illusions are both born and seen through.

4. The Rising Dream Orbs – Initiate's Ascent Above Laolys, transparent spheres carry fragments of him into higher realms. These orbs represent the planes of the mind, now accessible through integration of shadow. His awakening is beginning to touch the Netic realms of multiversal truth.

5. The Distillation Veil – Thin Boundary of Worlds Between hut and sky floats a vaporous veil, barely perceptible, where all separation dissolves. This is the boundary between pain and peace, illusion and insight. Laolys no longer tries to escape—he lets it pass through him.

Alchemical Stage: Albedo (Whitening) This chapter is pure Albedo. Having endured the shadow trials of Nigredo, Laolys now confronts his pain not by resisting it, but by letting it evaporate. The albedo phase is not glorious—it is pale, gentle, reflective. But within it, sorrow loses its density, and clarity begins. The lesson here is purification through tenderness: the inner wound no longer fights—it exhales. From the exhale, the ascent begins.

Storm at the Gate of Return

Storm at the Gate of Return

Laolys and the sage remain confined within the humble mountain hut, as an enormous storm lashes the exterior. The storm is more than weather—it is a Netic barrier, summoned not from above, but from within. Laolys lies awake, suspended between descent and continuation. He nearly chooses to leave the mountain, to return to the world unchanged. But the storm blocks his passage—a storm of resistance, fear, and the sacred refusal of premature return. The sage reads by darkness. The silence teaches louder than words.

1. The Lightning Bolt – Intervention of the Æther The bolt strikes the lower trail—a physical warning. It is the alchemical *Hand of the Æther*, stopping Laolys from descending before his rebirth. The universe responds to misalignment with luminous correction.

2. The Reading in Darkness – Wisdom Beyond Light The Sage reads without visible light. This is the symbol of Inned Illumination—an alchemist who no longer needs external tools. In Netism, this is the Second Sight: knowing without sensory crutches.

3. The Unopened Gate – The Path Yet Denied Outside, formed subtly in the clouds, is a monumental gate—a multiversal threshold not yet crossed. It appears only in lightning flashes, showing that true passage requires alignment, not intention alone.

4. The Silent Space – Contained Transformation The interior of the hut represents the sealed vessel—quiet, compressed, still. No ritual occurs, yet everything is happening. Alchemically, this is fermentation—when new essence stirs silently within.

5. The Storm as Mirror – Resistance of the Initiate The storm is not an obstacle, but a mirror of Laolys's inner resistance. His fear, hesitation, and unfinished transformation whip the winds into frenzy. He is both prisoner and warden of this weather.

Alchemical Stage: Fermentation (Bridge Between Albedo and Rubedo) Chapter XIV marks the hidden threshold. Laolys is neither dissolving (Nigredo) nor illuminating (Citrinitas), but undergoing silent chemical activation. Fermentation is when the spiritual essence first breathes, but has not yet animated the full self. He is suspended. If he leaves now, the Work remains unfinished. But by staying within the sealed hut, he permits the next stage to gestate. The sage does not stop him. The storm does. The atmosphere cries in opposition.

The Great Current of Becoming

Laolys is suspended within a great stream of Æther, body relaxed but alert, arms slightly open. He is no longer walking, sitting, or resisting—he is carried, surrendered. Around him are orbs of colored light, blending softly through the ink-dark waters of this dreamlike current. Above and below, celestial patterns flicker in the distance, hinting at other realms. A faintly discernible face in the current gazes with compassion—not a deity, but a higher version of Laolys himself.

1. The Æther Stream – River of Becoming The current Laolys floats through is not water, but the fluid of the multiverse—the same stream seen by mystics, poets, and prophets. It is not a place but a process—carrying him toward integration. The lesson: surrender is not passivity, but trust in deeper forces.

2. The Colored Orbs – Vibrational Gateways Each orb represents a layer of multiversal experience—joy, grief, fear, wonder. Laolys does not grasp them; they orbit and pass. This reflects the stage of *observation without identification*. The self becomes the witness.

3. The Silent Face in the Current – Ætheric Self A subtle face appears in the folds of current—*Laolys's higher self*, watching without interference. This is the *Netist principle* of simultaneous embodiment and transcendence: one can be within and beyond at once.

4. The Great Fish Below – Wisdom from Below Large dream-fish swim beneath him, symbolic of forgotten truths rising. They echo the big fish metaphor used throughout the story. These are not threats— they are *elders of the unconscious*, watching his courage.

5. The Lighted Horizon – Portal to Continuance In the distance is a barely formed doorway, glowing in soft gold-white. It represents what is coming: transformation not by choice, but by consequence of surrender.

Alchemical Stage: Rubedo (Reddening) This chapter is the final transmutation. Laolys has passed through blackening, purification, fermentation—and now enters the phase of the Philosopher's Stone. Rubedo is not a destination but a union of all stages: fire and water, mind and body, chaos and cosmos. The current no longer resists him because he no longer resists himself. He is becoming the truth he sought. While much still lies ahead of him, he has crossed the threshold to becoming. He is aligned with the Great Process.

About the Author

Nora Spinnor is an author, philosopher, and lifelong alchemist. Her work draws deeply from ancient texts—especially the wisdom of Ancient Egypt—while also echoing the voices of Plato, Nietzsche, and Thoreau. She credits her inspiration to both the great thinkers of history and her ability to pull from the subtle threads of the Net.

Her debut work, *The Young Man and the Sage*, mirrors her own inner journey of transformation. Blending science, philosophy, and mysticism, Nora's writing revives the spirit of ancient storytelling to illuminate the challenges of the modern world. Through timeless symbols and metaphysical insight, she explores what it means to awaken in an age of disconnection.

Nora's aim is to inspire readers to question their assumptions and rediscover the value within themselves. Each soul carries a distinct frequency—an essential tone in the harmony of the Net. Her work documents the spiritual trials we all face as we learn to accept the self in its entirety, drawing scattered fragments into coherence, and remembering our role in the greater whole.

Also by Nora Spinnor

All Titles Coming Soon

The Old Man and the Student
Book Two of The Herald's Trilogy

Fifty years after his own ascent, Laolys is no longer the student; he is the one sought out. A young physicist climbs the mountain, desperate to uncover the secrets that could save a collapsing world. In their unfolding dialogue, ancient truths resurface: energy flows from a unified source field, water holds memory, and the Cosmos speaks through geometry. A poetic and philosophical journey into hidden science, sacred responsibility, and the soul's longing to restore harmony.

The Visitor and the Native
Book Three of The Herald's Trilogy

Laolys travels as a visitor to a distant land, fulfilling a request from a friend. There, he finds himself once again in the role of the student, learning his last steps to ascension lie in community. He must step outside of his isolation to live by the philosophy of *ubuntu*—*I am because we are.*

Cosmic Alchemy
A Guide to a 12 Energy Center System Spanning Multiversal Awareness

Inspired by systems that pre-date the seven-chakra model, this book outlines 9 bodily centers along with an additional triad that expands into the multiversal Net. By balancing each center, readers will learn to tune their spirit and access higher planes of consciousness. A unique synthesis of physics, metaphysics, and psychology.

About Netism

Netism is a sacred metaphysical philosophy that reveals the hidden architecture of existence through the living pattern of the Net. At its heart, Netism teaches that all things, people, events, thoughts, stars, and even timelines are interconnected through a vast, conscious lattice that vibrates across dimensions.

This lattice is the Net, and it serves as both the memory and motion of the multiverse, the structure through which energy weaves itself into form and experience.

Rather than worshipping a deity or adhering to dogma, Netism invites a direct relationship with the energies of life. It honors stillness, balance, and the deep harmony between opposites, while also embracing movement, creation, and change.

Everything in the universe has its place within the Net, and every moment is part of a greater weaving. The more attuned we become, the more clearly we can sense the threads that bind all things together and learn to weave them with intention.

Netism speaks through symbol, energy, and resonance. It integrates ancient knowing with modern insight, offering a system of thought that is both mystical and grounded.

It teaches that each being carries fragments of a greater whole—

what is called soul shards—and that through love, memory, sacred union, and spiritual discipline, we can reunite those fragments across lifetimes, dimensions, and even universes.

To live Netism is to listen. To align with the deeper harmonics of life, to move with care, to speak with precision, and to act from the center of one's being.

It is a path of remembering, reconnecting, and restoring the sacred balance that holds the cosmos together. Whether read as philosophy, practiced as energy work, or lived through daily choice, Netism offers a way to awaken the threads of the self and weave them into the living field of all.

www.netism.org

Made in the USA
Coppell, TX
10 February 2026

71011060R00187